ST. FURSEY'S LIFE AND VISIONS

AND

OTHER ESSAYS

BY

SARAH ATKINSON

AUTHOR OF

LIFE OF MARY AIKENHEAD

Dublin

M. H. GILL & SON, LTD.

( )

M. H. GILL AND SON, LTD.,
DUBLIN

ST. FURSEY'S LIFE AND VISIONS

THERE appears to be no doubt that the Vision of St. Fursey is the oldest of all the Celtic legends treating of the experiences of the Christian soul in the regions beyond the grave. "Tracing the course of thought upwards, through the visions of Alberic and Owain Miles, and the other compositions of a like nature, we have no difficulty," says Sir Francis Palgrave, "in deducing the poetic genealogy of the *Inferno* and the *Purgatorio* to the Milesian Fursæus."[1]

Moreover, this prose poem of the seventh century is doubly interesting, as bearing the mark of its high antiquity in the lyric simplicity and artless form of the narrative. And as St. Fursey's name and story are not so well known in his native land as assuredly they ought to be, I will give, at the same time, a rapid sketch of his career,—first in Erin, then in East Anglia, and lastly in that glorious France where his memory is still held in grateful veneration.

The important position held by St. Fursey, and the authenticity of his history, are stated in a few words by a very distinguished archæologist, the Rev. Dr. Reeves, Protestant Dean of Armagh. "Among the Irish saints," writes the learned dean, "who are but slightly commemorated at home, yet whose praise is in all the Churches, St. Fursa holds a conspicuous place. With Venerable Bede as a guarantee of his extraction, piety, and labours, and above a dozen different memoirs, of various ages, which were found on the Continent in Colgan's time, the history of this saint is established on the

[1] Palgrave, *History of Normandy and England*, vol. i. p. 725.

firmest basis."[1] And this testimony is more than confirmed by another high authority, the late Protestant Bishop of Brechin. "The reputation of St. Fursey," writes Dr. Forbes, "extends far beyond the limits of the Scoto-Irish Church. Not only is he one of the most distinguished of those missionaries who left Erin to spread the gospel through the heathen and semi-heathenised races of mediæval Europe, bridging the gap between the old and new civilisations, but his position in view of dogma is a most important one. He has profoundly effected the eschatology of Christianity; for the dream of St. Fursæus and the vision of Drycthelm contributed much to define the conceptions of men with regard to that mysterious region on which every man enters after death."[2]

Venerable Bede, born not more than twenty-five or thirty years after the death of the Irish saint, sketches, in few but weighty words, the character of the holy man named Fursey, who came out of Ireland, and preached the gospel in East Anglia while Sigbert still governed that kingdom. This man, he continues, was of noble Scottish [*i.e.* Irish] blood, but much more noble in mind than in birth. From his boyish years he had particularly applied himself to reading sacred books and following monastic discipline, and, as is most becoming to holy men, he carefully practised all that he learned was to be done. Renowned he was for his words and actions, and remarkable for singular virtues. He was a man thought worthy to behold the choirs of angels, and to hear the praises which are sung in heaven. The father of English history says a good deal more about the saint's life and mission, and also gives an abstract of the vision in which the seer not only beheld the greater joys of the blessed, but also extraordinary combats of evil spirits. In fact, the nineteenth chapter of the third book of the *Ecclesiastical History* is occupied exclusively with Fursey, the author being desirous, as he says, that the sublimeness of this man may be known to the readers. Still, he would have no one remain satisfied with the curtailed narration he transcribes, but counsels all to read the little book of Fursey's life already written, from

[1] Manuscript account of St. Fursey, quoted in Webb's *Compendium of Irish Biography*.

[2] *Kalendar of Scottish Saints*, p. 352.

which they will, he says, be sure to reap much spiritual profit.[1]

The "little life" thus commended is supposed to be still extant. If so, it is only one of a hundred. A long catalogue of codices, in which various versions of St. Fursey's acts are preserved in the chief public libraries of Europe, is given by the Rev. John O'Hanlon in his exhaustive life of the saint, and a comprehensive list is added of the more modern authors who have, in various languages, treated of the same subject; this array of writers showing, as the laborious compiler observes, how greatly the fame of St. Fursey extended among the learned.[2] Mr. Wright also refers to several ancient manuscript versions of the Visions, and indicates where they are to be found;[3] while he has rendered an important service by publishing[4] the legend from an Anglo-Saxon manuscript preserved in the Bodleian Library. Lack of material does not offer any difficulty to the industrious student in this field; rather, to quote the Rev. Dr. Lanigan, so much has been written about St. Fursey, that it has served rather to darken than to illustrate his history.[5]

Towards the close of the sixth century, according to the most trustworthy authorities, Fintan, the son of Finlog, king of a territory in southern Munster, found it necessary, on account of some troubles in the little State, to absent himself for a while, and took advantage of the opportunity thus afforded to make a tour in Erin, visit the provincial kings in their royal raths, form friendships with distinguished men of the day, and perfect himself in such branches of letters and polity as might be useful to him in after-life. He was an accomplished prince, as young men of his position were expected to be after a prolonged course of education in the

[1] *Ecclesiastical History*. Bohn's edition. Venerable Bede was held in great esteem by the ancient Irish, as the author of *Ogygia Vindicated* thus quaintly testifies: "He (Bede) greatly obliged the Irish nation by his writing; and they, in recompense, were not forgetful of his memory in their annals, honouring him with this eulogy in the year of his departure, *Beda Saxorum Sapiens quievit*—'Bede, the Sage of the Saxons, rested.'"

[2] *Lives of the Irish Saints*, vol. i. pp. 224, 225.

[3] *St. Patrick's Purgatory*, ch. i.

[4] In *Reliquiæ Antiquæ*, vol. i

[5] *Ecclesiastical History of Ireland*, vol. i. ch. xvi.

schools of the Druids and the bards. Received with distinction in Leinster, he passed into Connaught, where a like success awaited him. Among the local magnates who gave him a hospitable welcome, was the Prince of Hy-Brinn or Breifne, Aedfind, the ancestor of the O'Rourkes and O'Reillys. While sojourning in this part of the country, he fell in love with Gelesia, the daughter of Aedfind. She, a Christian, won him over to the true faith, and then, under very romantic circumstances, though much to her father's displeasure, married him.

Authorities are not agreed in assigning the birthplace of Fursey, the illustrious issue of this alliance. Some will have it that he first saw the light in an island of Lough Orbsen (Corrib), whither his parents had fled to escape the wrath of Aedfind;[1] while others, with more probability, state that Munster was his *patria* or country, and that he was not born until Fintan had brought his wife home to his native place.

However this may have been, his childhood was passed in the south, and his education carefully attended to in his father's house. Very early in life he received a call to dedicate himself to religion, and when the proper time came, he set out for the shores of Lough Corrib, with a view to pursue his sacred studies in a district famous even then for the saintly men sojourning within its bounds, and for the monastic establishments flourishing on the bosky mainland, and in the islands dotting the broad expanse of the lake.

The goal of his pilgrimage was the island already alluded to, lying, with its primeval woods and holy solitudes, about a mile off the eastern shore. A special halo invested this sanctuary, owing to the fact that the great St. Brendan had chosen it for the home of his venerable age; and, after his mystic voyage on the Western Ocean, his missionary wanderings in foreign countries, his apostolic labours in Erin, and his arduous government of immense monasteries and colleges, had built a chapel and a cell on the island, and retired thither to await the hour of death and of deliverance. The "Patriarch of Monks" was not alone in this retreat. St. Moeni, who had

[1] The Rev. J. O'Hanlon, with good reason, excludes from his account of St. Fursey's parentage a wild legend in relation to the circumstances preceding and accompanying the saint's birth. The curious story, however, will be found in *The Irish Builder*, May 15, June 1, 1884.

been with him on his seven years' voyage, was also with him on the island. St. Meldan likewise became his disciple, and took up his abode in the same retreat. Probably these were not the only companions of his solitude. But whether the cenobites were few or many, the place must still have been a solitude when compared with the religious and scholastic colony he had governed at Clonfert, where three thousand monks dwelt in one community, and a vast concourse of students attended the schools.[1]

After St. Brendan's demise, the governance of the cœnobium devolved on Meldan Mac Ui Cuinn, under whose rule it grew into a large monastic establishment, famous throughout the country. Meldan was of royal extraction, being of the race of Con of the Hundred Battles, Monarch of Ireland in the second century. The sept of Hui Cuinn, as the descendants of Con were called, had possession of the country about Lough Corrib; and the island we are speaking of was a part of their patrimony. Meldan therefore, "Abbot and Bishop of Lough Orbsen, in Connaught," was, in every sense of the word, on his own ground when he trod the pathways of the holy isle. Doubtless many of his kinsfolk joined the recluses, and dwelt under the abbot's paternal rule. His brothers were undoubtedly of the number of his spiritual sons, for history records that the monastery was built about 580 by St Meldan and his brothers.

It is not expressly mentioned that a school formed part of the establishment on the island; but we may be tolerably certain that this settlement formed no exception to the general rule at a time when Irish monasteries were seats of learning, and when even anchorites in their lonely cells, and religious women secluded from the world, were subject to the visits, and

[1] St. Brendan did not die on the island, but on the mainland, not far off, at Annadown, whither he had gone to visit his sister, St. Briga, for whom he had built a nunnery in that place, under the invocation of the Blessed Virgin. After the oblation of the sacrifice, as an ancient life of the saint records, he said to his sister: "Commend my departure in your prayers." And Briga said. "What do you fear?" "I fear," he replied, "if I go alone, and if the journey be dark—the unknown region, the presence of the King, and the sentence of the Judge." The saint was called to his reward on Sunday, the 16th of May 577 His remains were removed for interment to the great monastery near the Shannon, of which he had been the first abbot. Tradition has it, that the funeral procession extended the whole way from Annadown to Clonfert, a distance of more than twenty miles.

not indifferent to the claims, of those who sought instruction at their hands Strange it would have been if the abbot were not called upon to train the youth of his clan in sacred and secular knowledge. His insular domain was within easy access of the frail, hide-covered coracles in which the natives of that region skimmed the translucent waters. The sound of St. Meldan's bell could be heard on the wood-fringed shore; and across the placid lake the chant of the Gaelic monks—those masters in sacred song—was borne far and wide by the wandering wind. Not, indeed, that the convenient situation of their seminary made much matter to the eager students. When youths began their school-life, they encamped in wattle huts (the work of their own hands), close to the cashel or circular wall enclosing the group of monastic cells and the little church of primitive construction; and there they remained until they had got the instruction they required in doctrine, in arts, and in industry. For, nurtured as they were on piety, poetry, and "grammar," they were, nevertheless, put through a healthful course of industrial training. They had all—the chieftain's child as well as the clansman's—to follow the example of the monks, and contribute by the labour of their hands to the support of the establishment. No college fees were exacted, nor was the community burdensome to any. Work and study, high thinking and low living, comprised the rule alike of professors and scholars in those old-world academies.

Meldan's monastery became so celebrated that the island shared in the renown of the founder, and was distinguished from the neighbouring isles by the appellation of *Inis mac Hua chin*, the Island of the Sons of Con Even Lough Orbsen received a reflected honour, and was sometimes called by a name signifying that it was the lake that bore on its breast the island of Inchiquin.[1]

The monastery founded by the descendants of Con of the Hundred Battles was already in a flourishing condition when the youthful Fursey arrived from southern Munster to complete his education under the monks, and embrace the religious life in the island monastery.

[1] For many succeeding ages St. Meldan's festival was celebrated in this island on the 7th of February A moat or rath is the only feature of antiquity now marked on its surface, which, moreover, has been denuded of its natural [illegible]

Though the abbot may have early discerned the gifts, and augured well from the virtues, of his disciple, he could hardly have divined that be himself should become famous in far-distant lands as the spiritual father of St. Fursey; or that his relics would be carried abroad and enshrined in the banks of the Somme by the loving hands of that illustrious son. Having remained for several years under St. Meldan's tutelage, Fursey, according to some authorities, repaired to the islands of Arran for study and edification, and sojourned for a while with the holy recluses dwelling in those ocean solitudes. Returning to Inchiquin a greater proficient in the science of the saints, he was advised by the abbot to build a monastery of his own and assemble a religious community around him. Following this counsel, Fursey, early in the seventh century, formed a settlement at a place called Rathmat, now identified as Killursa or Kill-Fursa (Fursey's Church), situated nearly opposite Inchiquin, and about two miles from the lake. To build a monastery in those days was by no means a stupendous undertaking. Nothing more was necessary than to clear a site, fell some trees, construct huts or cells of the wattles and timber, and encompass the cluster of rude edifices with a hedge or a wall, as the case might be. The little church, standing in the midst, would be of a superior style, constructed of planed timber, or, in rare instances, of cyclopean masonry. Of course, in districts where stone abounded, in exposed situations on the sea-coast, on the precipitous islands lashed by the Atlantic surge, the monastic settlements assumed a far greater solidity. But the wattle encampment was the usual style. It is quite possible that Fursey may have erected the small church, many ages ago incorporated with a larger structure, which, now in ruins, attracts the attention of the curious, and beguiles the feet of archæologists to Kill-Fursa. The original cyclopean west gable, with its Egyptian-looking doorway, is embedded in the later, yet still ancient, masonry; and the learned in such matters are of opinion that this vestige of primæval architecture cannot be less than twelve hundred years old [1]

When the settlement at Rathmat, or Kill-Fursa, was suffi-

[1] For a description of the ruins of Kill-Fursa, see Sir W. Wilde's *Lough Corrib*, and an article on the Cyclopean Churches of Loughs Corrib, Mask, and Cara, in the *Journal of the Historical and Archæological Association of Ireland*, July 1868.

ciently established, the pious founder resolved to make a journey to the home in Munster, which he had left so many years before and had not since revisited. Some changes had taken place meanwhile in the little kingdom. Finlog had died, and his son Fintan, elected according to the custom of the country, reigned in his stead. In this expedition, the abbot's purpose seems to have been to promote the spiritual welfare of his own people, and to induce some of his kinsfolk to join him, on his return to Rathmat, and place themselves under instruction at the monastery.

Fursey had not long arrived at his destination when a sudden illness seized him. He became so enfeebled that his friends fancied his last hour was at hand. Recovering himself, however, he arose, and, supporting himself with difficulty on the arm of a companion, went out, walked a few steps from the house, and began to recite the evening office. Completely absorbed in prayer, his lips murmured the words of the sacred psalmody. Suddenly he felt himself enveloped in darkness. All power of movement forsook him, and he was carried back into the house apparently in a dying state.

Presently, in the midst of the dense obscurity, he perceived that four hands stretched downwards towards him, caught him by the arms, and bore him aloft. After a while, becoming more accustomed to the darkness, he plainly discerned four great wings expanded upwards, and white as the driven snow. The hands and wings he could now distinctly see, but the rest of the angelic forms were only dimly visible. But when they had ascended still higher, he was able to distinguish the beauteous faces of his conductors, illumined with a wondrous glory, or rather, his eyes were filled with the radiance emanating from their faces, though he could not, on account of the excess of brilliance, distinguish any corporeal form. At the same time he became conscious that a third angel walked on before him, clothed in luminous vesture, carrying a white shield, and armed with a sword keen as a flash of lightning. The marvellous splendour of the angels, the harmonious rustling of their wings, the melody of their songs, and the divine beauty of their aspect, penetrated his soul with inexpressible delight. For, as they moved along they sang—the first angel intoning the opening phrase, the others joining in and continuing the chant. And the burden of their song was this—*The saints shall advance from virtue to virtue, the God of gods shall be seen in Zion.* Higher and higher rose the voices, the psalmody rolling on in ever-increasing power; and then the music sank in dulcet modulation, and seemed to die away in the ethereal distance, until, caught up again by myriads of angelic voices, the strain burst forth into a resounding chorus, of which Fursey could distinguish one verse only—*They shall come out before the face of Christ.* All the heavenly faces which he now beheld seemed to him alike, but the light was so dazzling that it veiled the corporeal form and hid it from his view.

Fain would he have tarried in this world of indescribable splendour and harmony, but it could not be,—he must fill up the term of his earthly probation; and the angels, promising to return to him before long, led him back to life

Meanwhile the night had passed away, and the crowing of the cock announced the rising morn The music of the heavenly choirs no longer filled his ear. Nothing was audible but the dissonance of human voices wailing and lamenting. At that moment those who were standing round the inanimate body uncovered the face; a faint blush mantled the pale cheeks, and the servant of God, opening his eyes, addressed the mourners, and asked them wherefore they lamented and why so great a rout was made. Thereupon the men related all that had occurred,—telling him how on the previous evening he had expired, and how they had remained ever since in the same spot, watching beside his corpse. Then Fursey arose. The splendid and gracious presence of the angels came back to his remembrance, and, recollecting that they had promised to return, he regretted that he had not beside him some wise and prudent man to whom he might recount all that he had seen and heard. And in order that the angels on their return might not find him unprepared, he asked to receive the Communion of the Body and Blood of the spotless Lamb Thus he remained all that day and the next in a state of great exhaustion

But in the night, about the hour of tierce, while relatives, friends, and several of the neighbours were assembled in the house, he was again wrapped in sudden darkness His feet grew stiff and cold; and extending his hands in the attitude of prayer, he awaited death in joyful expectation, for he remembered the enchanting vision of which these signs had been the forerunners once before. Overpowered, as it were, with sleep, he fell back on his couch. Immediately his ears were assailed with terrific cries, as of countless voices shouting and bidding him depart out of the body and come away. But, opening his eyes, he saw only the three angels standing at his side. The voices of men were hushed, and their forms had vanished. Already the heavenly orchestra and the beauty of the celestial visitants filled him with delight. The angel at his right hand said to him: "Be not afraid; you shall be defended."

They bore him upwards, ascending higher and higher, until the roof of his dwelling sank out of sight. Onwards he went, amidst the outcries and howlings of demons calling to one another to stop his progress, while he could distinctly hear one of the infernal spirits summoning the rest to come on and wage war before his face. On his left he saw, as it were, a dark cloud sweeping onwards—a whirlwind of hellish shapes twisted together in horrible confusion. Presently these writhing forms became disentangled, and marshalled their ranks in battle array before him. As far as his eye could reach, the figures of the demons showed black and terrible; while their long distended necks, their lean visages, and great bullet heads awakened feelings of the utmost loathing. When they flew hither and thither, or rushed to battle, he could distinguish nothing but a sinister shadow, an incompact mass of dreadful shapes, enough to make the soul wither away with fear. Moreover, their features were obscured by the denseness of the shadow in which they were immersed; just as, on the other hand, he had not been able to discern the traits of the angelic faces in the excess of light that surrounded them.

Forthwith began the onslaught of the satanic hosts. The demons shot their fiery arrows against the servant of God; but the darts struck the white buckler of the warrior angel, and fell away, innoxious and extinguished. In the presence of the angel equipped for the contest, the hostile ranks were overthrown. "Bar not the passage," said the angel, remonstrating with his adversaries, "it is of no avail. This man has no part in your perdition." But the devils, awfully blaspheming, clamoured for their prey, crying out that it was unjust of God to save sinners from damnation when it was written, that: *Not only they who sin, but they who agree with sinners are worthy of death.* Still the contest continued, and it seemed to Fursey that the thunder and clash of the combat must be heard throughout the whole earth.

Satan, though vanquished, raised his head again like a serpent crushed but venomous. "Many times," he shrieked, "has this man spoken idle words, and he must not enjoy eternal life without expiating his sins." "Not so," replied the guardian spirit; "if you can bring up no capital accusations against him, he shall not perish for venial faults." Then urged the reviler: "*If you will not forgive men, neither will your Father forgive you your sins.*" "When did He take revenge?" replied the angel; "or whom did He ever injure?" "It is not written," said the demon, "that you must not revenge yourself, but *If you do not forgive from your heart.*" "Forgiveness was in his heart," answered the angel, "though, yielding somewhat to a human custom, he did not outwardly show it" Then, persisted Satan. "Since he has contaminated himself with the sinful habits of men, he shall receive sentence from the Supreme Judge." "Be it so," concluded the angel. "He shall be arraigned before the Lord."

Repulsed for the third time, the old serpent's venom was not yet exhausted. "If God is a just God, this man shall never enter into eternal life; for it stands recorded: *Unless you be converted and become as little children, you shall not enter into the kingdom of heaven.* Fursey has by no means fulfilled this precept." "He shall be judged before the Lord," was again the angel's answer. And then the signal for the fight once more was given, and the battle raged until the hosts of hell were overthrown.

Then the angel on the right desired Fursey to look back upon the world. Casting his eyes downward, he beheld a dark and obscure valley underneath him, and saw four great fires kindled there at some distance from one another. And as he could not, in answer to the angel's query, tell what these fires might signify, his heavenly conductor said: "These are the four fires that consume the world, even though all sin was effaced by baptism, by faith in Christ, and by renouncing Satan with all his works and pomps. The first is falsehood; for men fail to fulfil the engagement they made in baptism to renounce the devil and his works The second is covetousness, which sets a higher value on the riches of the world than on heavenly things. The third is dissension; for men do not hesitate, even in needless matters, to injure the soul of their neighbour. And the fourth is iniquity; for they think little of dealing deceitfully and despoiling the poor."

And while they were yet speaking, the fires spread far and wide, until, uniting in one vast conflagration, the flames approached to where Fursey and the angels stood. Filled with dread, he cried to the guardian spirit "See, the fire rushes on to destroy me!" But the angel, reassuring him, bade him have no fear. "The fire you have not kindled," he said, "never will consume you. Great and terrible as these flames are, they burn only in proportion to the measure of each man's sins For all iniquity shall be consumed in him; and as the body is inflamed with sinful desires, so shall the soul feel the scorching pain in just retribution." Then one of the angels, going before, opened a way through the furnace,—the flames rising up like a wall on either hand,—and the other protecting spirits, spreading their wings and shielding him, on each side. The fires were alive with unclean spirits flying about, exciting a horrible commotion in the midst of the flames, and arming for a new contest. Immediately the battle began again. One of the devils, raising his voice, cried out: "Surely, *The servant who knows the will of his Lord, and doth it not, shall be beaten with many stripes?*" "And in what," inquired the angel, "has this man failed to do the behests of his Master?" "He has accepted the gifts of the wicked," was the rejoinder. "But he believed they had repented of their sins," said his defender. "He ought to have waited," retorted the accuser, "until they gave proof of the sincerity of their repentance before he received their presents; for *Gifts blind the eyes of the wise, and destroy the words of the just.*" The angel answered: "He shall be judged before the Lord."

Once more the arch-deceiver, worsted in his attack, vomited forth blasphemies against the Creator. "Hitherto we used to believe in a God of truth," he shrieked, "but we were mistaken Did not the prophet Isaiah affirm that the sin which was not punished on earth should be purged in the next world when he cried to the Jews: *If you be willing and will hearken to me, you shall eat the good things of the land But if you will not, and provoke me to wrath, the sword shall devour you?* Now this man did not expiate his sins while on earth, and he is not receiving chastisement here. Where, then, is God's justice?" "Cease to blaspheme," broke in the indignant angel; "you know not the secret judgments of the Lord." "What secret is there here?" persisted Satan. "As long as there is hope of repentance," rejoined the angel, "the Divine Mercy never abandons the human soul." "But there is no time here for repentance," objected the Evil One. "Perchance there may be," observed the heavenly spirit; "you cannot fathom the depth of the mysteries of God." Then the demon, silenced on this side also, shouted to his satellites to depart and leave them, since there was no justice to be expected.

But another of the accursed troop broke in: "Wait; there is still a narrow gate, which few succeed in passing through. Let us lie in ambush for him there. It is written: *Thou shalt love thy neighbour as thyself.*" The angel answered, that Fursey had done good to his neighbour; but the adversary rejoined, that it was not enough to do good, unless he loved his neighbour as himself. To which it was replied, that the performance of good deeds was the fruit of charity, and that God would render to everyone according to his works. But the demon insisted that the man's charity did not fulfil the precept, and that he had earned damnation. Then the infernal host hurried forward to give battle. But the heavenly spirits came off victorious in the contest.

Defeated for the sixth time, the demon, still according to his wont, flew into a passion of impious rage, saying that if God was not unjust, if falsehood and the breaking of promises were really displeasing in His sight, Fursey could not escape condemnation; for though he engaged to renounce the world, he had loved the world, contrary to the precept of the apostle when he said. *Love not the world, nor the things which are in the world*; he had been deterred neither by his own promise nor by the command of the apostle. To which the angel replied, that Fursey valued not the goods of the world for his own advantage, but that he might distribute them to the needy. "No matter in what way the riches of the world are prized," insisted the the old serpent, "it is against the law of God and contrary to the Christian obligation of baptism."

Again the angels prevailed, and their adversaries retreated before them. But Satan returned to pursue his insidious attacks: "*If thou wilt not announce to the unjust man his iniquity, I will require his blood at thy hand.* Thus it stands written," he said; "and this man has not preached repentance to sinners, as he was bound to do." Answering him, the angel said: "Yet also it stands written: *The prudent shall keep silence at that time, for it is an evil time*; and when hearers despise the word, the teacher's tongue is tied." But the wily enemy urged: "The truth must be preached despite of suffering, despite of death. One should neither consent nor hold his peace."

Thus, fiercely disputing and fighting, the demons raged, until at length, by the judgment of God, victory remained with the angels, and their adversaries were utterly routed.

Then around the saint a flood of light was shed; and the angels and the elect burst forth into a canticle, singing of the shortness of time and the lightness of labour when compared with the eternity of glory that is won by the faithful soul. Fursey was transported with delight; and raising his eyes, he beheld a multitudinous host resplendent as the sun; and the shimmer of their wings was like the rippling of waves on a luminous sea. These blessed ones drew near and surrounded him; and the trouble and the terror into which the fire and the demons had thrown him were banished far away. And also appeared two venerable men of his own nation, whom he knew on earth and thought were dead. Approaching, they told him they were Beoan and Meldan, and entered familiarly into conversation with him.

At this moment, in the serene distance of the heavens, an ethereal gate opened wide its portals. Two angels entered in through the opening; and immediately the celestial radiance encircled them with a still greater intensity, while the pure spirits abiding in that inner heaven sang, in four alternate choirs,—*Holy, holy, holy, Lord God of Hosts.* And while his soul was inebriated with the ineffable joys and enchanting psalmody of paradise, the bright cohorts of the celestial army marshalled their ranks on each side of him. One of the blessed spirits asked him if he knew whence issued these joyous acclamations; and as he could not tell, the angel said: "It is from the choirs of heaven, of which we form a part." The song meanwhile rose higher and higher, with a more thrilling and penetrating harmony; and Fursey, bewildered with joy, supposing that the music was for his delectation, said to the guardian spirit: "My soul is enraptured in listening to these heavenly sounds." "It is a delight," replied the angel, "of which we are oftentimes deprived while engaged in the service of men. And yet, after all our labour, the Evil One destroys our work by corrupting the human heart. In this realm of peace and purity," he added, "no judgment is pronounced except against the wickedness of mankind." Fursey's soul was completely absorbed in the transports and festivities of heaven.

And now, from the invisible paradise, came forth Meldan and Beoan, clothed in glory like the angels; and, drawing near to Fursey, they directed him to return to the earth and resume his mortal life. In speechless tribulation this order was received, and while the angels were engaged in restoring their sorrow-stricken charge, the saints said to him. "Why are you afraid? Your earthly course will seem no more than a single day's journey. Go forth and announce to mankind that the day of justice draws nigh." Fursey then inquired of them whether the dissolution of the world was at hand. They replied that the time had not yet come, though it was not far off; that famine and pestilence would first afflict mankind; and that a sign should be seen in the sun.

Beoan continued for a long time speaking to Fursey, showing how the anger of God was hanging over the people, threatening especially their princes and teachers. In grave discourse, worthy of God and of heaven, he imparted salutary counsels and instruction, which he charged Fursey to transmit to Ireland. "Depart now," he said in conclusion, "and tell the princes of the land that they must renounce iniquity, do penance, and work out their salvation. Declare to the rulers of the Church that God is a jealous God when the world is preferred before Him, and that to neglect the care of souls is to serve the world."

Then the multitude of the blessed who had been with Fursey vanished, and he remained alone with his three angels. Immediately they began their earthward journey, and soon approached the fiery furnace. As on the first occasion, the angel walked in advance, opening a passage and driving back the flames on the right hand and the left. But behold! from the midst of the flames a human form, hurled by the demons, struck against the saint's shoulder, and the reprobate's cheek touched the living man's jaw. Fursey felt his shoulder and cheek burn, and he understood that this was the person who on his deathbed bequeathed to him a garment. The angel seized the lost one and cast him back into the fire. But the malign spirit cried "Why do you reject what you once accepted? You had a share in this one's goods; take now your portion of his punishment." The angel replied, that it was not from avarice that Fursey had accepted the gift, but for the good of the man's soul. The fire approached no nearer. However, the angel said: "The fire you kindled has burned you; if you had not accepted the present of the man who died in his sins, you would not have felt in your body the fire of his chastisement." And then the heavenly guardian exhorted him in his turn to preach repentance to mankind.

Fursey now found himself near to the earth, and directly over his own dwelling; yet he recognised neither the house nor the crowd of mourners, nor even his own body lying before him. And when the angel commanded him to assume again his mortal vesture, he feared to approach, not knowing in the least what corpse that was. "Shake off this fear," said the angel, "even in this earthly tenement you can keep yourself from infirmity and evil. You have triumphed, even now, over the assaults of the Wicked One; he shall never prevail against you." Casting his eyes on the inanimate form, he saw the breast opening as if to receive his soul. Bidding him farewell, the angel said: "Pour spring water over your limbs, and you will feel no pain, except in the place where the fire touched you. Devote yourself to good works all the days of your life. We shall follow your steps without ceasing, and in the end receive you with joy into our company in heaven."

Awakening as if from the deep repose of death, Fursey arose, and looking around, saw a crowd of his relations and neighbours, and the people of the church, standing in the place. Then he sighed, thinking of the magnitude of human folly. And considering how perilous and difficult a passage death is, and how divine the reward of those who reach the abode of the blessed, he related in order all the things he had witnessed. He asked to have fresh water from the fountain poured over him, and this being done, the mark became visible of the burn which the damned one inflicted on him. Strange that the body should bear the mark of the pain which the soul alone had suffered![1]

[1] This version of St Fursey's vision is nearly altogether translated from M. L. Tachet de Barneval's *Histoire Légendaire de l'Irlande.* The

Obedient to the instructions he had received in his marvellous vision, Fursey lost no time in retracing his steps to Lough Corrib, and preparing for the mission he now must undertake. His journey to South Munster had not been fruitless—a warm welcome had been given to him by his kinsfolk; and on his departure from the principality, he had the consolation of being joined by his brothers Foillan and Ultan, who resolved to dedicate their life to the service of God under monastic discipline. Leaving these young men in the care of the monks, and resigning the government of Rathmat into competent hands, the abbot bade adieu to the solitudes he loved, and set forth to preach to princes and prelates, to gentle and simple alike,—exhorting all to do penance, save themselves from the evils to come, and aspire after the blessedness of which he himself had lately had so astonishing a revelation. Eloquence, prompted by the awful experiences of a soul assailed by satanic wrath and wile, and inspired by the ineffable joys prepared for the victors over sin and sorrow, could not fail in power to exhort, entreat, arouse, and win to God. During a year he preached assiduously, spending himself in labours for the salvation of the people, and reaping a rich harvest wherever he sowed the good seed.

On the anniversary of the memorable day when the terrors that encounter the disembodied soul and the glory that awaits the just had been disclosed to him, he fell again into a trance, and, save for a feeble fluttering of the heart, he seemed to die. That night the angel of the Lord appeared to him, instructed him minutely in the manner of announcing the doctrine of salvation, and informed him that his labours in Ireland should be continued for twelve years. Strengthened and consoled by converse with God's messenger, Fursey was able to receive the divine command, and to face the difficulties, the toils, and the long-enduring course of this onerous apostolate. Traversing a great part of the country, he carried on his ministry with the zeal of an apostle and the self-oblation of a saint,—the multitude hanging on his words, and miracles confirming the doctrine which he taught. Trials,

accomplished author of that work has, in the chapter devoted to our saint, drawn his material from the earliest sources. For this reason, it appears to me that his presentment of the legend is at once more interesting and more genuine than later and "improved" renderings.

however, were not wanting. Envy stirred up hostility in certain quarters, seeking to frustrate the efficacy of his mission; while, on the other hand, the pressure of the crowd, insatiable in their desire to hear his exhortations, and urgent for his help and counsel, became so excessive as to be well-nigh unendurable. When, therefore, the appointed term of his missionary labours in Ireland had been accomplished, he was glad to be released from the cares and distractions of the public ministry, and sought refuge once more in solitude.

Taking with him his brothers and some other companions, he retired to a little island lying off the coast, founded a religious settlement within its bounds, and, protected from the inroads of the greater world by the stormy defence of winds and waves, enjoyed for a happy interval the meditative calm from which he had been too long estranged.

After some time, however, the call of God was again heard summoning him away, and bidding him carry the light of the gospel to populations sitting in the darkness of infidelity, or lapsed from the practice of the faith which their fathers had received. Setting his sails towards Britain with a detachment of disciples, including his ever-faithful and pious brothers, he touched at the isles that lay in his course, sowing the good seed as he went. Having reached the mainland, these missionary exiles proceeded still in the same manner, working, that is to say preaching, their way from post to post, receiving a welcome wherever they turned, and leaving behind them a salutary influence and a grateful remembrance. At length they reached the kingdom of East Anglia, on the farther coast of Britain [1]

We are not told whether the Irish monks were invited to evangelise East Anglia, or whether their steps were directed thitherward by a secret inspiration. Probably they were pressed to come; for Sigebert II., surnamed the Learned, who then ruled that territory, was exceedingly zealous for the welfare of his subjects, and had already done much for the promotion of Christianity and civilisation throughout his dominions. Some time before, he had requested that a man of learning and sanctity should be sent to him from the famous monastery flourishing at Canterbury, to aid him in carrying out plans for the education of the people. Felix, the Burgundian, a man of

[1] St. Fursey arrived in England some time between 633 and 639.

note and capacity, was despatched on this mission. Teachers were procured, a school was opened, and Felix, having been appointed bishop, fixed his see at Dunwich. To carry on the work so dear to king and prelate, and to ensure that the population at large should be instructed in the truths of salvation, and trained in the practices of Christian life, a colony of missionary monks was indispensable. None knew better than Sigebert how qualified for the task were the Irish religious of this vocation; for, while an exile from his native land in his earlier years, he was himself converted and baptized in Gaul by St. Columbanus, and witnessed the apostolic zeal and marvellous success of that great missioner and his companions. He saw how welcome to princes anxious for the improvement of their subjects were a company of those saintly pioneers fresh from the Western Isle.[1] In fact, his great desire on succeeding to the throne was to see inaugurated in his own dominions the missionary work so successfully carried on in foreign countries. At anyrate, whatever the manner of their coming may have been, there is no doubt of the welcome the

[1] Dr. Wattenbach, an eminent historical antiquary, in a tract on the Irish Monasteries in Germany, translated by Dean Reeves, and published in the *Ulster Journal of Archæology*, describes the striking appearance of the Irish monks as they presented themselves in larger or smaller companies to evangelise the nations. "Their whole outfit," says this author, "consisted of a *cambutta*, or pilgrim's staff, a leathern water-bottle, a wallet, and (what was to them the greatest treasure) a case containing some relics. In this guise they appeared before the people, addressing themselves to them everywhere with the whole power of their native eloquence." In another passage he observes that these poor pilgrims, who always settled in cities or large towns, were in general revered and liked by the citizens, and were on the same friendly terms with them that the mendicant friars afterwards were "They first supplied the defect in the organisation of Christian society which arose with the development of cities, for, until their time, monasteries had been founded only in the solitude of the country, excepting such as were attached to episcopal seats." The French historian, Augustin Thierry, bears testimony to the popularity of the Irish missioners, pilgrims, and scholars who resorted to the Continent, and who "always gained the hearts of those whom they visited by the extreme ease with which they conformed to their customs and way of life" The monks asked nothing from prince or potentate but a plot of ground on which to form their encampment of huts. But the great delighted to honour the pious settlers, and oftentimes considerable grants were bestowed on them. The whole country of Glarus was given to St. Fridolin, Mount St. Victor was made a present to the monastery of St. Gall by Charles le Gros, and more than one island in the Rhine belonged to Irish [illegible].

abbot and his disciples received in East Anglia. Every facility was given them in carrying on their mission, and forthwith, to quote Venerable Bede, "Fursey began to perform his usual employment of preaching the gospel, and, by the example of his virtues and the efficacy of his discourse, converted many unbelievers to Christ, and confirmed in His faith and love those that already believed." Furthermore, in order that a permanent settlement might be made and the good work secured, the king gave a plot of ground to the monks."

At this juncture the saint's angelic friends appeared to him as of old, admonishing him "diligently to proceed in the work he had undertaken, and indefatigably to continue his usual watching and prayers." Being confirmed by this vision, continues the historian, "he applied himself with all speed to build a monastery on the ground given him by King Sigebert, and to establish regular discipline therein."

The plot of ground referred to, though moderate in extent, was yet amply sufficient for the requirements of a religious settlement constructed in the manner of the Irish. But its position and its associations rendered it a gift worthy of the generous prince who bestowed it on the strangers. Situated not far from the sea at the juncture of two rivers, backed by natural woods, and commanding a wide view over land and water, the field, some five acres in extent, was enclosed on three sides by a massive wall, flanked with solid circular towers apt for watch and ward, while on the fourth the flowing stream formed a scarcely less effective bulwark. In a word, St. Fursey found himself in possession of what was once the Roman station and camp of Garianonum, a fortress built in the reign of the Emperor Claudius by the Pro-Prætor Publius Ostiorius Scapula when he conquered the people inhabiting the country, afterwards subdivided into the counties of Suffolk, Norfolk, Cambridgeshire, and Huntingdonshire.[1] The area on which the monks now raised their huts had been the quarters of a body of cavalry called the Stablesden Horse, whose command-

[1] Castles and towers ranged along the walls constructed by the Romans as a defence against the unsubdued tribes that surrounded their colonies in Britain. These fortresses were constantly garrisoned by armed men. The stations were so near to each other, that if a beacon was lighted on any one of the bulwarks the warriors who garrisoned the next station were able to see and to repeat the signal almost at the same instant, and the next onwards did the same, by which token they announced that some

ing officer was styled Ganionnensis. When the Imperial Legions vanished from the scene, the lofty walls indeed remained, but the name of the fortress was forgotten. Ganianonum of the Romans became Cnobbersburgh of the Saxons, and by this designation, derived from a neighbouring village, St. Fursey's monastic establishment was known. From his headquarters in the Roman castrum he also in his turn directed operations—levying war against the powers of evil, and pushing on the conquests of Christianity and civilisation throughout the East Anglian territory.[1]

Bede speaks of Cnobbersburgh as a noble monastery, and says that after Sigebert's death his successor and the nobility of the province embellished it with more stately buildings and donations. Many of the young men of the country joined the monks; and the community was increased, no doubt, from time to time, by accessions from Ireland

Offshoots from the central station were established in different parts of the country; and among the foundations made at this time by St. Fursey were examples of the so-called double monasteries—institutions which, originating in Ireland, and subsequently introduced into other countries, have left some interesting traces in history In these monasteries communities of men and women dwelt within the same enclosure, though, of course, in separate domiciles. In some instances

danger was impending. The coast was protected with equal care against any invading enemy; and the ancient maritime stations, Ganianonum and Portus Rhutupis, may be instanced as fine specimens of Roman skill and industry.—*History of the Anglo-Saxons*, ch. i.

[1] After the Norman Conquest the place fell into the hands first of Robert de Burgh, and secondly of Gilbert de Wischam, and received the name of Burgh Castle, by which it is known at the present day. Henry III. gave it to the priory of Bromholm in Norfolk, where it remained until the dissolution. Some years ago the castle was purchased by Sir J. P. Boileau, Bart, with the design of preserving a monument which recalls so powerfully the later days of Roman dominion in England. A plan of the fortress and a distant view of Burgh Castle, taken in 1775, may be seen in Grose's *Antiquities of England*, vol. v. A nearer view, showing the Roman masonry and one of the towers tufted with elder bushes, is given in the *History of the Anglo-Saxons* already quoted. No trace of St Fursey's monastery is discoverable within the fort: but somewhat to the north, remains of an ecclesiastical group of buildings still exist. Probably the Irish monks after some time transferred their nomadic settlement to this position *extra muros*. In an abbey church in Norfolk, not far from this place, was a chapel dedicated to St. Fursey.

the abbot was the ruling power, in others the abbess held the jurisdiction. Besides religious women and priests ordained to perform sacerdotal functions, there were brethren charged with the duty of attending to external affairs,—cultivating the farms, managing the granges, and so forth.[1]

During this period of his life, St. Fursey appears to have been favoured with visions of a similar nature to those which have been already narrated. Bede expressly mentions that this heavenly intercourse was enjoyed by the saint while dwelling in the fortress-monastery of Cnobbersburgh, and that after these sublime revelations he always took care, as he had done before, to persuade all men to the practice of virtue, as well by his example as by preaching. "But as for the matter of his visions, he would only relate them to those who, from holy zeal and desire of reformation, wished to learn the same. An ancient brother of our monastery is still living," continues the venerable historian, with a precious realistic touch, "who is wont to declare that a very sincere and religious man told that he had seen Fursey himself in the province of the East Angles, and heard those visions from his mouth; adding, that though it was in most sharp winter weather and a hard frost, and the

[1] An interesting account of certain monasteries of this kind established in England in the twelfth century may be read in a volume, now unfortunately very scarce, entitled *Lives of the English Saints*, and published in London forty years ago. In the life of St. Gilbert of Sempringham, written, it is well known, by Father Dalgairns before he entered the Catholic Church, we are told that the saint, having failed in founding a community of monks at Sempringham turned his thoughts to the young maidens of the parish, and built a cloister for seven virgins adjoining the church. He then established a community of lay brethren to dig, plough, and labour for the support of the nuns, turning every farmhouse on his estate into something like a monastery, where, throughout all the appurtenances of cow-houses, stables, and barns, all should be subject to religious discipline. These brethren were clothed almost like Cistercian monks, were taught to read, and had a chapter of their own. In the granges around the nunnery the lay brethren were distributed; and there might be seen the blacksmith at his forge, the carter with his horses, etc. Gilbert joined to his nunneries an Order of canons for the spiritual direction of the nuns. France possessed some monasteries of this kind, the most celebrated being the great abbey of Fontefraud, where the abbess held jurisdiction over the monks as well as the nuns Originally the establishment was humble enough, and the description of it reminds one of the far more ancient double monasteries of the Irish, consisting of a collection of rude huts, with two separate oratories,—one for the brethren and the other for the sisters.

man was sitting in a thin garment when he related it, yet he sweated as if it had been in the greatest heat of summer, either through excessive fear or spiritual consolation."

Hardly any of his supernatural experiences would have seemed stranger to the saintly seer than a revelation, had he received such, of the keen interest that should be exhibited in his life and in his dreams by studious antiquaries walking this earth more than one thousand years after his departure from terrestrial scenes. Nor indeed is this fact much less surprising to the reader when for the first time he becomes aware of the association that links St. Fursey's name so intimately with the poetry and devotion of succeeding ages. "The stranger on the dank, marshy shores of the oozy Yare," says a modern historian, "contemplating the lichen-encrusted walls of the Roman castrementation . . . scarcely supposes that those grey walls once enclosed the cell of an obscure anchorite destined—so strangely is the chain of causation involved—to exercise a mighty influence equally upon the dogma and genius of Roman Christendom." The Milesian-Scot Fursæus "there became enwrapped in the trances which disclosed to him the secrets of the world beyond the grave." He "kindled the spark which, transmitted to the inharmonious Dante of a barbarous age, occasioned the first of the metrical compositions from which the *Divina Commedia* arose."[1]

Modern research has not discovered the name or local habitation of the "inharmonious Dante" who reduced to writing the wondrous narrative first orally communicated by the saint himself. But the date of the transcription must be somewhere in the third quarter of the seventh century, not many years after the death of St. Fursey; and the writer we may fairly assume to have been one of his Anglo-Saxon disciples. When the learned author above quoted speaks of the mighty influence of the anchorite of Burgh Castle on the dogma of Roman Christendom, he means, no doubt, to refer to the singular impetus given to the devotion to the souls in purgatory by the teaching of the Milesian monk, and by the vivid way in which he brought before his auditory the reality of the judgment which awaits the disembodied spirit in the other world. Sir Francis Palgrave attributes to St. Fursey and his followers, and to the Irish monks generally, the merit

[1] Palgrave, *History of Normandy and England*, vol. i. p. 163.

of popularising the devotion to the faithful departed, and gives the credit of its systematic extension to the brethren of the monastery of St. Gall and its offshoot at Richenau. What he says precisely is this :—

"Fursæus was followed by the Anglo-Saxon Drithelm, similarly gifted, similarly raised up, as it was supposed, to convince the faithful that sin is a fearful reality. Sermon and homily repeated these legends; and the curious archæologist still recovers from the walls of the East Anglian churches the fading traces of the grotesque designs by which the same lessons were imparted. The well-known festival for the dead, the Feast of All Souls, was not formally instituted till the eleventh century; but the dreams of the night, presented to the Celtic and Saxon recluses, had long before instigated the members of various monastic bodies to agree upon periodical commemorations, enabling them to join in common prayer for the repose of the deceased, under chastisement, but not lost,—and the earliest community which practised this work of faith and charity were the monks assembled in the venerable sanctuary founded by the countryman of Fursæus the Scot, St. Columbanus, the monastery of St. Gall. The neighbouring house of Richenau followed this influential example. In the same year, during which Charlemagne received the imperial crown, St. Gall and Richenau united themselves for this pious observance into one sodality"[1]

Picturesque legends connected with this period illustrate St. Fursey's possession of that faith which can remove mountains, and his well-founded trust in the miraculous aid promised to the successors of the apostles in their work for the conversion of nations. One of these legends relates how, on a certain occasion when famine prevailed in the country, and some of the monks showed signs of apprehension lest they might be left without the necessaries of life, the abbot reprehended them for their want of confidence in God's supporting providence, and enforced with striking effect the lesson he had

[1] *History of Normandy and England*, vol. i. pp. 164, 165 A few pages earlier the author thus speaks of Richenau "Just where the Rhine rushes away with youthful vigour through the Lake of Constance, is the island of Richenau, the *rich meadows* . . . . The monastery, in the Carlovingian era, was one of the chief colleges of the region, imparting religion and instruction, light and knowledge, to all the nations and tribes around."

often given them on the text, that those who for the love of God embrace a state of poverty shall never be deserted in the hour of need. Taking with him his countryman, St. Lactain, he went into a field belonging to the monastery, and, though the sowing time had long gone by, began to dig the ground, and cast seed into the furrows. Lookers-on were puzzled to guess what this unseasonable diligence might mean; but far more were they astonished when, three days later, the brother-saints betook themselves to the field once more, and, sickle in hand, began reaping the full-eared harvest that had ripened in the interval.

According to another legend, when the monastery at Cnobbersburgh had been erected and the church furnished with the first requisites for religious worship, there still was wanting one desideratum, namely a bell. An Irish abbot without a bell was an unheard-of thing; and the wonder is that among the brethren were none of the skilled artificers usually found in such communities, whose business it was to design and fashion the sacred vessels required at the altar the utensils needed in the kitchen and refectory, and the indispensable bells. One day, however, as the corpse of a widow's son was carried into the church, and the requiem service was proceeding, a stranger—a heaven-sent envoy—suddenly appeared, and in the presence of the assembled mourners presented a bell to St. Fursey. At the first sound the whole scene changed. The young man came to life, and the funeral train, transformed into a triumphal procession, filed off by the ramparts, giving glory to God. The bell that begun its mission thus happily rang on for ages with a blessing in its voice, and it was believed that the country over which it was audible suffered no injury from lightning or storms.[1]

[1] Bells, first used in Christian churches about the beginning of the fifth century, were introduced into Ireland by St. Patrick, who employed native artificers, skilled in metal-work, to make them. Wherever he preached and made a religious settlement, he left a bell. It is particularly mentioned that he carried with him across the Shannon, to leave in new places, a goodly supply of patens, chalices, altar books of the law, books of the gospel, and *fifty bells*. The bells which belonged to the early Irish saints, often the work of their own hands, were preserved with religious veneration, either in the monasteries they founded or elsewhere, under the care of hereditary keep[illegible] They w[illegible] from

( )

Having laboured incessantly for twelve years in East Anglia, St. Fursey felt the old longing after a solitary life return with irresistible force. He became desirous, says Bede, "to rid himself of all business of this world, and even of the monastery itself, and forthwith left the same and the care of souls to his brother Foillan and the priests Gobban and Dieull, and, being himself free from all that was worldly, resolved to end his life as a hermit. Some time earlier in our history, Ultan left the monastery in order to lead a more retired life in a lonesome part of the woods. Thither his brother now followed him, and there he dwelt for a year, devoting his mind to heavenly contemplation, and procuring by the labour of his hands such things as were necessary for the support of existence.

But a longer term of the coveted solitude was not vouchsafed him. About this time an inroad of the pagan Mercians, under King Peuda, interrupted the peace of East Anglia, laid waste the country, and led, it is supposed, to the temporary dispersion of the Cnobbersburgh monks.[1] Whether St. Fursey's hermitage was in danger of discovery and destruction by the enemies of the Christian name does not appear, but the apparition of a friendly stranger on the scene proved, as it turned out, quite as inimical to the recluse's dream of lifelong seclusion. Count Vincent Hannonia, returning to France from Ireland, whither he had gone on an embassy from King

four inches to fourteen inches in height, made of plates of hammered iron fastened with rivets, and brazed or bronzed. In after times they were enclosed in costly, elaborately-wrought shrines, and in some parts of the country it was customary, when a particularly solemn oath was administered to swear persons on these consecrated relics. Several saints' bells, together with their curious and beautiful cases, are preserved in the museum of the Irish Academy and in other antiquarian collections. St. Gall's bell is still shown in the monastery he founded on the banks of the Steinach.

[1] Sigebert, desiring to end his days in religious seclusion, had some time before left his kingdom under the care of his kinsman Egric and retired to one of the monasteries he had founded. Some are of opinion that Cnobbersburgh was the place where he received the tonsure, others maintain that he chose Bury St. Edmunds; however, the probability is that neither of these abbeys, but a third house, was his retreat. On the invasion of the Mercians, his subjects carried him by force into the battle-field, trusting that his presence would animate the Christian soldiers to deeds of valour. Mindful of his religious profession, the king would carry nothing in his hand but a wand. The pagan invaders prevailed, Sigebert and Egric were slain, and the East Anglian army was dispersed.

Dagobert, travelled out of the direct route to visit St Fursey, whose eminence as a missioner and fame as a preacher had no doubt reached his ears while in Ireland. So deeply was Count Vincent impressed by the saint's extraordinary gifts of intellect, eloquence, and grace, that he became extremely anxious to persuade him to pass over into Gaul and undertake a mission to the Franks. Strenuously urging his appeal in behalf of the multitudes sitting in darkness, the zealous nobleman gained his cause. The hermit's missionary ardour was aroused. Renouncing all that he held most dear,—freedom from external engagements, and his hut in the woods,—and choosing some companions to assist him in the work he was about to undertake, he bade adieu to England, and, under the escort of Count Vincent, set sail for a foreign shore.

So loose is the chronology of the seventh century that it is impossible to fix the date of St. Fursey's arrival in France, or ascertain the duration of his mission in that part of the world. We are led to infer from the reference made to Count Vincent's return to the Continent from an embassy to Ireland, on which he had been despatched by Dagobert I, that this monarch was still king regnant when the Irish missioners landed in Normandy. If this were the case, it would establish the date of Fursey's arrival as not later than 638, the year usually assigned for the death of Dagobert, but this would seem too early to synchronise with other events in our saint's history. However this may be, it is certain that his most important work was accomplished during the lifetime of Dagobert's sons, who reigned simultaneously—the one, Clovis II, over Neustria and Burgundy up to 655 or 660, the other, Sigebert II, over Austrasia to 656, as generally stated.

Whether the newly-arrived monks followed any settled plan in the conduct of their mission we are not told; but it would appear that in the first instance they proceeded overland to the territory of Haymon, Duke of Ponthieu, in the maritime parts of Picardy. On approaching the village of Mazerolles, where the duke had a residence, the sounds of lamentation struck their ears, and they learned on inquiry that the nobleman's only son lay dead at the castle. Touched with compassion, Fursey entered the house of mourning, and, as we read in an ancient record, he prayed over the [illegible] Lord to show mercy to the afflicted parents. The prayer of faith prevailed, and the boy was restored to life. Words could not describe the joy of the family and the amazement of the people. The multitude entreated the servant of God to take up his abode with them. The duke presented gifts of gold and silver, and offered to surrender his estate at Mazerolles to the abbot and his monks. But Fursey, though grateful for the princely presents and generous proposals, declined to accept them; and as he believed that his mission at that time lay elsewhere, he would not make a settlement in the place. However, he willingly engaged to remember Duke Haymon in his prayers, and to visit him at some future time if Providence should permit; or, if this might not be, and he should be called out of the world without revisiting his friend, he promised to signify to him his departure to the other world. "When three lights shall be placed before you," said the holy man, "take it as a sign that I am no longer a sojourner on the earth." After a short stay, during which he preached the word of God to a willing audience, he blessed the ruler, the people, and the land, and then, continuing his journey, he spread the light of the gospel and worked miracles wherever he went.

In course of time Fursey and his little band approached the borders of the kingdom of Austrasia, where, as already said, Sigebert, the son of Dagobert, occupied the throne. This monarch, one of the most interesting of the Frankish princes, cannot have been more than a stripling then, and yet he was already confessor as well as king. His father, who perhaps at no time made himself remarkable by the practice of domestic and Christian virtues, refused at first to allow the boy to be baptized, but at length, by the advice of St Ouen and St. Eligius, who were then laymen holding office at his Court, he recalled St. Amandus, the great apostle of Belgic Gaul, whom he had banished for reproving his vices, and requested the holy man to baptize the child and regard him as his spiritual son. The ceremony took place at Orleans, Charibert, prince of a territory on the farther side of the Loire, and a generous protector of the exiled apostle, standing sponsor at the font. Sigebert's education was intrusted to another eminent servant of God, Pepin of Landen, the founder of the family of Charlemagne and the head of a race of saints. Dagobert built high hopes on this child, whom, at the age of three years, he invested with the kingdom of Austrasia or Eastern France. On the death of Dagobert, the prince being still a minor, Pepin conducted the affairs of Government as mayor of the palace, while the spiritual interests of a considerable part of the kingdom were attended to by St. Amandus, whom Sigebert held in the highest veneration, and obliged to accept the bishopric of Maestrich. When grown to man's estate, Sigebert gave ample proof of capacity to defend his rights and hold his own in warlike contests But the arts of peace were his delight. "His munificence in founding churches and monasteries, his justice in ruling, and the spotless virtues of his private life, made him to be regarded as a model of a saintly king."[1]

As soon as Sigebert learned that the illustrious missioner, Abbot Fursey, was at no great distance from his territory, he set out to meet him, accompanied by a splendid retinue. Dismounting from his horse, he knelt to receive the saint's blessing; and then, with every mark of honour, conducted him to Court, and offered him magnificent presents. On this occasion also the costly gifts were refused. But the king, understanding that a small plot of ground, such as would answer for a monastic settlement, would be accepted, called his nobles into council, and with their assistance made choice of a fine site, with abundance of wood and water, and placed it at the disposition of the pious strangers. The simple constructions were then commenced,—the nobles and the people of every degree vieing with one another in their generous efforts to second the good works the monks had undertaken.

"All the inhabitants, according to their means and opportunities, presented offerings to the servants of God for their immediate and future support. A church was also constructed in a high style of art for the period, both externally and internally. To St. Fursey some gave village property, others offered woodlands, others again provided him with fish-abounding rivers; while from other donors he received flocks and herds, comprising different kinds of animals. Some grant him silk ornaments and materials, woven in various designs and wrought with gems and gold, others tender gold and silver vessels suitable for various offices of the Church; while some again assign their men and women-serfs as heritages of the monastery, others resign themselves to the service of God, with

[1] Rev. S. Baring-Gould, Festival of St. Sigebert. February 1.

all their possessions, having likewise assumed the religious habit."[1]

During his mission in Austrasia, St. Fursey became acquainted with one of the most remarkable and saintly personages of the time, Gertrude, daughter of Pepin of Landen, and Abbess of Nivelles. After the death of Pepin (variously stated as having occurred between 640 and 649), his widow, St Itta, founded the monastery just named, and retired to it with her daughter, whom, though young in years, she soon appointed abbess. Gertrude held large territorial possessions in her own right, and, being closely connected with magnates of the day, exercised a wide personal influence. Simple and mortified in her manner of life, as became a religious, she was deeply versed in the Sacred Scriptures, munificent in her charities, and great in all her undertakings. Under her rule, Nivelles was constituted as a double monastery, with an Order of canons to perform priestly functions, instruct the nuns in spiritual matters, and manage the temporal affairs of the establishment. Asylums for widows and orphans, and houses for the reception of pilgrims and travellers, were supported by the monastery and intrusted to the discipline of the canons and canonesses of the institute.[2] In a word, the monastery of Nivelles became the centre of an immense field of religious work, extending throughout Brabant and the neighbouring countries; and the saintly abbess exercised over the mother-house and its dependencies a regal sway, directed by singular wisdom and prudence. It is easy to imagine the veneration in which St. Gertrude held the Irish abbot and his band of missioners,—so rigidly austere in their life, so magnificent in their self-devotion, so marvellously successful in spreading the light of faith. She consulted

[1] Rev J. O'Hanlon, *Lives of the Irish Saints*, vol. i.

[2] "From the saint having established large hospices for the reception of pilgrims and travellers, whom she entertained with great liberality, arose the custom of travellers drinking a stirrup-cup in her honour before starting on their journey. She became the patroness of travellers. Then, by a curious superstition, she was supposed to harbour souls on their way to Paradise. It was said that this was a three days' journey. The first night they lodged with St. Gertrude, the second with St Gabriel, the third was in Paradise. She therefore became the patroness and protector of departed souls."—Rev. S. Baring Gould, Festival of St. Gertrude, March 17.

St. Fursey in weighty matters, and aided him in the work of his apostolate.[1]

Time passed on, and Fursey returned to Western France, where Clovis II., the brother of St. Sigebert, reigned as King of Neustria. Like Sigebert, he was a minor when he ascended the throne; but, unlike that pious prince, he left behind him no particular reputation for ability or sanctity. He was the first of the Rois Fainéants or sinecure kings of France. However, he did not neglect to advance the spiritual interests of his subjects; and his wife, Bathilde, was a saint. His mayor of the palace was Erchinoald, a capable and energetic ruler, and eventually one of Fursey's most powerful and devoted friends. Erchinoald's residence was at Peronne, and he invited the abbot to visit him at his castle and baptize his infant son. This request was complied with, and during his stay the man of God preached to the people and healed their bodies and souls. Peronne appears to have had a singular attraction for him, and he took particular delight in visiting a little chapel dedicated to SS. Peter and Paul, situated near the castle, on an eminence called the Mont de Cignes. Here he passed whole days in prayer, whole nights in vigil; and here he enshrined the relics of his venerated friends St. Bœan and St. Meldan,[2] together with those of St. Patrick and other

[1] After the death of St. Fursey the abbess sent to England to invite his brothers, St Foillan and St. Ultan, to come over and instruct her community in sacred psalmody. "For," says Frederick Ozanam, "the Irish excelled in the ecclesiastical chant, and it was among them that the Frankish princesses sought masters to teach the nuns of their monasteries to sing in a becoming manner the praises of God." The invitation was accepted. Foillan remained at Nivelles, but Ultan after some time was appointed Abbot of Fosses, a monastery which St. Gertrude had built and endowed for Irish monks. When the abbess felt that her last hour was approaching, she sent one of the canons of her monastery to Fosses to ask St. Ultan when she must die. "Then," to quote the Rev. S. Baring-Gould, "the saint replied to the messenger, 'To-morrow, during the celebration of the Holy Mass, Gertrude, the spouse of Jesus Christ, will depart this life, to enjoy that which is eternal. Tell her not to fear, for St. Patrick, accompanied by blessed angels, will receive her soul into glory.' And it was so, that after she had received extreme unction, and while the priest was reciting the prayers before the preface in the Holy Sacrifice, on the morrow, the second Sunday in Lent, she breathed forth her pure soul." Fosses long maintained its character as an Irish monastery, and was much resorted to by pilgrims from Erin.

[2] Of St. Bœan, whose appearance in an earlier part of our narrative cannot have been forgotten, nothing further is known about what Dr.

saints, which he had carried with him from his native land. He is said to have expressed a wish to repose in death in the same hallowed spot, and even to have predicted that such should be the case.

Meanwhile Clovis, hearing that Fursey wished to form a monastic settlement in Neustria, and being himself anxious that his subjects should enjoy the advantage of having such a centre of civilisation established in the land, issued a command to the effect that whatever place in his dominions might be selected should at once be granted to the missionary monks. Thereupon Fursey, taking as his companions three prudent counsellors, undertook a journey with the object of selecting a plot of ground. Their choice did credit to their taste and sagacity. It was a noble site, on an eminence in the midst of a fertile, well-wooded country between Paris and Meaux, watered by the river Marne, and enjoying a healthy climate. Here then the pious exiles pitched their camp, and in so doing laid the foundations of the celebrated abbey of Lagny-sur-Marne. From this post of vantage they conducted their missions in the neighbouring territory, and the monastery itself, being easy of access, was resorted to by the surrounding population, eager to hear the preachers of God's word, and curious to see the abbot—"the mysterious stranger who had tasted death."[1] Another attraction to the pious crowd was a fountain of pure water near the monastery, said to have sprung up when Fursey struck his staff into the dry soil, and connected, no doubt, in the popular mind with the angel's admonition concerning the use of spring water to heal the hurt inflicted on the saint by the son of perdition. A copious and ceaseless stream filled the reservoir, served the wants of the monastery, and supplied the people who dwelt around.

Lanigan records, namely, that he was a native of Connaught, and no less renowned than his countryman and contemporary, St Meldan. Concerning the latter there is not much to add to what has already been said. Owing probably to his having been the spiritual father of St. Fursey, he continued to be held in particular honour at Peronne, taking rank as one of the patrons of the city. Many churches are dedicated under his invocation, and his festival is kept on the 7th of February.

[1] See Ozanam, *Études Germaniques*, chapter on the preaching of the Irish. This incident reminds one of what happened nearly seven hundred years later, when the women of Verona stood at their doors to see Dante pass—the man who had been in hell!

Moreover, being endowed with certain curative properties, the Well of Lagny acquired a widespread reputation, and was resorted to by pilgrims from distant parts.

Soon the abbot's work of love and zeal extended over a wider field than that included in the immediate neighbourhood of Lagny. Many churches in that part of France owed their foundation to him. One of these was dedicated to our Divine Saviour, another to the Prince of the Apostles, and a third was, in after times, dedicated in his own name. Audibert, Bishop of Paris, invited him to establish missions in his diocese and act as his assistant, and when the abbot had built a church at Compans, that prelate came in person to consecrate the new edifice. St. Landry, his successor in the see, showed in an equally marked way the singular esteem he entertained for the Abbot of Lagny. Some years later, when St. Fursey had gone to God, St. Bathilde, widow of Clovis and regent of the kingdom, rebuilt the convent of Chelles, near Lagny, and, through reverence for the deceased abbot, instituted there a double monastery, after the Celtic manner, for monks and nuns.[1]

In modern times it might seem an ordinary achievement thus to build churches and found religious houses. Not so, however, in the seventh century of the Christian era. To build a church in those days meant literally to plant the standard of Christ in a new territory; and to found a monastic settlement was to enlarge the frontiers of civilisation. The abbeys of the seventh century, to quote a high authority, with their populations of three, four, or five hundred monks, were so many fortresses, forming a barrier against the inroads of paganism. They were also securely-planted colonies, stationed in the midst of the fluctuating rural population. These religious societies were not subject to extinction by death, like the bishops, nor could they abdicate their office. Neither were they capable of being led away in the retinue of kings. Consequently, they were in a better position to oppose fraud and violence. Subject to obedience, leading chaste and laborious lives, these pious settlers astonished the barbarians, whom they attracted and retained by the benefits they conferred. In fact, they accomplished the first step towards civilisation, fixing in a permanent abode the nomadic tribes.

[1] Cardinal Moran, *Irish Saints in Great Britain*, ch. xii.

The abbeys were centres of science, sacred and secular, and at the same time schools of industry and agriculture. In their workshops all the arts of the antique world were taught, and from their cells went forth the men who opened up a way through the impenetrable forest with the indomitable perseverance of the ancient Romans.[1]

Considering the constant intercourse kept up at that period between Ireland and the Continent, it is not surprising that the fame of Lagny and tidings of the abbot's missionary enterprises spread through the Western Isle. Many of Fursey's countrymen, on their way to Rome or Jerusalem, and some who set out purposely to visit in foreign lands the religious settlements founded by the monks of their nation, directed their steps to the banks of the Marne, to claim the hospitality never denied by Irish cenobites, congratulate the abbot on the conquests won for Christ, and draw edification from the spectacle of the fruitful labours of the self-exiled saints.[2] Over and above the joy of welcoming the pilgrims of Erin to his home in Neustria, Fursey had the happiness of receiving from Ireland aspirants to the monastic and missionary vocation desiring to take part in his hallowed labours. Among others came Æmelian, who had been a disciple of his own in former days, accompanied by a band of younger men ready to adopt the austere but glorious life of the monks of Lagny. This accession of strength from the Sacred Isle was particularly welcome to Fursey, who, moreover, recognised in Æmelian a man after his own heart,—one to whom the

[1] Ozanam, *Etudes Germaniques*, vol. ii. ch. iv.

[2] Somewhere about this time, St Faro, Bishop of Meaux, founded a celebrated hospice at the gates of his episcopal city. He had known Columbanus in his youth, and held his memory in the highest veneration. The illustrious missioner's countrymen were made specially welcome at this pilgrim's home; and in *Lives of Irish Saints* particular mention is made of it. We read, for instance, that St. Kilian, the apostle of Franconia, rested there, and that St. Fiacre, honoured as one of the principal patrons of the diocese of Meaux, sojourned within its walls for a considerable time. It is more than probable that many of the Irish visitors to Lagny were received and refreshed at St. Faro's hospice. In France and Germany several institutions of this kind were founded by princes and bishops specially for the Irish pilgrims and travellers who passed through these countries in such numbers One of these, situated in an island of the Rhine near Strasburg, was founded early in the eighth century by an Irish bishop, and enjoyed the patronage of the monarchs of the Carlovingian dynasty.

monastery might safely be intrusted during any temporary absence of the abbot, and one who was destined, in all probability, to be his own successor in its government.

Meanwhile Erchinoald, mayor of the palace, directing the affairs of the kingdom from his castle at Peronne, though rejoicing in the progress of Christianity and civilisation throughout Neustria, was far from being satisfied to see his own place of residence deprived of the advantages which a settlement of missionary monks would confer. He therefore undertook a journey to Lagny, laid the matter before his venerated friend the abbot, and besought the latter to accompany him on his return to Peronne, begin at once the erection of a monastery in the vicinity of the fortress, and transport thither in due course a community from the parent house. Fursey gave a willing consent to this proposal, and soon after laid the foundation of his new settlement at a place situated higher up than Erchinoald's stronghold, and called Mount St. Quintin. As soon as the buildings were ready, a band of monks migrated from Lagny, and a great concourse of the clergy and nobility of France assembled to congratulate with the mayor of the palace, and to assist at the consecration of the monastery. The officiating prelate was the illustrious Bishop of Noyon and Tournay, St. Eligius.

It was a happy event, this meeting of the Abbot of Lagny and the Bishop of Noyon on so auspicious an occasion. They were kindred spirits, and in some ways similarly gifted, similarly blessed. If Fursey had preached to his tens of thousands in the isles and on the Continent, converting by his impassioned eloquence hosts of pagans and a multitude of relapsed Christians; then also had Eligius evangelised the idolaters of Belgium, and overcome, by the suavity of his character and the irresistible persuasiveness of his oratory, the fierce barbarians of Ghent and Courtray. Fursey may have possessed the poetic faculty in larger measure, but the bishop, on the other hand, was an artist of high attainments. In his youth he had distinguished himself so much by the beauty of his designs and his skill as a gold worker, that King Dagobert invited him to his Court and appointed him Master of the Mint. Clovis retained him in the same office until, being ordained for the sacred ministry, he was soon after raised to the episcopal dignity. Even now with the charge of the vast united dioceses on his shoulders, he did not altogether give up the pursuit of his original vocation; only, devoting his rare talent to purely sacred objects, he employed his leisure upon the holy vessels of the altar, the shrines of the saints, and the decorations of the tombs of great servants of God.[1]

In the establishment of the monastery at Peronne, Erchinoald's main object was happily fulfilled; but with his characteristic munificence he continued to give proofs of the esteem in which he held the saintly founder, and the importance he attached to the establishment in his district of a colony of such apostolic men. About this time he undertook the erection of a fine church in connection with the little chapel dedicated to SS. Peter and Paul, in which Fursey had loved to watch and pray on the occasion of his first visit to Peronne.

Years having now been spent in the fruitful labours of the Frankish mission, and secure foundations made in important places, Fursey began to think seriously of returning to East Anglia and visiting his beloved brothers, Foillan and Ultan, from whom he had been now a long time separated. In furtherance of this design he set out, and entering into that part of the country where his apostolic work on the Continent first began, arrived at the village of Mazerolles, the scene of his memorable meeting with Duke Haymon, lord of the soil. Here a heavenly messenger, one of the blessed spirits with whom he had been long familiar, came as of old to reveal to him the will of God: the apostle's mission was accomplished, the labours of his life were ended; before long he should pass away from earthly scenes, and reach, under the angels' escort, the judgment-seat of God. Making, therefore, his preparation with all humility and fervour, he received the Viaticum for his

[1] The account of St. Eligius (in French, St. Eloy) in Butler's *Lives of the Saints* is very interesting, and so also is Mrs. Jameson's sketch of the artist-bishop in her *Sacred and Legendary Art*. The last-named writer, in observing that Eligius cut the dies for the money coined in the reigns of Dagobert and Clovis II., tells us that thirteen pieces are known which bear his name inscribed. Mrs Jameson enumerates several of the pictures in which scenes of his life are portrayed. One of these, a celebrated work of Pelegrino Piola, was about to be removed from Genoa, by command of Napoleon, to Paris; but the Company of Goldsmiths so resolutely opposed the removal of this picture of their patron saint that the emperor all[illegible]

Ui

final journey, and, commending his soul to the great Creator, happily departed.

Haymon was not at Mazerolles when the abbot expired. He was elsewhere at that hour, sitting at table with some guests. In the middle of the repast he beheld Fursey enter the banquet-hall, clothed in sacerdotal vestments and attended by his two deacons. They each held a lighted taper, and advancing to where the duke sat, placed the lights before him and silently withdrew.[1] Haymon, in amazement, turned to the friends around him and asked them whether they had seen the vision. They replied that they had not perceived anything unusual. Then, remembering Fursey's promise to inform him in this way of his dissolution, he related what the saint had said to him many years before, and declared his belief that the man of God had passed away. Immediately rising from table, and followed by his household, he hastened on horseback to Mazerolles, where he found his forebodings only too sadly realised. Abbot Fursey lay dead, and around his mortal remains were assembled the clergy, the monks, and the inhabitants of the village, singing the requiem office and lamenting their loss. Placing a military guard round the body, he joined in the devotions and bewailed his friend.

The report of St. Fursey's death spread with rapidity over the country, and soon reached Peronne. Erchinoald, divining Duke Haymon's design of enshrining the remains of the holy abbot at Mazerolles, instantly placed himself at the head of a royal guard and marched out with a determination to prevent, by force of arms if necessary, any such infringement of his own rights. Having arrived at the river on which the village was situated, he sent messengers to Haymon, setting forth his claims, and informing him that it was the king's pleasure that they should be allowed. The duke, considering that he himself had just as good a right to retain the precious remains in the spot where God had called his servant out of life, declined to comply with the request now made. A sanguinary contest seemed imminent over the body of the man of peace, when fortunately a more humane way of deciding the question was suggested. Finally, it was agreed that two young bulls,

[1] For hundreds of years three candles were kept constantly alight on the altar of the church at Peronne, in memory of this miraculous occurrence.

unused to the yoke, should be attached to the funeral car, and that the cortege of mourners and men-at-arms should follow whatsoever road the animals took of their own accord. The mayor of the palace, Duke Haymon, the military force which attended these magnates, the clergy and the monks, and the pious crowd, fell into a processional line, the saint's coffin was placed on the car, and the untamed oxen were yoked thereto. Greatly to Erchinoald's delight they took the road to Peronne. Over hill and dale the funeral train wound its way, the people coming from the neighbouring districts to testify their veneration for the holy dead, and to have their ailments healed through his intercession. Once a startling interruption took place. Another claimant appeared on the scene. Bercharius, Duke of Laon, escorted by an armed troop, stopped the procession, and demanded that the body should be delivered up to him, urging in support of his claim that he had accompanied Abbot Fursey on his voyage to France, that he had bestowed a great part of his means for the use of the saint's disciples, that he entertained the deepest love and veneration for the departed, and had been much beloved in return. Bercharius after some time was likewise pacified He joined company with the other noblemen, marshalling his soldiers in the rank-and-file of the attendant throng. Finally Peronne was reached. The remains of the abbot were deposited in the porch of the new church, which the mayor of the palace had from the first designed to be the resting-place of the illustrious dead.

Erchinoald meanwhile set all hands at work, and spared no cost to finish the church. At the end of thirty or forty days the edifice was sufficiently advanced to allow the solemn ceremony of consecration and the removal of St. Fursey's remains from the porch to take place. St. Eligius, and St. Aubert, Bishop of Cambray and Arras,[1] came to perform the sacred functions on the day appointed, an immense multitude assembled to witness the imposing ceremonies, the air was

[1] St. Aubert was one of the greatest ornaments of the seventh age and eminent promoters of learning and piety in the Gallican church. He was consecrated Bishop of Arras and Cambray in 633. His instructions, supported by the wonderful example of his own life, had incredible success in reforming his flock. By his zeal, religion and sacred learning flourished exceedingly in all Haynault and Flanders.—Butler's *Lives of the Saints*, Dec. 13.

Ul

filled with the harmony of the sacred chants, and the church was ablaze with light. The bishops took the remains of their brother saint in their arms and deposited them behind the high altar, near the relics of St. Bœan and St. Meldan, which he had himself borne over sea and land from the Island of the West, and entombed in that place.

However, all was not yet accomplished according to the magnificent plans of the mayor of the palace. A shrine was still wanting to enclose the treasure which the new church possessed, and Erchinoald was resolved that it should be costly in material, and wrought, if possible, by consecrated hands. He therefore sent a large amount of gold and silver to St. Eligius, praying him to design and execute the work that was required in honour of Blessed Fursey. The task was graciously undertaken; and in four years' time a sumptuous shrine, on which the artist-bishop had put forth his skill, was completed. Again St. Aubert was invited to repair to Peronne, and to assist the Bishop of Noyon and Tournay at the second translation of St. Fursey's remains; and St. Æmelian, Abbot of Lagny, was likewise requested to be present. Another great festival was held on the Mont de Cignes, and the shrine, with the relics enclosed, was placed over the high altar dedicated to St Peter, Prince of the Apostles [1]

Peronne, a most important fortress-town in the middle and subsequent ages, owed its growth and renown to the entombment of St. Fursey on its commanding heights. The place became a centre of attraction to the religious world, and a constant stream of pilgrims flowed in from all sides to offer up their devotions before the shrine of the patron saint and use the waters of his famous well. For here, too, as at Lagny, and indeed in every place where the holy man dwelt, a fountain sprang up endowed with virtue to relieve the ailments of those who used the healing tide with faith. Throughout succeeding ages the veneration in which the saint was held continued to be manifested from time to time in an exceptionally marked way. Thus, to quote Archbishop Moran, six hundred years after the entombment of our saint, St. Louis, King of France,

[1] Full details relating to the first and second translations of St Fursey's relics are given in the second volume of the *Lives of the Irish Saints*, by the Rev. John O'Hanlon, to whom the present writer has been much indebted all throughout this lengthy article.

solemnised his return to his kingdom, after six years' absence, by the gift to the church of Peronne of another rich shrine for the relics of St. Fursey. It was of gilt metal, enriched with precious stones, and adorned with statues of the twelve apostles; and the king himself, with several bishops, assisted at the translation of the sacred relics, on the 17th of September 1256. Again, the small portion of the relics saved from profanation amid the demoniac scenes of 1793, was placed in the church of St. John the Baptist, where they are now preserved. Lastly, on the 12th of January 1853, the bishops of the ecclesiastical province of Rheims, then assembled in Provincial Synod at Amiens, proceeded to Peronne, and once more enshrined in a rich case the relics of its great patron saint.[1]

During far more than a thousand years, therefore, this sainted exile of Erin has been an object of extraordinary veneration in the place where his relics are laid, and of honour throughout France generally. He is usually regarded as a French saint, and is far better known abroad than in the land of his birth. In fact, his insular fame has been absorbed in the superior splendour of his continental renown. The personality of the Milesian Fursæus is not always recognised in that of "St. Farcy of France," or "St. Furse of Peronne." That his name is now more frequently heard amongst us than it was for generations past, is due to the extension in these our days of the study of Dante. After a laborious and reverential study of the great Florentine, extending over six hundred years, Dantean scholars have reached the poetic sources of the Divine Comedy, and at the fountainhead they find the Celtic spring—the Vision of St. Fursey.

[1] *Irish Saints in Great Britain*, ch. xii.

THE RAPT CULDEE

"Such wondrous sight as once was given
In vision to the Rapt Culdee."—THOMAS D'ARCY M'GEE.

AENGUS, like many another of the early Irish saints, sprang from a noble and even regal stock. His family, Chiefs of Dalaradians of Ulster, traced their descent in unbroken line through Coelback, Monarch of Ireland in the middle of the fourth century, up to Ir, the third son of Milesius. It seems probable, however, that Aengus, the most illustrious scion of the proud Ultonian race, was born, not in the northern province, but in some part of Lagenia. At anyrate, it is certain that his birth took place about A.D. 750, and that at an early age he repaired to the monastic schools of Clonenagh, in Offaly, where he applied himself with extraordinary energy to the study of the arts and sciences which formed the curriculum in the seats of learning for which the island of saints and scholars was at that time celebrated. When the long academic course came to an end, he was well versed in Greek and Latin, a distinguished Gaelic scholar, profoundly learned in the Sacred Scriptures, and a poet thoroughly skilled in the "art of the Irish," that is to say, in the use, according to the laws of a varied and elaborate versification, of the copious, sonorous, and exquisitely melodious language of the Gael.

Nor was his progress less conspicuous in a still nobler field; for, having joined the religious community at Clonenagh, he advanced by giant strides in the narrow way of the saints. His brethren, noting the ardour of his zeal and the fidelity of his observance, the sincere depth of his humility and the transcendent [illegible] of his devotion, bestowed on him a name full of sweetness and significance, calling him *Angus Kélé-Dé*, meaning Angus the servant or lover of God.

To have acquired thus early so high a reputation for sanctity and learning at Clonenagh was indeed remarkable, seeing that the monastery was famous for its religious discipline as well as for the number of its learned teachers, at the head of whom was at that time the erudite and holy Abbot Malathgenius. From the monastery to the well-frequented schools, and from the schools to the circumjacent territories, the fame of Aengus spread with rapidity. He was thought to excel all others in Ireland, he was regarded with singular veneration, people came to consult him on different points and in weighty matters, and soon he had a numerous following of friends, admirers, and disciples.

Fame, albeit of so high and holy a description, was not only distasteful to the professor of learning, whose serious and absorbing pursuits required leisure and seclusion, but was uncongenial to the spirit of humility which the pious monk strenuously cultivated. He therefore asked and obtained permission to withdraw to some extent even from community life, and to fix his abode in a retired place where, safe from distraction, he might continue his studies, and devote himself more than ever to meditation and prayer.

The retreat he made choice of was a solitary spot in the midst of woods on the north bank of the Nore, six or seven miles from the monastery, and not far from the present town of Mountrath. There he erected a little wooden oratory, and constructed a rustic hut for his habitation. Surrounded by the primeval forest stretching down to the brink of the "cold clear Nore," he spent long intervals of time poring over ancient folios, storing his memory to an extent well-nigh incredible with entire books of the Sacred Scriptures, abstruse writings of the Greek and Latin fathers, and records of the lives of saints who had flourished in every age and in every clime. Three hundred times a day he adored God on his bended knees, and the entire Psalter he sang between one sunrise and another,—fifty psalms in the little oratory, fifty in the open air under a wide-spreading tree, and fifty while standing in cold water. Disappointment awaited him, however. He soon found that the difficulties of a journey through the pathless woods were made very light of by his admirers and disciples, and that the river was only a highway for visitors, who floated their coracles down the current or paddled them up the stream until the hermit's fastness no longer remained inviolate.

Under these circumstances it seems to have struck the Culdee that better success might attend an attempt to hide in a crowd, and that a safer hermitage might be discovered in the open inhabited country. Something like an inspiration urged him at the same time to forego, at least for an interval, his ardent pursuit of knowledge, and to throw himself into a life of practical humility, hard obedience, and severe manual toil. He had heard of a large monastery with a numerous community situated a good way off, in a fine open tract extending between the terminating spur of a chain of mountains and the eastern seaboard of Leinster, and he made up his mind to go to that place, and, without revealing his name and condition, present himself before the abbot, craving admission to serve at the monastery in a menial capacity. In such a position, thought he, the world would leave him unmolested, and he should have ample opportunities for perfecting himself in all the lowly and essential virtues dear to God. He would mortify his love for the higher studies, hide in ashes the flame of poetic aspiration, and relinquish the exercise of his bardic accomplishments. One thing only was he now ambitious of, and this was that he might become an abject in the house of his God.

We cannot doubt that Aengus had taken good counsel and obtained the blessing of his lawful superior when he entered on an undertaking so unusual, and set out on his journey as the poorest of Christ's poor,—alone, without money in his purse, or scrip for his journey, or two coats, or even a name. Steering his course in a north-easterly direction, he proceeded pilgrimwise, receiving a meal and a night's shelter now at a chieftain's rath, and again within some religious enclosure. One only incident of the journey has been related, and that was a memorable one. Coming to a place called Coolbanaher (near the present town of Portarlington), the traveller turned off the road and entered a church to pray there. When he had finished his devotions, he noticed in the cemetery a newly-made grave, and beheld a wondrous vision—legions of bright spirits, angels of heaven, descending and ascending and hovering over the spot, while their heavenly songs filled the air with an ecstasy of joy. Desiring to know who it could be that the ministers of God thus honoured at his place of sepulture, Aengus went to the priest of the church and asked who was buried in that grave. The priest answered that it was a poor old man who formerly lived in the neighbourhood. "What good did he do?" asked the Culdee "I saw no particular good by him," said the priest, "but that his practice was to recount and invoke the saints of the world, as far as he could remember them, at his going to bed and getting up, in accordance with the custom of the old devotees." "Ah! my God," said Aengus, "he who would make a poetical composition in praise of the saints should doubtless have a high reward, when so much has been vouchsafed to the efforts of this old devotee!"

Suddenly it flashed through his mind that he should do this thing as a work pleasing to God, edifying to his brethren, and beneficial to his own soul, and he saw at a glance how a metrical hymn might be composed in honour of all the saints, which he should himself recite every day as long as he lived, and bequeath as a rich legacy to the land of his birth.

Here then was an idea as vivid as an inspiration and as holy, whirling him once more into the high latitudes of poetry. The impulse to attempt this undertaking had an urgency not to be gainsaid; he felt conscious of possessing the power to accomplish it, and he was lifted as by the hair of the head into a region where neither fear nor misgiving, neither distrust nor diffidence, leave a blight or cast a shadow. Yes, he would raise his voice and sing a glorious song in honour of the hosts of heaven!

But how it was to be done, or when, he knew not, for it did not occur to him that he should turn aside forthwith from the path on which an earlier inspiration had set his feet. The Lord, who had bestowed on him the gift of song, would doubtless provide for the doing of His own work! And so, with the prelude of the new chant re-echoing in his soul, and the joy of the new possession elating his heart; with the thought of the old devotee in his mind, and the rustle of the angels' wings in his ears, the Culdee came out again on the track that served as a highway, and continued his journey towards the goal he had in view. At length, having crossed St. Brigid's pastures (the Curragh of Kildare), and passed through the woods enclosing that tract on the north, he turned the mountain range at the upper extremity and came out on the open country gently sloping to the eastern sea.

There he beheld the monastery of Tamlacht or Tallaght, whither he was bound, standing in all the holy simplicity of the antique time when high thinking and low living were the order of the day. A cluster of wattle huts, with a timber church in the midst, stood within the circuit of a low fence; outside, a considerable area was occupied by farm buildings and groups of rustic huts which the scholars had built for themselves; and farther off the mill, the kiln, the fishing weir, and other appurtenances of an extensive rural establishment could be observed; while along the river banks and the higher ground, ascending towards the adjacent hills, the cultivated fields and well-stocked pastures testified to the industry and good management of the religious colonists. The only thing wanting was that air of antiquity which some of the larger monasteries could boast of, but this Tallaght had not had time to acquire, for its origin dated only a few years back, when in 769 St. Melruan founded the church on a site and endowment "offered to God, to Michael the Archangel, and to Melruan," by Donnoch, the pious and illustrious King of Leinster. Already, however, the monastery enjoyed a high reputation throughout Erin for piety and scholarship, the saintly abbot ranking among the most learned men of the day, and his community following close in the wake of their father and founder.

Weary and travel-stained, Aengus, presented himself before Melruan as a poor humble stranger, and with all the earnestness which another might show when supplicating for a special favour, besought the abbot to take him into his service as a menial, and appoint him to do the rough work of the monastic farm. Surprised, perhaps, that this stranger should ask so little, the abbot nevertheless discovered nothing in the applicant's speech or manner suggestive of a higher capacity. He granted the prayer of the willing drudge, sent him to take charge of the mill and the kiln and desired him to turn his hand to any kind of labour that might offer in the fields and works. And so, as it is related, he set to his task with right goodwill, reaping the corn, carrying the sheaves on his back to the barn, thrashing them with a flail, loading himself with the sacks of grain, and trudging like a beast of burden to the mill. With his face begrimed with sweat and dust, his hair all tangled, and his clothes covered with chaff and straws, the Culdee looked very unlike a man of letters and "a master of verses." He hardly looked like a man at all, but he did look like what he wanted to be—an abject, and the last of human kind.

One might reasonably wonder whether he had time to say his prayers. And, indeed, if praying depended altogether on church-going, there would have been but a short account of his spiritual exercises. Out early and late in the barn and the fields, his opportunities for meditation cannot have been frequent, and, as an old panegyrist observes, "It was not a condition meet for devotion to be in the kiln constantly drying." But this man of contemplation, this lover of deep study, this poetic soul, had not in vain spent his youth in a school of religion and learning. His well-stored memory now served him in good stead. He had subject-matter for meditation in abundance, and he knew more prayers off book than many a manual contains Moreover, like all the holy men of Erin, and for that matter a vast number of the common of the faithful too, he knew by heart the spiritual songs composed and sung by the early saints, and preserved as a glorious heirloom by succeeding generations. Most of these poems were indulgenced or privileged, and the chanting of them was regarded as a truly instructive, devotional, and meritorious exercise. The sublimity of the thoughts and the rhythmic elegance of the diction made the recital of the verses at once easy and delightful. Several of the hymns in constant use were of the kind called by the Irish a *Lorica*, or breastplate, -in other words, a defensive armour fashioned to keep the heart pure and to make the darts of Satan glance away. The Christian people thus buckled on their spiritual armour, and, chanting the sacred psalmody, felt ready to confront the dangers of the day and the darkness of the night. These sacred compositions, frequently of considerable length, were not merely read or spoken; they were intoned or musically recited, the Irish, like the Greeks, holding poetry and music to be inseparable. Moreover, they were sung out in full voice, not only in the church, the monastery, and the home, but in the fields and by the shore and on the mountains,—

wherever, in fact, the prayerful heart might sigh or sing towards heaven.

First in favour, as in date, written in the most ancient dialect of the Irish, was St. Patrick's poem, "In Tarah to-day, at this awful hour, I call on the Holy Trinity"; a hymn believed to be the best protection in all dangers of soul and body, a safeguard against sudden death to the person who was in the habit of devoutly reciting it, and an armour to his soul after death—a hymn which ought to be sung for ever!

Next, perhaps, came St. Sechnall's piece in praise of Patrick, "Audite omnes amantes Deum," probably the first Latin hymn composed in Ireland. An angel, it is said, promised heaven to everyone who should recite the last three stanzas at lying down and at rising up, and this it was the practice of the Irish saints to do.

The *Altus* of St. Columba, "Alone am I upon the mountain, O God of heaven! prosper my way," composed and sung in an hour of danger, was another favourite prayer, and was used with great faith by travellers as a protection when setting out on a journey. Angels are present while it is sung, says an old commentator, the devil shall not know the path of him who sings it every day, and moreover there shall be no strife in the house where it is frequently sung. Some had the pious habit of reciting the *Altus*, a poem of seventy lines, no less than seven times daily.

St. Coleman's hymn, "May the Son of Mary shield us," composed at the Saint's School in Cork while a pestilence was raging,—the abbot giving the first and last stanzas, and his pupils supplying the intermediate verses,—was intended as a shield of protection against the perils of the hour, and continued to be fervently recited by the pious under all circumstances, but especially in visitations of epidemic disease.

Many other poems of the kind were popularly known and generally recited; and so when the Culdee, drying and grinding, and digging and delving, sang out his Gaelic and Latin hymns in measured cadence, he attracted no observation,—he simply did as others did, while thereby he fed his spirit with the highest and holiest thoughts, solaced his poetic soul, and fulfilled to the letter the divine precept of praying always.

( )

And as the drudgery of his daily occupations proved no obstacle to the intimate union of his heart with God, so in like manner the penitential course of his bodily servitude seems only to have set his soul free for surer flight into the heaven of poetry and song. Although at first sight it might appear that his surroundings were anything but inspiring, it must be allowed, on further consideration, that the situation was not without its balance of compensation. Wherever he turned, a scene of beauty met his gaze, something suggestive met his fancy. Close by were the picturesque groups of the monastic buildings and the students' shanties, sheltered by ancestral trees. Now and then a chorus of youthful voices burst upon the silence, the abbot's bell rang out from time to time, at the canonical hours the psalm-tones of the divine office, resounding from the choir, brought heaven and earth together in holiest harmony. Far and wide spread cornfields and pastures watered by a stream which, having left its wild ways in its native glens, glided past in peaceful flow. South and west extended a screen of gentle hills, rising from a wooded base, and backed by a mountain range. Viewed from the upper tract of the terman lands, these loftier eminences displayed their sides and summits, royally vested in dusky purple, gold, and green, with veils of blue-grey mist and down-falling bands of silvery streams. From the same vantage ground the prospect north and east presented a still more magnificent spectacle—for a wooded plain with wide clearings extended on one side to the open sea, with its islands and headlands and changeful surface, and stretched away in another direction towards the fertile territories of Oriel and Meath.

Again, the country round the monastery was full of associations interesting to a poet and antiquary. On the hill just above the monastery ground were strewn the sepulchral monuments of Parthelon's race, many thousands of whom fell victims to a pestilence that devastated the territories round the bay in pre-Christian times; the original name of the district of Tallaght, *Tamlacht Muntire Parthalen*, signifying that it was the plague grave of Parthelon's colony. Not far off, in a southern direction, at Bohernabreena, were the ruins of a great court or mansion of hospitality, kept by a chieftain called Da-Derga, about the time of the Incarnation of our Lord. Conary-more, the just and valorous monarch of Ireland, while enjoying the hospitality of the master of the Court, was slain by a band of pirates, who attacked and demolished the habitation. The story of the destruction of the Court of Da-Derga formed the subject of one of the celebrated historic tales preserved in the ancient books of Erin. Incidents less tragic, though equally striking, had invested the adjacent glens with a poetic interest, and the Thrushes' Valley (Glenasmole), through which the stream came dancing down from its fountainhead on the slopes of Kippure, was the very home of legend and romance.

Like all the old Irish saints, Aengus was fond of animals. The harmless denizens of the fields and woods were liked for their innocent demeanour and interesting ways, and even the beasts of wilder nature received kindness for the sake of their Creator. History is not silent with regard to the friendship that existed between the Culdee and the birds. No doubt, both at the mill and in the cornfields, the holy man had many opportunities of doing his feathered favourites a good turn, and they, as in duty bound, would have a song and a welcome for him whenever he came within view of their airy dwellings. How delightful it must have been in "the vocal woods," when thrushes and blackbirds, and a chorus of minor minstrels, poured in "full-throated ease" their tide of song, while "Aengus of the festal lays" chanted in resounding tones his praises of the hosts of heaven! Once, so runs the legend, when the disguised poet met with a severe accident while cutting branches in a thicket, the birds became excited in an extraordinary manner, and by their screams and cries seemed to lament the calamity that had befallen their comrade and benefactor.

But whatever be inferred or surmised, one thing is certain, namely, that during his servitude at Tallaght, and amidst such surroundings as these, the saint composed his famous metrical Festology of the Saints.

The poem is divided into three principal parts, with subdivisions, consisting altogether of 590 quatrains. The Invocation is written in what modern Gaelic scholars call English chain verse; that is, an arrangement of metre by which the first words of every succeeding quatrain are identical with the last words of the preceding one. The following literal translation gives the dry bones, as it were, of the Invocation, while leaving out all the colour and harmony of the verses, which ask grace and sanctification from Christ on the poet's work :—

"Sanctify, O Christ! my words :—
    O Lord of the seven heavens!
    Grant me the gift of wisdom,
    O Sovereign of the bright sun!

"O bright sun who dost illuminate
    The heavens with all their holiness!
    O King who governest the angels!
    O Lord of all the people!

"O Lord of the people,
    O King all righteous and good!
    May I receive the full benefit
    Of praising Thy royal hosts

"Thy royal hosts I praise
    Because Thou art my Sovereign;
    I have disposed my mind
    To be constantly beseeching Thee.

"I beseech a favour from Thee,
    That I be purified from my sins,
    Through the peaceful bright-shining flock,
    The royal host whom I celebrate."

The Invocation is followed by a poem, giving in beautiful and forcible language an account of the sufferings of the early Christian martyrs, and telling how the names of the persecutors are forgotten, while the names of their victims are remembered with honour, veneration, and affection ; how Pilate's wife is forgotten, and the Blessed Virgin is remembered and honoured from the uttermost bounds of the earth to its centre. Even in our own country (continues the poet) the enduring supremacy of the Church of Christ is made manifest; for Tara had become abandoned and deserted under the vain-glory of its kings, while Armagh remains the populous seat of dignity, piety, and learning, Cruachan, the royal residence of the kings of Connaught, is deserted, while Clonmacnoise resounds with the dashing of chariots and the tramp of multitudes to honour the shrine of St. Kieran, the royal palace of Aillinn, in Leinster, has passed away, while the Church of St. Brigid, at Kildare, remains in dazzling splendour; Emania, the royal palace of the Ulstermen, has disappeared, while the holy Kevin's church, at Glendalough, remains in full glory;

the Monarch Leaghaire's pride and pomp were extinguished, while St. Patrick's name continued to shine with glowing lustre. Thus the poet goes on to contrast the fleeting and forgotten names and glories of the men and great establishments of the pagan and secular world with the stability, freshness, and splendour of the Christian churches, and the evergreen names of the illustrious, though often humble founders.

Then follows the chief poem, the Festology, beginning with the Feast of the Circumcision of our Lord, for, says the poet—

> "At the head of the congregated saints
> Let the King take the front place."

This Festology is not confined to the Saints of Erin. The author tells us that he has travelled far and near to collect the names and history of the subjects of his laudation and invocation; that for the foreign saints he has consulted St. Ambrose, St. Jerome, and Eusebius; and that from "countless hosts of the illuminated books of Erin" he has collected the festivals of the Irish saints. The main body of the composition is divided into twelve monthly parts, and the various saints are mentioned on their respective days, with allusions to their lives, their characteristics, and the localities they were connected with. Thus, when St. Adamnan of Iona is named in September, allusion is made to his band of brilliant associates; and his countryman does not forget to say that it was he whom "the glorious Jesus besought to free permanently the Irish women." On June 3rd occurs the festival of a "Soldier of Christ in the Land of Erin," a "noble name over the billowy ocean"—Kevin, the chaste, noble warrior, whose dwelling was in the "glen of the two broad lakes." May 3rd brings "The Chief Finding of the Tree of the Cross of Christ, with many virtues," the death of the noble Chief Conleath, and the great Festival of the Virgin Mary.[1] The Calends of February are "magnified by a galaxy of martyrs of great valour; and Brigid, the spotless, of loudest fame, chaste head of the Nuns of Erin."

Having mentioned and invoked the saints at their respective festival days, the poet recapitulates the preceding subject, and

[1] The Conception, honoured on the 8th of December in other martyrologies, was commemorated on the 3rd of May by the Irish.

( )

invokes the blessed ones in classes or bands under certain heads or leaders—the elders or ancients under Noah, the prophets under Isaiah, the patriarchs under Abraham, the apostles and disciples under Peter, the wise or learned men under Paul, and the virgins of the world under the Blessed Virgin Mary. And then follow the holy bishops of Rome and Jesusalem, Antioch and Alexandria, under their great chiefs, the bands of monks and learned men under Anthony and the gifted Benedict, and a division of the saints of the world under Martin. Lastly are invoked once again the noble saints of Erin under St. Patrick, the saints of Scotland under St. Columba, and the great division of the saintly virgins of Ireland under the holy St. Brigid of Kildare.

Lastly, the sacred bard in eloquent strain beseeches the mercy of the Saviour for himself and all mankind, through the merits and sufferings of the saints whom he has named and enumerated, — through the merits of their dismembered bodies, their bodies pierced with lances, their wounds, their bitter tears, through all the sacrifices offered of the Saviour's own Body and Blood, as it is in heaven, upon the holy altars, — through the blood that flowed from the Saviour's own side, through His humanity, and through His divinity in unity with the Holy Spirit and the Heavenly Father. Enumerating, still in the full swing of his melodious verse, the conspicuous examples of God's mercy as shown forth in the Scripture history, the poet returns once more to the beloved saints of Erin, whom he regards with such extraordinary veneration, and beseeches Jesus again, through the heavenly household, to be saved as He saved St. Patrick from the poisoned drink at Tara, and St. Kevin of Glendalough from the perils of the mountain.[1]

Such in outline is the sublime song the Culdee composed in his heart, committed to memory, and chanted in the hearing of the woods, the birds, and the heavens, as he trudged through the furrows and cut wattles in the woods of Tallaght. No doubt, as already said, he intended it for something more than the fervent expression of his own piety and faith. He intended and hoped that the people of Erin would in his own day, and

[1] The above is an abstract of the analysis of the Festology in O'Curry's *Manuscript Materials of Ancient Irish History*, with some particulars from the Rev. Matthew Kelly's Martyrology of Tallaght.

in succeeding ages, glorify God in His saints in these very words. This is evident from certain stanzas of the poem in which he recommends it to the pious study of the faithful, and points out the spiritual benefits to be gained by reciting it. But when and in what manner it should be made known to the world he could not imagine. This cause, with all else, he commended to *the faithful Creator*.

Years passed on in this manner, until at length the scene changed suddenly. The identity of the man at the mill with the famous Aengus of Clonenagh was discovered in a strange way. On a certain day, the Culdee being at work in the barn, one of the children of the school rushed in, frightened and breathless, and hid himself in a dark corner. Aengus spoke gently to him, and asked what was the cause of his trouble. The boy answered that, having failed to learn his lesson, he was afraid to appear before his teacher, who would be certain to punish him severely. He was then soothed and encouraged, and bidden to come forth from his hiding-place. Doing as he was desired, he crept forward, laid his head against the saint's breast and fell asleep. After some time he awoke, and was then told to repeat his lesson. Immediately, without hesitation or mistake, he did so; and having received an injunction to say nothing of what had just occurred, was directed to go and present himself before his master. The latter was surprised to find a usually dull boy acquit himself so well on that occasion and the following days, could not understand how such a remarkable change had been effected, and mentioned the matter to the abbot. St. Melruan sent for the boy, and, suspecting that something strange had happened, obliged the reluctant scholar to relate exactly all that had taken place in the barn. A light flashed on the abbot's mind, and he exclaimed: "This can be no other than the missing Aengus of Clonenagh!" Hastening to the barn, he joyfully embraced the Culdee, reproached him affectionately for having deceived him so long, and, bidding him join himself forthwith to the religious community, welcomed him as a heaven-sent friend and brother. Aengus, overwhelmed with confusion, threw himself at the abbot's feet and implored forgiveness for whatever cause of complaint he might have given.

From that hour until death parted them, these two gifted and saintly men continued to be fellow-labourers and bosom friends. The Culdee was appointed to lecture on the higher sciences in the upper schools, and to teach theology to the young religious; and moreover, in spite of his humility, was obliged to receive priestly ordination. For some time past, Abbot Melruan had been engaged in compiling a prose martyrology, and he now hastened to secure the co-operation of his new friend in the prosecution of the work. The task was a difficult one, but the pious antiquaries achieved it, and the result of their joint labour is generally known as the Martyrology of Tallaght. According to the best authorities, it is the oldest Irish martyrology in existence, and the most copious of the kind written in any country at that period Its full title is *Martyrologium Aengusii filii Hoblenii et Moelruanii.*

After some years had been spent in this way the abbot died, and received a tribute of esteem and affection from his friend, who, in the Festology, made a commemoration of Melruan, the "Bright Sun of Ireland" Tallaght having lost its principal attraction when its founder was called away, Aengus returned to his old home at Clonenagh, where he ruled for many years as abbot, while exercising at the same time episcopal functions. Literary aspirations, however, were by no means relinquished. The Festology was finished at his own monastery, and thence made known to the world, A.D. 804, with all the form and éclat proper to the publication of a singularly beautiful and valuable work. The occasion was an interesting one In the course of the year just cited, Aedh, Monarch of Ireland, undertook an expedition against the men of Leinster, marched his forces through Offally, and encamped at no great distance from Clonenagh. Fothad, Chief Poet of Ireland, surnamed the Canonist from his knowledge of the Church canons, accompanied the king on this expedition, and Aengus took the opportunity thus afforded to submit his Festology to the judgment of the Chief Poet, the highest literary authority in the kingdom. The result was a cordial and just recognition of the extraordinary merits of the poem, a solemn approval of its publication, and an official recommendation to the nation at large to peruse and study its pages. In courteous return for a copy of the Festology presented to him by the author, Fothad gave Aengus a poem which he had himself lately written with a very important object in view. This interchange of literary amenities was the beginning of an enduring friendship between the Culdee and the Chief Poet of Ireland.

Many other works of great value, whether in plain prose or in elegant metre, are included in the list of the Culdee's writings Among these are a collection of pedigrees of the Irish saints; the *Saltair-na-Raun*, or Psalter of Verses, consisting of 150 poems on the history of the Old Testament, written in the finest style of the Gaelic language of the eighth century; and a variety of Litanies, in which, among a vast number of saints invoked, are several Italian, Gallic, British, and African saints who lived and died in Ireland. A very curious tract, giving an account of the mothers of some of the most remarkable Irish saints, is also attributed to the same authorship.

Authorities are not of accord as to the date of the saint's death. In all probability he departed out of this world towards the close of the first quarter of the ninth century. Clonenagh undoubtedly was the place of his decease, and he died the death of the saints on Friday, the 11th March. Another poet, his namesake, countryman, and contemporary, Aengus, Abbot of Clonfert-Molua, surnamed the Wise, wrote the Culdee's panegyric in a poem which tenderly laments the departure of a Master of Verses, the Sun of the Western World, the Poet of the Hosts of Heaven.[1]

The works of St. Aengus are, at the present day, held in as high esteem by the historians, the philologists, and the Celtic scholars of the great European centres of learning as they were in Ireland a thousand years ago. It is a wonder to all that they have not long since been collected from old books difficult of access, and issued with a translation. They are, says the editor and learned annotator of the Martyrology of Tallaght, the best, and often the only authorities, on the brightest period of the history of Ireland, and a still more competent authority, Eugene O'Curry, doubts whether any country in Europe possesses a national document of so important a character as the Festology of St Aengus. How much longer, we may ask, are these treasures to remain practically overlaid and hidden amidst the mass of Ireland's unutilised resources?

[1] In a lecture delivered at Oxford, Professor Matthew Arnold, referring to this poem, said that though it was composed by no eminent bard, yet a Greek epitaph could not show a finer perception of what constitutes propriety and felicity of style in composition of this nature.

HOGAN, THE SCULPTOR

"IRELAND gave me birth," said Barry, "but never would have given me bread." So little was it thought, one hundred years ago or thereabout, that native talent was likely to produce a noticeable work of art, that when Barry exhibited in Dublin his picture of St. Patrick baptizing the King of Cashel, it was not for a moment supposed, by a crowd of admiring spectators, that a young Irishman might be the painter. Timidly venturing to announce himself, he was met with so contemptuous a sneer that he burst into tears, and rushed out of the room in which was being held the first exhibition of the Society, then recently established, for the Encouragement of Arts, Manufactures, and Commerce in Ireland. Barry's genius was of a kind that no discouragement could crush. He was resolved to sacrifice everything in the pursuit of what others, as well as his father, considered wild and unprofitable nonsense. Despairing, and with good reason, of finding appreciation and reward in his own distracted land, where the arts of peace had not for centuries flourished, he left this "miserable isle" in early manhood, and having settled in London after a period of study on the Continent, made himself known before long as a courageous art critic, and an illustrious member of the British School of Painting.

Nearly sixty years after Barry left Ireland, without much hope of visiting its shores again, and possibly without much regret, another young enthusiast went forth in search of higher culture than could be obtained at home, but with no reproachful or final adieu to the country of his birth. The general state of affairs had improved in the interval,—the country had begun to recover from the pitiable condition to which it had been reduced, and a taste for art had shown itself, though in a fitful way. There was, at anyrate, sufficient hope to animate the courage of a young man of original genius, whose ambition it was to become not only a sculptor, but so distinguished a sculptor that his own people should take pride in his excellence—should intrust him with great works, and associate his name with national and noble monuments. Hogan was twenty-three years of age when he left Ireland for Rome. Six years later he revisited his country, bringing with him works which, having gained him great credit in Rome, now obtained him the applause of all lovers of art in Ireland, and procured him commissions to undertake important works for Cork and Dublin. Thenceforth he was characterised as "the Irish Sculptor"; not merely because he was born in the land, and was the first Irishman who had greatly distinguished himself in that noble art, but principally because his best works were executed for Ireland,—to beautify her churches, personify her nationality, and perpetuate in marble the form and the features of her leaders, her poets, her men of learning, and her men of worth.

Barry, in all probability, could never have gone to Italy to study as a painter without the generous assistance of Edmund Burke, who allowed him an annuity for the three years he was thus engaged. On the other hand, Hogan owed the opportunity of improving himself in Rome to the zealous exertions of a few friends, who stirred up men of taste, brought the matter under the notice of one or two public societies, and by dint of untiring perseverance succeeded in collecting subscriptions enough to keep the wolf from the student's door while he pursued his vocation in the capital of art itself.

Just fifty years have passed over since young Hogan was sent to Rome. An idea of the progress we have made since then may be formed if we fancy for a moment that a youthful genius like Barry, hungering and thirsting after excellence, or an enthusiastic student like Hogan, dreaming of the delight of being one day an hou our to his country, should come before the public, and the project of sending him to some great centre of art be started. It requires no stretch of the imagination to fancy the applause that would greet the young man's efforts, the encouragement his aspirations would receive, the glow of

( )

nationality that would be enkindled, the liberal subscriptions that might possibly be offered. At anyrate, some very eloquent speeches would be pronounced,' and the young aspirant would be told to recollect what his countrymen have already accomplished. He would, if a painter, be reminded of Barry's renown, of Maclise's good fortune, of Mulready's success, of Danby's and Elmore's reputation, of the admiration elicited by every production of Burton's exquisite pencil. Or if not painting, but the severer art of sculpture had fired the enthusiasm of the young artist, he would be excited to the pitch of "fine frenzy" by allusion to the honours Rome conferred on Hogan, and the tribute, in the form of overwhelming commissions, which the three kingdoms bestow on Foley.

Having thus advanced from blank incredulity in the likelihood of the country producing anything of acknowledged excellence in the higher walks of art, to a jealous eagerness to claim, as national property, the talent which owes most of the fostering and patronage it receives to other nations, it is not unnatural to hope that another half-century may find us still farther advanced, perhaps with a distinct school of our own to boast of. There is nothing unreasonable in such an expectation, for art, in whatever form, and at whatever time, it flourished in Ireland, invariably displayed a marked originality. In architecture, we can point to our stone-roofed oratories and our round towers. In ornamental design, we have the *opus Hibernicum*. Our illuminated manuscripts of the sixth century are unique in style as well as unsurpassed in beauty. Everyone knows that our music is original, characteristic, and inimitable.

If ever we have a School of Art, it is certain we shall be no way loath to talk about it. In other words, we shall want to have a history of its origin, development, and, let us hope, ultimate perfection. Meanwhile, the more knowledge and taste we acquire, the more value we shall set on these remarkable men, Barry and Hogan, and that not merely for the works they produced, but also for the good example of their lives. Not that they were faultless—Barry, in fact, bristled with faults; but they possessed, each of them, in an eminent degree, the qualities which ought to accompany, direct, and control genius—qualities, too, with which we as a people are not usually credited. Their enthusiasm, for example, was by no means of a fitful, evanescent order—it had the solid strength of a principle, and was kept at a white heat for the length of a lifetime. Untiring industry and intense mental application characterised the painter and the sculptor, who took good care, each of them, that study should keep pace with work. In fact, they held the same opinion as that enunciated by a great thinker of our own day who has defined genius to be *an infinite capacity for taking pains.* "If I should chance to have genius or anything else," wrote Barry in his youth, "it is so much the better; but my hopes are grounded upon an intense, unwearied application, of which I am not sparing." Hogan expressed the same idea when he said: "Labour is the only price of solid fame; whatever a man's force of genius may be, there is no easy way of becoming a great artist." They were temperate in their habits, strictly accurate in money dealings, and independent to a degree that is at least uncommon. It was said of Barry, who lived in penury that he might paint in peace, that he was never known to borrow money nor to want it. And when Hogan's friends, wishing in his latter years to lessen the strain of severe work and enable him with more ease to educate his children, suggested that a Government pension might be obtained for him, he would not listen to the proposal. "I want nothing," he proudly said, "but work." Both these men were sincere Catholics. Among Barry's disagreeable peculiarities, his contemporaries reckoned his "bigoted attachment to the doctrines of the Church of Rome." Hogan was not so belligerent as Barry, who had a taste for theological studies, and did not shrink from controversy, but he had a proud way of professing the faith, especially when he was likely to lose by the avowal.

Several, and tolerably full, biographical sketches of Barry are to be found in most libraries; and as a member of the social circle that included Johnson, Burke, Reynolds, and Goldsmith, his name is familiar to all acquainted with the literature of the latter part of the eighteenth century. There is much less known of Hogan, though his story is well calculated to interest his own countrymen in every part of the world, and to stimulate young men of genius to a hearty and honourable emulation. Not long after his death, a biographical notice, founded on original materials obligingly intrusted to the writer by Mr. Hogan's family, appeared in the *Irish Quarterly Review*. From this memoir, long since out of print, we shall take (having, it may be well to observe, an unquestionable right to do so) all that may be required for the following brief sketch of the sculptor's career.

The first twenty-three years of John Hogan's life were passed in the south of Ireland, principally in Cork, whither his father removed with his family from Tallow in the County Waterford soon after the birth, in 1800, of this his eldest and afterwards distinguished son. The elder Hogan, a very worthy man and a builder by trade, was descended from an old Tipperary tribe mentioned in the *Annals of the Four Masters*. He had married a young lady of much superior position to his own, Miss Francis Cox of Dunmanway, great-granddaughter of Sir Richard Cox, Lord Chief Justice of Ireland in the reign of William and Mary, and Lord Chancellor under Queen Anne. She had met the young man at the table of her guardian, whose mansion was at the time undergoing alterations. Her fortune of £2000 was withheld by the indignant family, and her husband appears to have been too proud to urge his claim to the money. The home of the Hogan family, in Cove Street, Cork, though somewhat humble, was a refined and happy one. The children grew up with a taste for intellectual cultivation, and the family affections were cherished with remarkable warmth and constancy. At fourteen years of age the eldest son, John, who had been for six years at Mr Cangley's school in Tallow, and became a proficient not in classics, but in the study of history and mathematics, was brought home and placed in the office of Mr. Michael Foote, an attorney. Legal business, however, was not congenial to the lad's disposition, and much of his time was spent cutting figures in wood, drawing fancy sketches, and copying any architectural designs that came in his way. His brother Richard, whose tastes were also artistic, encouraged him in his stolen studies, and so likewise did Dr. Coghlan, an eccentric but able physician, who having on one occasion surprised the idle apprentice making sketches at his desk, praised his efforts and rewarded him with a bright crown-piece. Subsequent visits to the office on the part of the good doctor had the same pleasurable result to the bright spirit chained to the desk

Before long, however, he was set free by a happy accident.

Certain plans and specifications required to be copied for a contractor's office within a limited term, and no one was found in Cork ready to undertake the task. The self-taught artist was thought of, and he was pressed to do the work. Day and night he laboured,—had the copy ready by the appointed hour, and received the highest encomiums from his employers for his quickness and proficiency in outline drawing. Immediately he was removed from the attorney's office to the workshop of Messrs. Deane & Co., to be employed as draughtsman and carver of models. His mind had been bent on architecture; he did not think of being a sculptor until Mr (afterwards Sir Thomas) Deane placed the chisel in his hands, but from that day forward neither he himself nor anyone else had a doubt of his vocation.

With extraordinary industry he employed himself, during the next few years, in mastering the principles of his art, and practising every kind of drawing and carving. He attended diligently Dr. Woodroffe's anatomical lectures, thus laying the foundation of his subsequent success in modelling. While so engaged he carved a human skeleton in wood, life-size,—an achievement that excited the astonishment of his fellow-students, and was turned to account by the doctor, who long afterwards used the figure in demonstrating to his pupils. All the time that remained after business hours in his employer's workshop, and many stolen hours of the night, were spent in severe study and careful practice of the hand. In the year 1818 the young artist and his band of sympathising friends were thrown into a state of delightful excitement by the arrival in Cork of a selection of fine casts from the antique, which had been taken under the superintendence of Canova, and sent as a present to the Prince Regent by His Holiness Pius VII., as a mark of gratitude for the services rendered by the English Government in the removal from the Louvre, and restoration to their places in Italian churches and galleries, of the works of art plundered by the First Napoleon. Through the interest of some energetic friend—the Marquis of Connyngham, Lord Ennismore, or perhaps John Wilson Croker—these casts were obtained for Cork, and consigned to a society lately established for the encouragement of talent in that city. The gallery, or rather loft, in which the casts were placed became the centre of attraction to young Hogan, and the scene of his labours. He copied everything, from masks to life-size figures,—chiselling in stone, cutting in timber, or drawing in chalk.

Mr Paulett Carey, a writer on art and zealous encourager of genius, visiting the gallery on one occasion, had his attention attracted by a small figure of a Torso, carved with remarkable skill in pine timber and bearing marks of recent workmanship, which had fallen under one of the benches. In answer to his inquiries, he was told the history of the talented young man who so assiduously studied among the casts, and was directed to an adjacent apartment, where he found the sculptor surrounded by the works of his chisel in every variety of taste and every stage of progress. Mr. Carey's experienced judgment enabled him to recognise the genius thus struggling towards development. His determination to help was as fixed as his appreciation was just. With a view of obtaining subscriptions to enable the young sculptor to go to Rome, he began to write letters to the newspapers, and to interest private friends and patrons of art in the enterprise he had taken so kindly to heart. The result of this gentleman's exertions was the collection of a sum of money sufficient, if managed with severe economy, to keep the young man in Rome for two or three years, and allow him to pursue the study of the higher branches of his art without interruption. To this fund Lord de Tabley, then Sir John Fleming Leicester, contributed twenty-five pounds, giving at the same time a commission for a statue in marble. The Royal Dublin Society, restricted from granting premiums to an artist not a student of the Dublin Academy, voted twenty-five pounds for the purchase of some figures the young artist had carved in wood. The Royal Irish Institution gave one hundred pounds.

With the least possible delay all necessary preparations were made, and the young sculptor left his happy, pious home, to enter, for the first time, the great world of life and art. In Dublin and London he was kindly received, got plenty of advice, and also some letters of introduction. Everything was new to him, and he walked at the rate of twenty miles a day, seeking out whatever was specially interesting to him in his professional capacity. He was not pleased with Paris,—the streets were so narrow and so dirty, and one ran such a risk of being run over by the coaches driven quite close to the shops! However, he saw "pictures that are originals indeed, and in a gallery as long as the Parade of Cork!" On the Italian part of the road he lingered a while, especially before the gates of Giobertı in Florence, and finally arrived in Rome on Palm Sunday, 1824.

Hogan began forthwith to work in right earnest, attending the schools of St. Luke, studying in the halls of the Vatican and the Capitol, and modelling in the life academies of the French and English artists. He could not begin at once to model the figure for Sir John Leicester, for he was not able to hire a studio, and pay, as was required, a year's rent in hand. His pension was barely sufficient to support nature, and he had to study economy with hardly less attention than sculpture. It would need, he wrote home, at least one hundred a year to study as he liked. With that he could take a studio, pay living models, cut marble, model in clay, cast in plaster, and at last arrive at excellence. But such a sum was not forthcoming from the old land. Doubtless, poverty saved him from many temptations, as likewise did the isolation in which he found himself in Rome. The Duchess of Devonshire, to whom he had an introduction from Sir Thomas Lawrence, died before he could present his letter. His best friend at this time was Signor Gentili, afterwards the priest and preacher so idolised in Dublin, but then practising law in the Eternal City. He taught Italian to Hogan, who was anxious to learn the language perfectly, but who was so infatuated with his art that, coming home one day, after a study in the Vatican Museum, and finding Signor Gentili in the midst of his books awaiting him, he sprang at the table, seized the books, and flung them out of the window. "There is nothing in the world but art," he cried; "so here goes!" However, master and pupil always continued great friends. The English and Scottish artists living in Rome, Hogan found less congenial. They were too fond of sneering at the Catholic religion, talking of the misgovernment of Catholic countries, and so on. The everyday life of Rome presented enough to interest the solitary student, and when he could get out for a ramble over the Campagna, or among the hills, he was supremely happy. He may have lived in what would be considered no better than a garret elsewhere; for he had his lodging in the Vicolo dei Greci, off the Corso, for two and a half crowns a month. But there was a beautiful garden at the rear. the rich Pergolese grapes he and the birds were welcome to taste; branches bearing ripe figs reached up to his window, and of these he ate full many a score; the air meanwhile being full of the odour of ripening oranges and lemons

After some time the artist's prospects began to brighten, or at anyrate he took more courage. A studio offered for sale in a good situation, and this he secured at a very reasonable rate. It was expected that Rome would be crowded with English nobility during the approaching winter, and he thought it would be well to model a figure in plaster, and have something to show by the time these patrons of art should arrive. The subject chosen was a shepherd boy recumbent, with a pipe in one hand and a goat by his side. A stout Sabine lad was the model,—employed for fifty hours, remunerated when the work was done with five crowns, and refreshed with a draught of wine. Twelve scudi were paid to a *formatore* to cast it in *gesso*. Cammuccini, Gibson, and all the English artists in Rome went to see the group, and pronounced it to be very like nature, and modelled with a good deal of spirit, breadth, and force. The next undertaking was a *basso-relievo* of the Dead Christ laid at the foot of the Cross; which work he hoped to be enabled to cut in marble and send home to Cork as a proof to his friends that their encouragement had not been abused or misapplied. Then, having begun to consider what subject he should choose for the figure he was commissioned to execute for Sir John Leicester, he decided on adopting an idea from Gesner's idyl, The Death of Abel, and modelled the figure known as Eve startled at the sight of Death. The English artists congratulated the young sculptor on the purity of sentiment and gracefulness of outline exhibited in the model; and Albigini and Rinaldi expressed their astonishment at the mastership of the chisel he displayed when, shortly afterwards, he cut the figure in marble. The block he had purchased was unusually hard and perfect, and he worked on it with great care and caution; doubtless pleasing his fancy the while with the thought of the pleasure his work would give his generous patron when it should be sent him from Rome But just as it was receiving the final touches of the chisel, the news of Lord de Tabley's death was brought to the artist, who, with his usual delicacy of feeling, considered it would be "wrong and unmanly" to put in a claim on his successor for the acceptance of the statue "which his lordship had ordered for his advancement" Mr. Carey, however, was too watchful of his young friend's interests to be dictated to by such over-refinement. The work was paid for and sent home. For a number of years the case in which the statue was packed remained unopened At the Manchester Exhibition of Art Treasures, 1857, the Eve was seen for the first time

Soon after the completion of Lord de Tabley's commission, Mr. Hogan, calculating on receiving a considerable remittance from Cork, purchased a block and set a *scarpellino* to rough out the Shepherd Boy, while he himself continued his studies at the English Life Academy, and began to model what he called "an active, light, and strong figure of a fawn." This was the afterwards well-known Drunken Fawn,[1] one of the most remarkable of Mr. Hogan's works, and worthy of the highest praise for originality of design and masterly execution. Camuccini and the other Italian artists were delighted with it, and gave the sculptor, ungrudgingly, a meed of praise that acted, he said, in the same manner as the sound of a trumpet to the ears of a war-horse. Thorwaldsen likewise went to see the Fawn, and pronounced the figure worthy of an Athenian studio. "Ah!" said he, striking the artist familiarly on the shoulder, "you are a real sculptor—*Avete fatto un miracolo!*" Greatly as the Danish sculptor admired the Fawn, he was still more pleased with a second figure of the Dead Christ modelled not long afterwards, and pronounced by that very high authority the Irish artist's *capo d'opera*. The form, proportion, dignity of character and expression, were universally admired; the head has been pronounced one of the finest known in sculpture. Of the pathetic and religious character of the composition, an idea may be formed from the avowal of the artist, who, writing home to his father, said that although it was his own work he had been once or twice deeply affected by it himself. All he wanted now was an order from Cork to execute the figure in marble. He would be content, he declared, to live on macaroni *al sugo* and polenta, so that he could purchase a fine block, and return with flying colours to Ireland to exhibit a work he need not be ashamed of.

Encouragement sufficient to enable him to proceed having been received from home, the Dead Christ was finished, and

[1] A cast of it is in the [illegible]

Mr. Hogan resolved to visit his own country. Having packed up his marble figure of the Dead Christ, his cast of the Drunken Fawn, some busts and a few studies in plaster, and having seen the brig containing the cases safe down the Tiber, he stowed into a soldier's knapsack his small stock of wearing apparel, a guidebook, notebook, and passport, and set out by the cheapest route on his homeward journey; leaving, not without regret, the charmed precincts of *Vecchia Roma*, where he acknowledges "a frank and familiar intercourse with professors of all nations opens a man's eyes," and where "there is felt a certain stimulus in the air which makes a person think and fare like an artist."

Mr. Hogan received a gratifying reception on his arrival in Dublin, in the month of November 1829. The members of the Royal Irish Institution placed their board-room at his disposal for the exhibition of his works. The Royal Dublin Society awarded him a gold medal. He was warmly received by the Dublin artists, and visitors of every degree hastened to admire the Dead Christ and wonder at the Fawn. The Archbishop, the Most Rev. Dr. Murray, was anxious to purchase the Dead Christ for the Cathedral, but there was probably a difficulty in setting on foot a subscription for the purpose. The Carmelite community offered £400 for the figure, and though the sum was considerably below the value of the work, the offer was accepted. The money was paid at once, and the statue placed beneath the high altar in the Clarendon Street Church. Before leaving Ireland, Mr. Hogan received the earnestly desired commission to execute a figure of the Dead Christ in marble for Cork, and an order for a group for Francis Street Church in Dublin.

On his return to Italy he repaired to Carrara, and remained two months in the neighbourhood of the quarries, in search of a spotless block for the Dead Christ. He completed an entirely new cast for this work, making several important alterations in details, and considerably improving the design. Immediately on his arrival in Rome, he commenced the group for Francis Street Church. This was the Pieta, of which a cast now occupies the place over the high altar. In Rome, it was thought a matter of certainty that this work had only to be seen in Ireland to obtain him a commission to do it in marble. The artist himself cherished hopes on this score that turned out sadly delusive. We had not made such progress in Ireland as to expend £1000 on a work of the kind, and it would have cost no less a sum to finish it in marble. The original cast continued for many years to occupy the most prominent position in Mr. Hogan's Roman studio. The classic character of the composition always obtained for it enthusiastic admiration. An outline engraving appeared in the *Ape Italiana*, and a highly appreciative description of the composition may be found in Count Hawks le Grice's *Walks through the Studii of the Sculptors at Rome.*

In 1837 Mr. Hogan received a commission for a monumental group to the memory of the illustrious Dr. Doyle, Bishop of Kildare and Leighlin, having carried off the palm from ten competitors. The genius displayed in the design and execution of this group obtained for the sculptor the honour of being elected a member of the Society of the Virtuosi of the Pantheon. This, the greatest distinction an artist can enjoy, was never dreamt of nor sought for by Mr. Hogan. Great, therefore, was his surprise and joy when the secretary of the society, an archbishop, announced to him by letter that he had been unanimously elected. His diploma was presented to him by Signor Fabris, the personal friend of Gregory XVI., and afterwards director of the Vatican and of the Museum of the Capitol. The uniform worn by the members is a splendid one. On the buttons are represented the compass, chisel, and pencil, with the motto, *Florent in Domo Domini*, and the wearer is entitled to carry "a true Toledo, silver mounted." No British subject had ever been enrolled among the members of this select society. Our countryman became a member, under equally flattering circumstances, of the Academy of St. Luke.

The Doyle Monument was brought to Ireland by Mr. Hogan in 1840, and exhibited for some months in the Royal Exchange. Crowds of people went to see the work, and gazed with a feeling akin to veneration on the majestic figure of the bishop, and the pathetic yet dignified form of Hibernia.[1] The artist

[1] A writer in the *Pallade*, a Roman journal dedicated to the Arts, enters into a minute description of the group. Among other things he says — "In this work the sculptor has represented Ireland, by personification, in an attitude of submission, as one patiently supporting the burden of the unjust and oppressive laws which had been imposed upon her. She is plunged in profound and yet dignified melancholy, but her countenance, bent towards the earth closely, indicates an inward feeling of [illegible] hope

himself was rather overwhelmed by the personal attentions he received. Invitations to viceregal banquets, and the continual reappearance of "couriers booted and spurred, sweating with despatch from the Castle," together with similar attentions bestowed on him by other distinguished and influential parties, nearly exhausted his patience and good humour. He used to complain of all it cost him on these occasions for car-hire and other expenses, and would characteristically express a wish that they would send him, instead of a polite invitation, a ready boiled or roasted turkey, which he might eat at home in peace with a pleasant friend or two. One thing, however, did afford him some consolation, and that was the pleasure and pride he felt in appearing on these festive occasions in the full uniform of the Virtuosi of the Pantheon. No other British subject, he knew very well, could do so. Unfortunately, the admiration bestowed on his work, and the magnificent hospitality extended to himself, were no compensation to the artist for the want of prompt and sufficient payment. Mr Hogan considered himself extremely ill-used by the Doyle committee. He had at one time to apply to the Roman banker, Torlonia, for money to go on with the work, no remittances having been forwarded from Ireland,—and some years after the commission was given, more than £400 remained still due to the sculptor. However, before his departure for Rome, he received another commission, and under circumstances both complimentary and satisfactory.

Captain Drummond, Under-Secretary for Ireland, having died in the spring of the same year (1840), it was resolved to raise a subscription for the erection of a monument to the man whose loss was justly regarded as a public calamity, and whose love for Ireland had exhibited something of romance in its tenderness and tenacity. It was not forgotten, that when on

blended with gratification arising from the knowledge that one of her own beloved children has undertaken with strenuous and powerful efforts the assertion of her cause before the empire. The bishop, in a posture expressive of tenderness and emotion, his left hand approaching her back below the left shoulder, and his right raised in dignified and earnest supplication, with his face to heaven, stands by the drooping figure of his country, as it were, to raise her from the anguish and distress in which for so many ages she had groaned, his confidence fixed above—thither he addresses the fervent aspiration of his soul for the welfare of his beloved Ireland Such is the philosophical conception of the work—a conception which has an intimate connection with the history of that fertile and unhappy la[illegible]"

his deathbed he was asked where he wished to be laid to rest,—in Scotland, his native country, or in Ireland,—his immediate answer was, "In Ireland, the land of my adoption. I have loved her well, and served her faithfully, and lost my life in her service." The erection of a colossal statue was decided on, and it was resolved to give the commission, without competition, to the sculptor of the Doyle Monument. The terms offered were liberal—£500 in hand, £200 to be paid in Rome when the work was modelled and cast, £500 on the arrival of the statue in Dublin, the artist not to be at any expense in the matter of freight, insurance, pedestal. The terms were kept to the letter; Lord Morpeth proving on this occasion, and not for the last time, a good friend to Mr Hogan. The statue was finished early in the year 1843, but was detained till spring in the Roman studio, where it created somewhat of a sensation on account of the spirit of the execution and the sentiment which it breathes.[1]

At this period Mr. Hogan had several important works on hands. Among others, Lord Cloncurry's Hibernia; a statue for Cork of one of his own earliest and best friends, Mr. Crawford, on which, as he said himself, he poured out all his soul, and the colossal figure of O'Connell, ordered by the Repeal Association. When the model for the Liberator's statue was completed, the artist made a journey to the marble quarries or caves of Saravezza, distant about two hundred and fifty miles from Rome, and spent a considerable time searching for a faultless block for the gigantic figure.

The block he selected was of an immense *grossezza*, and proved immaculate indeed. The moment he saw it on the mountain-side he was able to perceive within the rough contour of the huge mass his intended colossal figure, concealed from all eyes but his own, in the vast block just hewn from the bowels of the mountain. When *purgato*, that is to say, cleaned from the worthless portions, it was shipped for Rome. The immense mass was dragged from the Ripa Grande, on the Tiber, through the city by a long train of oxen, and representa-

[1] "When I went to Ireland in 1852," writes Miss Martineau, "one of my first objects in Dublin was to see the statue of my poor old friend in the Royal Exchange. It was a far more pathetic sight than I had imagined. It was the same face,—but I should hardly have known it without looking for it,—so worn, almost haggard in comparison with what it had been! It justified his closing words, 'I die for Ireland.'"

tions were made to Mr. Hogan about the danger of injuring the streets by dragging over them so weighty a mass. An addition had to be made to the studio in preparation for the reception of the block, which was got in through a breach made on the occasion in the outer wall of the building. A correspondent of the *Art Journal*, writing home in terms of the highest admiration of the Hibernia then completed, and of the O'Connell in progress, remarked that the marble in which the latter figure was being cut was, for its size, of a most remarkable quality: "Its colour beautiful and without a speck, and so hard that, as they chisel it, it rings like a bell."

Though Mr Hogan not unfrequently visited Ireland, Rome was his home from 1824 to 1848. These twenty-four years were the busiest and the happiest of his life. During the greatest part of the time his studio was in the Vicolo di S. Giacamo, a small street running from the Corso to the Ripetta under the walls of the Great Hospital of S. Giacomo. It had been part of Canova's studio, vacated a short time before Mr. Hogan's arrival in Rome by the death of the great Italian. As the original casts of their works are always preserved by sculptors, their studii are generally places of considerable interest. In Rome they are the common resort of all travellers, literary people, and persons of taste. If the artist himself be not occupied with his living models or sitters, he generally receives his visitors and accompanies them, or at least gives them perfect liberty, to inspect his works. The Irish sculptor was himself a striking figure in the studio. His tall, lithe, powerful frame, and his noble head and eagle look were eminently characteristic. He was full of gesture and vivacity, yet withal was simple in manner and direct in speech. Among the visitors at Mr. Hogan's studio were often to be seen a group of Irish students from the Franciscan College of St. Isidoro, or from the Augustinian house of Santa Maria in Posterula, or of Irish Dominicans from San Clemente. Students from the Irish College of St. Agatha would sometimes drop into their countryman's studio to see some work in progress: the majestic figure of Dr Doyle, or O Connell, or Davis, or Drummond; the monumental effigy of Dr. Brinkley, or Peter Purcell, or Father M'Namara; the portrait-busts of Father Mathew, Father Prout, or some other distinguished countryr[illegible] visiting Mr. Hogan's studio could fail to observe that the subjects that had most attraction for him in the ideal order were the group of the Pieta, the form of the Dead Christ, and the personification of his country in the figure of Hibernia.

His brother artists, as we have said, were to be met with from time to time in the Irish sculptor's studio. Among the Italians of the same profession he had many friends, notably, besides those already mentioned, Tadolini and Rinaldi, and Tenerani, whom the Italians called the Goliath of sculptors. But most of all he valued the friendship of Giovanni Benzoni. With Gibson, Wyatt, Macdonnel, and Theed, Mr. Hogan was on friendly terms. The greatest of them all, Thorwaldsen, had, as already stated, the highest opinion of our countryman. When about to return to Denmark he took leave of Mr. Hogan, embracing him warmly. "My son," said he, "you are the best sculptor I leave after me in Rome."

Mr. Hogan, who was always a hard-working man, was to be found every morning in his studio at five o'clock if there was light, and generally during the summer still earlier, and his *siesta* was never a long one. The men employed by him to rough out his works in marble were frequently assisted by him in the operation of "taking the points," which, according to the old system still used in Italy, and unaided by mechanism, required the nicest accuracy; and when the block of marble was reduced by them to a tolerable approximation to his model, he was in the constant habit of taking the chisel into his own hands and bringing out himself all the fine developments of muscle, and all the critical details of the drapery, without waiting to content himself with giving merely the last touches. In this way he took upon him a great deal of additional labour —labour which few sculptors have the mechanical skill to undertake. Many sculptors are utterly unable to handle their own works except in the plastic clay in which the model is first produced, and for every subsequent operation are obliged to depend on the skill and expertness of tradesmen. But it was not so with Mr. Hogan. He was generally his own *formatore*, making the waste-mold for the clay and casting the plaster model; and also, as we have said, when there was difficulty or nicety, he took upon himself the harder manual labour of the *scarpellino*. Thus to his own hands are to be attributed the delicate softness of the flesh and the peculiar grace of many a fold in his works in the rigid marble. It is said of Michael Angelo that he chiselled a statue out of a block of marble without the preliminary step of modelling it, and Mr. Hogan has often been known to deviate boldly from his model in transferring the work to marble,—a thing which would be impossible unless he held the chisel in his own hand, and which must have required great skill in guiding it, and no little courage in attempting an alteration in such a material.

After his marriage in 1838 to an Italian lady, Mr Hogan, to whom the dissipated style of life in which artists frequently indulge had always been distasteful, became more and more domestic in his habits, seldom going abroad for amusement except when accompanied by his family. In many things he had become a perfect Italian, and few Italians were more abstemious. About seven or eight o'clock in the morning he might be usually met at the large *café* near the Church of San Carlo in the Corso Here he came to sip a *tazza* of coffee, which, with about two mouthfuls of bread, constitutes the Roman breakfast, and to read *Galignani*, where he met an occasional paragraph of Irish news. In the evening he never exceeded a glass or two of sober *orvieto*, or of the bitter infusion the Germans call beer. Sometimes he walked in the evening with his family on the Corso, and sometimes he took them out for a holiday to Albano or some of the picturesque towns beyond the Campagna. He was hospitable to friends, and very frequently had young English or Irish artists at his table. For many years before he left Rome he occupied a spacious house in the Via del Babuino, one of the three great streets which diverge from the Piazza del Popolo, the other extremity of that street being in the fashionable thoroughfare of the Piazza di Spagna.

But the "continual round of peace" which, to use his own words, Mr. Hogan enjoyed at this time, was brought, as well as his twenty-four years' residence in Rome, to a disastrous termination. The revolution of 1848 shattered the peace of that happy household as it shook the foundations of the Eternal City itself The general despondency which followed the siege of Rome affected the artist's mind with perhaps too deep a gloom, and he resolved to return to Ireland. He had many times expressed a wish to have his children educated in the country of his birth; yet, were it not for the evil times that had fallen on Italy, he might have long hesitated to break up his home in a country to whose climate and manners he had long been naturalised, in which it is easier than elsewhere to support a family upon limited means, and where, as in matters of art the mind naturally turns to Rome, patronage would have more surely found him. It was indeed an evil day when Hogan stowed away among the casts of his works such articles of property as he did not care to remove, and, giving the key of his studio to his good friend Benzoni, turned his back on that beloved second home, and led his wife and young Italian children to his distant motherland.

The next ten years of the artist's life were saddened by many trials and disappointments. He had left the terrors of the revolution behind him in Italy only to encounter the horrors of the famine time at home. There was little artistic work to be done, and that little was, in some remarkable instances, not given to Mr. Hogan, but intrusted to incompetent hands. We need only refer in this place to the Moore Testimonial, which remains a memorial of the injustice done to an eminent artist, and can be regarded in no other light than as a national disgrace. The rejection of Mr. Hogan's models for the Moore Testimonial gave him a severe shock, and brought on a dangerous attack of illness. He could only account for the injury done to him on this and some other occasions by supposing that he must have had secret enemies bent on his ruin. He had lived so long out of Ireland that he forgot how often our unfortunate propensity for jobbing in committee leads to unjust and atrocious proceedings Nor did he remember the prevailing ignorance of artistic matters that accounted, as nothing else could account, for the want of consideration too often shown him by would-be patrons as well as by public bodies. It is also true that there was felt to be a certain prestige about getting a work done in Rome which did not attach to the execution of a similar work at home; and that some who would have been willing to give him a commission in Italy did not care to employ him in Dublin. Most of all was he irritated by a misapprehension which prevailed in some qurters as to the cause of his leaving Rome. It was erroneously supposed that because he had left Italy during the revolutionary period, his departure must have been attributable to political reasons. This injurious suspicion, Mr Hogan fancied, made him be regarded with a certain coldness on some occasions when he fully expected to meet with a cordial reception.

Certainly, to the artist's nature, sensitive to the verge of irritability, nothing could be more ungenial than the atmosphere in which during these years he was obliged to live. He had a host of small annoyances to bear beside the serious troubles that made his latter years unhappy. No doubt a little more patience with a people uneducated in art, and somewhat more tolerance for professional inferiority, would have tended to make his own life less uncomfortable. When a member of committee wanted to have spectacles put on a statue, the artist might as well have laughed as have become enraged; but when one of his exquisitely-chiselled figures, to remove the hue of antiquity it had already assumed, was scoured with freestone as a preparation for its appearance at an exhibition, we cannot blame him for fretting at an example of the way in which ignorance can inflict an injury as well as malignity. Unfortunately, instances were not wanting in his experience of hardship and injustice for which no plea of ignorance could be alleged. The owner of one of his *alto-relievos*, it is said, allowed the work to be copied three times for the profit of another sculptor; and all his attempts to obtain a settlement of the balance due for the Dead Christ in St. Finbar's Church in Cork proved unsuccessful.[1]

Happily, Mr. Hogan's devotion to art did not unfit him for the practical business of life. Though generous in affording help to others, he was never recklessly extravagant, nor even careless in the expenditure of money. His frugality and good sense enabled him to support his numerous family in comfort and respectability. He was admirable as the

[1] We believe that since Mr Hogan's death his family have received a considerable part, if not the whole, of the sum due for this work. At one time it was suggested that the sculptor should try to get possession of this statue, which would be certain to find a purchaser in America, if not in Ireland But he said, "No, I will not have the curses of the people, accustomed to pray before that statue, on my head; let it remain where it is." And, indeed, a most prayer-inspiring and beautiful object it is in St. Finbar's Church—excellently placed, and to be seen by all and at all times. The Dead Christ in Clarendon Street Church, Dublin, is also admirably placed, and [illegible]

head of a family, and the strength of the domestic affections ensured him an amount of happiness which consoled him for the disappointments he met with in other spheres. All his interests centred in his children,—he could not bear to be long away from them. He seldom accepted an invitation to spend the evening out, and, when he did, he was all impatience to get home again. It was his custom to gather his children round him in the evening, and while they were engaged in their studies he would read some amusing book, now and then translating a passage into Italian for his wife. At nine o'clock the household retired to rest, unless on festival days, when the family devotions would be somewhat lengthened. During the school holidays he always occupied himself in the studio, teaching his sons to draw from the round.

After a time the deep gloom that had overshadowed the country began to clear away, and Mr. Hogan's prospects also became brighter. His old friend Dr. Mulloch, Bishop of Newfoundland, gave him a commission to execute important works for the Cathedral of St. John's. He received several orders from private individuals. It was decided that the statue of O'Connell for Limerick should be given to him; and he was requested to prepare a model for a statue of Father Mathew about to be erected in Cork. There was a good deal of talk just then of a monument to Goldsmith for Dublin, and a statue of Sarsfield for Limerick, and there was little reason to doubt that Mr. Hogan would have had these works intrusted to him. The idea delighted him. He was fond of counting over with his friends the cities, towns, churches, and convents in Ireland which possessed works of his, and he now hoped that the list would be increased. In fact, he believed that what he had foreseen nearly thirty years before as the result of Catholic Emancipation was about to be accomplished, and that at last the arts would be "pushed on gloriously in Ireland" He was satisfied that if his life were lengthened a few years he should be able to leave his family in easy circumstances. In Rome his studio remained undisturbed, filled with casts of his works. His dream was to return to the genial land where he had lived and laboured for so many years, and near his dear friend Benzoni, and, with his eldest son, whom he was educating as a sculptor, beside him, to resume a life of peaceful study and noble productiveness.[1]

But this was a dream not destined to be realised. His health declined, and for a year before his death he was often restless at night and unfit for work by day. When unable to sleep, it was his habit to light a lamp and read a chapter of his favourite book, *The Imitation of Christ.* Sometimes he would arise, take a light and go down to his studio—to recall, perhaps, the inspirations that had once informed the shapeless mass, or to refresh the weary spirit with a vision of what yet might be accomplished. On one of these occasions he was found kneeling in prayer before his own figure of the Dead Saviour the same work which, twenty years before, he had told his father was greatly admired by the artists in Rome, and, though his own work, had sometimes affected himself. On the Sunday preceding his death he left his bed and stole down to the studio. He looked round on his unfinished works, and pausing in front of a work in marble which was being executed at the cost of a private gentleman for the then recently erected Church of St. Saviour in Dublin, he said to his son and to his assistant, "Finish it well, boys, I shall never handle the chisel more!"

When he lay down again, he directed a search to be made for an engraving of Thorwaldsen's statue of the Redeemer, which those about him had not been aware that he possessed. This he had pinned to the wall in such a way that his eyes could conveniently turn to it; and he seemed never tired of gazing upon a figure which he said would in itself have been enough to immortalise a sculptor—the gently outstretched arms and whole attitude so well expressed the idea, *Venite ad me omnes!* From time to time he spoke with the friends who were round his bed of times long gone by, and of the loved ones who had preceded him to life eternal. He talked of the father he had idolised, of the pious mother who had made his

[1] Lady Morgan, a very sincere friend of Mr Hogan, who presented to her a cast of the Shepherd Boy, left by her will a sum of £100 for a monument to Carolan, the Irish bard, to be executed by "Hogan the Younger." This work, a prominent feature of which is a portrait-bust in high relief of the harper, is, we understand, now on the way from Rome; and will before long occupy its destined position in St. Patrick's Cathedral. Judging from a photograph taken of the monument, we have no doubt it will be considered [illegible] sculptor

youthful days so happy, of the only brother who had died early, and of the sister who had devoted her life to God. He spoke of them as if they were not far from him. And then he would pray for his children, and taking his wife's hand, assure her that he would watch over her—most certainly watch over her For some hours before his death he seemed insensible, except that when they read the prayers for the dying he audibly made the responses, and for a long time the only words he uttered were—"Beautiful! how beautiful!"

On the 27th March 1858 the sculptor breathed his last, in the fifty-eighth year of his age. Three days after his death his remains were carried to Glasnevin Cemetery in a hearse open at the sides, so that as the procession passed through the city it was observed that on the coffin lay the hat and sword, scabbard and sword-belt, worn by the Virtuosi of the Pantheon—the insignia of the honours he had won and worn with pride in the city of arts. His four sons followed, and a long train of men distinguished in every calling—members of the bar and the press and the medical profession, literary men and artists, representatives of the secular clergy, the Friar Preachers, and the Jesuit Fathers. As the procession approached Trinity College, the students, wearing academic cap and gown, and headed by two of the Fellows, issued two by two from the inner entrance, and, lifting their caps as they passed the hearse, took up their position, and headed the procession in its passage through the city. As the *Europe Artiste* said "Genius had its triumph even in the vain, shallow city of Dublin, and the funeral car of Hogan, the great sculptor, who died poor as he had lived, was yet followed to the grave by a file of private carriages long enough to cover two of the Boulevards of Paris"

The committee of the Glasnevin Cemetery had offered a plot of ground in any part of the cemetery that might be chosen for the sculptor's grave; and in the old "O'Connell Circle" he was laid to rest, in a spot now covered by a plain slab, on which the single word HOGAN is inscribed.

A hope has more than once been expressed to see a monument raised over the remains of so distinguished an Irishman Departed genius may be honoured, we think, in other ways than in the erection of monumental structures, and Hogan's fame would hardly be much extended by the erection of a pile of masonry in Glasnevin, where mediocrity is wont to lie buried beneath a mountain of granite, and "mute inglorious" citizens are sometimes, and with too sharp an irony, distinguished by "a loud epitaph upon their marble." Perhaps at no distant day a statue of Moore, cast in bronze from Hogan's model so memorably rejected, may be erected in our capital. Perhaps that beautiful statue of Davis may also be cast in bronze, and set up in one of our provincial cities. Perhaps the Pieta may in course of time be executed in marble, and placed in one of the beautiful churches erected within the last half-century in Catholic Ireland. Meanwhile we would venture to suggest to the directors of the National Gallery in Dublin, the propriety of making some effort to secure one of Hogan's works, or a series of casts of his works, for that institution. Assuredly some tribute should in our generation be paid to the memory of a man of singular moral worth, gifted with undoubted genius, and inspired with that elevated and sustained enthusiasm without which art is lowered to handicraft and literature degraded to a trade.

"COMMONPLACE SAINTS"

OBSERVING the efficient and courteous way in which a lady of my acquaintance discharges the duties of a Sodality Librarian, I have oftentimes admired her tact in suiting the tastes and supplying the wants of readers who, though they may have a tolerably clear idea of what they should like, do not always seem to know precisely what it is they ought to ask for. Once only do I remember to have seen her at a loss, and that was on a certain occasion when a bright little maid, stepping up to the table in front of the book-shelves, delivered herself in the following terms:

"Please, ma'am, my mother wants something to read, and says she would be very much obliged if you could lend her the life of a commonplace saint!"

How our good librarian managed to meet so unusual a demand, I cannot now say, but I recollect that she remarked on the moment that it was to be feared the story of "commonplace saints" had never been written—except in the Book of Life. The incident, however, started a discussion, which was carried on with considerable animation for some time by a group of "heads of classes" who happened to be standing by. So quaint an association of the ordinary with the extraordinary suggested some interesting reflections, and examples were quoted as bearing on the case in point. Among other things, it was remarked that saints following vocations of an altogether exceptional character are recorded to have cherished an exalted idea of the perfection of devout persons who undoubtedly treaded their way to heaven along very humble paths; and that some, whose nimbus of sanctity was all but dazzlingly visible to those around them, had avowedly been impelled to "strive for the mastery" by the example of, perhaps, a relative or acquaintance, whose holiness the world at large seemed never to have divined. The question was, whether those unsuspected mirrors of perfection might not, if their simple story were told, answer completely to many a one's idea of "a commonplace saint."

"In the history of the Egyptian solitaries," said one of the interlocutors, "you will find, if I mistake not, an example of what might be called 'commonplace sanctity' held up to one of the great hermit-saints as a model on which to form himself to a still higher perfection than he had attained after years of penance and prayer in the wilderness."

"You need not travel quite so far as the African deserts," rejoined another, "to see how a lowly sanctity may pass unheeded even in the midst of a community of godly men, and yet win the delighted recognition of the angelic host, and stimulate an illustrious servant of God to undertake a memorable achievement. Recall the story of our own St. Aengus, and you will discover a pendant for the lesson taught by God to the famous anchorite of the East"

"After all," struck in a third, as if to clinch the argument, "what the little girl's mother really desires, for her own special edification and encouragement, is simply an account of the life of one of God's servants whom the children of this world would probably designate as quite a commonplace sort of person; while the sons of light would discern in him, or in her, as the case might be, a gem of the purest water Certainly, it would help us greatly if we kept well in mind the simplicity of the elements which constitute the perfection of those who are *saints according to God.*"

Mentally, I made a note of this suggestive conversation, and on my return home lost no time in looking up the desert saints, while postponing to a later day an antiquarian ramble on the track of "the rapt Culdee" The indicated illustration from Oriental sources was not long to seek. It turned up in the Life of St Macarius the Elder.

Far removed from commonplace, indeed, was the type of this man's sanctity. His early years were spent in watching flocks and herds with his father, a shepherd dwelling in Lower Egypt, at the beginning of the fourth century of the Christian era. From childhood he was distinguished for his singular holiness of life—he had ever before him a high ideal of religious conduct; and when he grew to manhood, he built for himself a hut near a poor village, and took up his abode therein, devoting himself to the austere routine of a prayerful, laborious, secluded life, and desiring nothing so much as to avoid the dangers of the world and the notice of his fellow-men. But his was a light that could not be hid The wisdom of his unstudied words, the charity of his simple heart, his heroic patience in bearing injuries inflicted on him by the malignity of a wicked neighbour, attracted the reverential regard of those among whom he lived. Many persons came to his little cabin to seek his counsel, solicit his help, beseech his prayers. He could not refuse anything that was asked of him for Christ's sake, nor could the Lord Himself, so it seemed, turn a deaf ear to His faithful servant's petition, whatever it might be. The efficacy of his intercession justified the confidence of his clients, and was oftentimes attested even by miracles.

All this, however, accorded in no degree with the humble hermit's estimate of himself He began to feel unsafe, and anxious to escape from his admirers; and, being now about thirty years of age, he resolved to forsake his hut, and go forth in search of a retreat remote, unknown, and inaccessible.

At that time the deserts of Egypt, the mountains of Syria, and the hills of Palestine, were peopled by a multitude of holy men, who had fled from a wicked world to follow in seclusion the perfect way of the ascetic life. Though associated in communities, and bound to assemble at stated times to hear Mass, receive the sacraments, and follow a disciplinary course of instruction, each of the cenobites dwelt apart in his cave or rustic cell, practising self-denial of the rudest kind, pursuing laborious avocations, and praying incessantly. Withdrawn though they were from the temptations and dangers that beset a secular life, they did not hold themselves exempt from the exercise of charity towards their fellow-men All who came from the centres of population to rest awhile in the desert, refresh their soul in the companionship of saintly men, and strengthen their spirit under the tuition of those masters of the penitential life, were kindly received at the cenobium — fed, sheltered, instructed, shriven, and set on a better road to the heavenly country than they had hitherto pursued. And as the persevering industry of those holy men compelled the reluctant soil to yield a produce far in excess of what was required to supply their own limited wants, they found themselves in a position to succour the necessitous, and even to undertake the charge of sick and infirm persons. We are told that in the heart of the desert the ascetics established refuges for the suffering members of Christ, asylums for cripples, and hospitals for sick children. It is hardly surprising to hear that, in course of time, paths were literally worn in the once trackless waste by the feet of innumerable pilgrims journeying towards the monastic settlements in search of counsel, instruction, consolation, and charitable aid in every variety of spiritual need and bodily ail.

But this sort of desert would not satisfy the aspirations of Macarius. It did not seem enough to *flee from the midst of Babylon.* He longed to bury himself in complete solitude with God. Passing, therefore, through Egypt, he directed his steps to the wilderness of Sceté, stretching within the confines of Lybia. Untenanted even by anchorites, this vast expanse exhibited a scene of unmitigated desolation. There were no roads, no landmarks of any kind. Travellers obliged to cross the unfrequented plain, depended on the stars for guidance in their course. Dangerous morasses, and lakes of brackish water, diversified, without relieving, the dreariness of the scene —a scene in every respect accordant with penitential rigour and merciless self-immolation. Here Macarius found the awful solitude he sought; here, accordingly, he took up his abode, and here he had his home during the remainder of his mortal pilgrimage of ninety years.

Gradually, however, a change came over the sombre face of Sceté. The fatality, as perhaps he would have called it, which overtook him in his younger days, still, it would appear, pursued Macarius in the years of his maturity. Hid though he was in the swamps, wrapped safe, as he fancied, in the stillness of the desert, his retreat and his identity were discovered; people came out from the luxurious cities and smiling pastures to tarry awhile for their soul's good in the neighbourhood of the hermit-saint; and many of these temporary refugees from the world of sin and sorrow, yielding to the fascination exercised in all unconsciousness by the [illegible] of God, and conquered by divine grace, declined to return any more to the arena of perilous distractions, declaring they must abide henceforth in the desert, and complete the course of their earthly pilgrimage under the direction of the holy man of Sceté. Communities, as if by natural growth, formed settlements within reach of the centre of attraction—the hut wherein Macarius dwelt; these, again, after a while, found others grouped without their bounds, until, in the end, it became necessary to erect four churches for the religious colonists, and appoint a priest to minister in each. Despite of his humility, the hermit-saint was himself compelled to enter the ranks of the priesthood, and assume the direction of the cenobium.

Although hitherto unused to the task of ruling men in organised associations, Macarius was singularly blessed in his government of the monastic family. He was called the god of the monks, so affectionate and ready was the obedience he received from his spiritual sons, while at the same time the pilgrims who still sought the desert in their spiritual needs, experienced the prevailing force of his exhortations, as if he had been specially ordained for the succour of those whose destiny it was to work out their salvation in the throng and conflict of secular life.

A thoughtful writer of our own day has somewhere said, that "there is no eloquence unless there is a man behind the speech"; and perhaps in the same way it may be laid down, that preaching can have little effect unless there is a saint behind the sermon. At anyrate, it is evident that the secret of the extraordinary influence of Macarius lay in the holiness and gentle charity of the man of prayer. Whether in the homilies addressed to his monks, or in the instructions given to the strangers who laid their hearts open before him, he made use of language suited to the meanest capacity, and, indeed, seemed to aim principally at simplifying the doctrines and practices of the spiritual life. Thus, when urging his disciples to persevere in their penitential course, he would exhort them to bear their hard lot by the thought that they must be crucified with the Crucified One, and that the human soul, which is the bride of Christ, must suffer with the Bridegroom. Or, when inculcating the duty of continual prayer, he would teach them short, easy methods, saying: "We need not use many or lofty words; we can keep God in our hearts and the Holy Ghost in our breast; and if we can do no more, we can often repeat, with a sincere affection, this ejaculation of perfect resignation and love—*O Lord have mercy on me, as Thou pleasest, and knowest best in Thy goodness.*"

He knew how on occasions to enforce a lesson in a striking and original way. For instance, when a certain young man came to him for advice and assistance in overcoming his spiritual enemies, he desired him go to a neighbouring burial-place and revile the dead! The young man returned when he had fulfilled this strange command, and being asked how the dead had received the abuse showered on them, he replied: "My father, they took no notice whatever." "Go back, then," rejoined the saint, "and flatter them." This also was done in simple obedience; and the dead having displayed an equal insensibility, answering never a word to the proffered adulation, the abbot pointed the moral with good effect. "Learn, therefore," he said, "to be moved neither by injuries nor flatteries. If you die to the world and to yourself, you will begin to live to Christ."

Humility, which another saint declares is the only virtue no devil can imitate, and the secret of the strength by which the saints have won their greatest victories, was, it need hardly be added, a main characteristic of Macarius. Satan himself acknowledged that the anchorite defeated all his efforts by this resistless weapon. "I can surpass thee in watching, fasting, and many other things," he said, "but humility vanquishes and disarms me." However, this all-conquering virtue had not been acquired without many a sharp encounter and much long-suffering in resisting temptation. Once he was so beset by the enemy of mankind with suggestions of vain-glory, and so worn out in the prolonged warfare, that he implored Almighty God day and night to give him a true humiliation, and free him once for all from the tantalising attacks of the evil spirit. Heaven heard his petition; and he received for answer a command to go to a certain city, a considerable distance off, where there were persons living who had reached a higher perfection than the hermit of the desert, and who would teach him the secret of their pre-eminent virtue.

And so we can picture to ourselves the servant of God, with his wan face and wasted form, taking his staff in hand and turning his steps once more towards the great world of sin and sorrow, out of which he and companies of saints had fled in affright, how many a long year ago! Across the marshy plains and by the margin of the brackish lakes he wended his way out into the vast yellow sands, marked here and there by the slow march of a labouring caravan, or startled into momentary life by the lightning passage of a train of dromedaries, until at length, suddenly rising from out a sea of shifting undulations, he beheld the city of his destination in its oasis of verdure.

If Macarius imagined that he would have no difficulty in finding the saints whom the Lord commended, if he thought the city must be filled with their renown, he soon discovered his mistake. The city was quite unaware of the treasure it possessed. No guide appeared to conduct the pilgrim to their abode. The saints themselves were personally known to few, and those few, in all probability, regarded them as commonplace persons. To a certainty this was the opinion of the pious souls themselves, who would have been the last in the world to suppose it possible that anyone would travel out of the desert to make their acquaintance.

In a word, the good and faithful servants to whose door the Spirit of God led the anchorite, turned out to be two homely married women, who for fifteen years had dwelt in the same house together in perfect peace, attracting no attention, having nothing remarkable in themselves or in their circumstances; but cheerfully obeying their husbands, taking the best care of their children, diligently labouring in their household affairs, speaking no rash or idle words, and making all around them happy.

Having learned thus much, Macarius besought those simple souls so dear to God to disclose to him their way of life "Oh! my father, it is not worth the trouble," they answered. But as he insisted, they told him that their endeavour was to keep themselves in the presence of God while engaged in their household affairs, that in a spirit of recollection they sanctified their actions by ardent ejaculations, striving thereby to praise God and to consecrate to the divine glory all the powers of their soul and body. "That is all we can do for love of Him," they added, "and it is, alas! very little."

This, then, was what Macarius came out of the desert to hear. But it was enough a lesson of humble fidelity and constant love, a revelation of the goodness of God, who, by lowly ways no less than by aspiring paths, leads the sincere soul to its heavenly destination, who makes a tabernacle for the children of the kingdom even in the midst of Babylon, and, in recompense for the modest sacrifices of a willing service and a loving heart, bestows the crown of life.

Glad that he had seen "saints greater than Macarius," with a mind enlightened and a heart consoled, the pilgrim took up his staff once more and turned towards the solitudes of Sceté. And as he wended his way, angel-guarded and star-guided, he thanked God for the souls, serene and steadfast, fulfilling their appointed course, whether in the world's tumult or the desert's peace, whether in the twilight of obscurity or in the noonday glare of recognition, hastening on to the heaven of full beatitude, where the just shall *shine like stars for all eternity.*

THE DITTAMONDO

Two or three incidental circumstances have led me to the conclusion that a short article written by me on Fazio degli Uberti and his poem, the Dittamondo, about two years ago, attracted some attention, and set more than one of its readers on a search for ampler information concerning the poet and his book. Certainly, I was not myself by any means satisfied with the meagre statements which contained nearly the sum-total of what I had learned up to that date of Fazio, his family, and his literary achievements. Since then I have had better success in the field of inquiry. One thing led to another, in the curious way not uncommon in pursuits of this kind, and, before the exploration ended, my acquaintance with certain pages of Italian literature and some chapters of Irish legendary and historic lore was considerably improved.

Comparing notes may sometimes be an interesting exercise. For my own part, I should greatly like to hear the result of other folk's rambles on this track. In the hope of inducing one or another of my unknown fellow-travellers, who may have advanced farther or succeeded better than myself, to share his garnered store, I will now set down in rough order the notes I jotted on the way.

And first, as regards the family referred to. In the thirteenth century the Uberti were of ancient standing in Florence, occupying that part of the city called the quarter of Porta Santa Maria, "where now stand," says Villani, "the Piazza de' Priori and the Palazzo del Popolo." The most renowned of the race up to that date, or indeed at any time, was Farinata degli Uberti, whom Machiavelli describes as a man of exalted

( )

soul and great military talents. Moreover, he was the most eloquent orator of his day. He was the foremost chief of the Ghibellines, that is to say, of the aristocratic faction in the republic, who paid an honorary allegiance to the emperor and carried on a constant warfare against the Guelphs, or party acknowledging the pope as their head, and claiming to be the supporters of the Church and Liberty. In the year 1250 the Guelphs acquired a complete ascendency over their opponents, established a popular government in the city, and compelled the neighbouring republics to espouse their cause. Meanwhile the vanquished Ghibellines intrigued and conspired, but to no good purpose; for in 1258 their designs were frustrated, and all their chiefs expelled from Florence.

Farinata, in exile, maintained the ancient strife on another stage and after a different manner. He persuaded Manfred, King of the Two Sicilies, to assume the position of acknowledged leader of the Ghibelline party, obtained from that monarch a considerable body of German troops, and, placing himself at their head, marched to Siena; which city, disregarding the treaty forced on its acceptance by the Guelphs, had already welcomed the Florentine refugees within its gates. These proceedings enraged the Signoria of Florence. Reinforced by their allies, the men of war marched out with their carroccio or battle-car and took the road to Siena, determined to draw Farinata, with his Germans and the Sienese and Pisan Militia, from the city, and annihilate at one blow the forces of their enemies. An encounter took place on the 4th of September 1260 a few miles south of Siena, on the banks of the Arbia, which stream, as readers of the *Divina Commedia* remember, on that day ran red with blood. The standard-bearer of Florence was treacherously cut down, and the army, seeing the colours fall, fled on all sides, leaving ten thousand dead on the field. The battle-car and the battle-bell and the fallen standard were carried in triumph to Siena, and consternation fell on the city seated on the Arno.

Self-exiled, the chief men of the Florentine Guelphs abandoned their dwellings, and, joined by those of Prato, Pistoia, Volterra, and San Geminiano, took refuge in Lucca; while the victorious Ghibellines, reinstated in their ancient supremacy, abolished the popular government, and set up an aristocratic régime in its stead.

At a diet of the Ghibellines held soon after at Empoli, the representatives of Siena and Pisa proposed, as a means of securing the advantages already acquired, that the walls of Florence should be razed to the ground and the inhabitants dispersed among the neighbouring towns,—urging that the populace were ingrained democrats, that no safety could exist for the Imperialists while the Guelph city stood within its ramparts, and so working on the passions of the assembled deputies that the merciless counsel was on the point of being adopted. But Farinata, fired with indignation and pouring out a torrent of patriotic eloquence, silenced the proposers of so ungenerous a policy Better would it have been to die on the Arbia than live to listen to such a discussion. He loved his country better than his party, and as long as he had life to wield a sword—even though he should stand alone among the Florentines—his native city would never be destroyed. He would, with those companions whose bravery they had witnessed at the battle of Arbia, join the Guelphs and fight for them sooner than to consent to the ruin of what was most dear to him in the world. Even if it were necessary to die a thousand deaths, he was ready to meet them all in the defence of Florence! "Farinata then rose and, with angry gestures, quitted the assembly; but left such an impression on the mind of his audience that the project was instantly dropped, and the only question for the moment was, how to regain a chief of such talent and influence."[1]

The Ghibellines were still supreme in Florence when Farinata died. Two years later, however, in 1266, their royal chief, Manfred, King of the Two Sicilies, was defeated and slain in the battle of Benevento by Charles of Anjou, the brother of St. Louis, to whom the championship of the Guelph party had been committed by the pope. Immediately the German garrison was driven out of Florence, the nobles and Ghibellines were excluded from any share in the government of the republic, and a decree of perpetual banishment was fulminated against the Uberti and their descendants.[2]

[1] Napier's *Florentine History*, vol. i

[2] "In every amnesty their names were excepted The site on which their house had stood was never again to be built upon, and remains the great square of Florence . the architect of the Palace of the People was obliged to sacrifice its symmetry, and to place it awry, that its walls might not encroach on the accursed ground"—Dean Church. *Dante an Essay.*

Not alone on the page of history does the magnanimous Farinata appear as a striking figure. The victor on the Arbia, and the saviour of the city of his birth and love, reappears on another stage, sadly immortalised by the great poet of his nation. Dante encounters the Ghibelline chief in the city of Dis, and the meeting of these citizens of the republic is the subject of a never-to-be-forgotten passage in Canto x. of the *Inferno*.[1]

Traversing with Virgil the fourth circle of hell, Dante is recognised by a fellow-countryman, Ciacco by name. While holding discourse together on the affairs of their native city, Dante, longing to know what has become of Farinata, Pegghiaio, and the rest "who bent their minds on working good," conjures Ciacco to throw some light on the matter—

> "Oh! tell me where
> They bide, and to their knowledge let me come,
> For I am prest with keen desire to hear
> If heaven's sweet cup, or poisonous drug of hell,
> Be to their lip assigned."

Ciacco removes all doubt when he replies—

> "These are yet blacker spirits. Various crimes
> Have sunk them deeper in the dark abyss.
> If thou so far descendest, thou mayst see them."

Pursuing their course along the fearful track, the poets draw nigh unto "the city that of Dis is named, with its grave denizens, a mighty throng." Framed of iron the walls seem to be; the minarets gleam vermilion under the action of the eternal fire raging through the valley, upon the gates as sentinels stand more than a thousand of the spirits "who of old from heaven were shower'd." Not without difficulty are the visitants admitted. Within is a vast plain, "thick-set with sepulchres" glowing like red-hot iron in the midst of scattered flames.

[1] Dante was born in 1265, the year after Farinata's death, and the same year in which the Guelphs regained their ascendency on the defeat and death of Manfred. His family were of the same party, and when about twenty four years of age he fought at the battle of Campaldino—the Uberti and other exiled Florentines being in the opposite ranks. Many years had not passed away when Dante himself became the victim of a faction in "the divided city." The sentence passed on him was exile, with the penalty of being [illegible]

None keep watch over these fiery vaults, above which hang suspended the lids—not to be closed until the entombed shades shall return from Josophat, bringing the bodies which they left behind on earth. Dolorous sighs and lamentable moans, "such as the sad and tortured well might raise," issue out of the sepulchres, wherein arch-heretics and "every sect their followers" lie buried, together with Epicurus and his disciples, "who with the body make the soul to die" Dante wonders whether he may see and speak with the occupants of these tombs. While he addresses himself to his guide, the Tuscan accent catches the ear of one of the unhappy dead, and suddenly from out the depths a voice proceeds—

> 'O Tuscan! thou, who through the city of fire
> Alive art passing, so discreet of speech:
> Here, please thee, stay awhile Thy utterance
> Declares the place of thy nativity
> To be that noble land with which perchance
> I too severely dealt."

Dante, thus adjured, presses closer to his guide in dread. But Virgil reassures him "Lo! Farinata there," he says, thrusting him to the tomb's foot, and bidding him let his words be clear. Raising himself from the girdle upwards, and erecting his breast and forehead even as if hell itself he held in scorn, the Ghibelline leader eyes the stranger from the upper world, and in disdainful mood inquires who were his ancestors. Then follows a long dialogue, in which Farinata alludes to the fierce hostility of these ancestors to himself, his family, and his party, and reminds their representative that twice he drove them out of Florence; while Dante rejoins, observing that although his progenitors were expelled from the city on more than one occasion, they nevertheless each time returned from all parts, displaying thus an art which the Uberti "have shown they are not skilled to learn." This allusion to the doom of exile, incurred by his noble race, strikes Farinata to the heart—

> "'And if,' continuing the first discourse,
> 'They in this art,' he cried, 'small skill have shown;
> That doth torment me more e'en than this bed'"

He warns Dante that he too shall learn, ere long, how

difficult is that art of returning from banishment, and bids him say why it is that in all its laws this people is so pitiless towards the Uberti. The poet answers that the reason is to be found in "the slaughter and great havoc that coloured Arbia's flood with crimson stain."

> "Sighing, he shook
> The head, then thus resumed · 'In that affray
> I stood not singly, nor without just cause,
> Assuredly, should with the rest have stirr'd ;
> But singly there I stood, when, by consent
> Of all, Florence had to the ground been razed,
> The one who openly forbade the deed.'"[1]

Dante, lately so reluctant to approach, now lingers, hoping to learn more from the renowned chief. But Virgil calls him away,—not, however, until he has learned that more than a thousand lie with Farinata in that one sepulchre. Two the latter names—"of the rest I speak not."

Not as a Ghibelline, be it observed, was this place of punishment assigned to Farinata. Guelphs were under the same doom as well · for even while the dead Imperialist and the living poet were discoursing, Cavalcante, a distinguished member of the popular party, rose from among the suffering throng to ask some news of his son, Dante's beloved Guido. No; not for political views was Farinata thus condemned, but for holding, with Epicurus, that the soul dies with the body, and that human happiness consists in temporal pleasures.[2]

Those who know anything of Italian poetry must remember a sonnet by Dante, beginning with this line—

> "Guido, vorrei che tu e Lapo ed io."

The Guido here named was Dante's friend, the son of the Cavalcante mentioned above. During a short interval of

[1] "The great Ghibelline had lain thirty-six years in his sepulchre of flame Yet the mere footfall of a Florentine, and the sight of the familiar habit, stir him to the interests of the upper world. . . . Perhaps no other poet than Dante would have dared to paint a spirit triumphing in the potency of factious pride over hell and the torments of 'this bed'"—J. A. Symonds, *An Introduction to the Study of Dante.*

[2] See the long and interesting notes to Longfellow's translation of the *Divina Commedia.* I have followed in the text Cary's rendering of Dante's v

reconciliation between the rival factions, some intermarriages of Guelphs and Ghibellines took place. On that occasion Guido Cavalcante was united to a daughter of Farinata degli Uberti. The Lapo named in the sonnet is in all probability Jacopo, commonly called Lapo, the son of Farinata. He was a poet of no mean repute, and highly esteemed by Dante. Fazio, or Bonifazio, the author of the Dittamondo, was the son of Lapo, and consequently the inheritor of an illustrious name, and the inheritor, also, of the exile's doom.

No one appears to have thought it worth while to note where Fazio degli Uberti was born. Filipo Villani speaks of him as a countryman and contemporary of his own, alludes to his gay and pleasant disposition, and adds, that the only fault he discovered in him was a disposition to frequent the Court of tyrants, and laud their life and ways. This implied reproach of singing the praises of princes probably meant nothing more than that the historian's politics were not of the same colour as those of Fazio, and that the latter adhered to the traditions of his family, preferring the society of the nobles to the company of the popolani. This exclusive association with men of rank is noticed by another Italian writer of the same period as a praiseworthy characteristic of the expatriated family. They had been, when he wrote (in Dante's time), "more than forty years outlaws from their country, nor ever found mercy nor pity, remaining always abroad in great state, nor ever abased their honour, seeing that they ever abode with kings and lords, and to great things applied themselves."[1]

Fazio's choice of great things appears to have been the pursuit of learning and the cultivation of poetry, and in these conjointly he distinguished himself not a little. Villani says that he was the first to compose in the style of the canzone, and that he used that form with great ability and discretion; adding that in his old age, following better counsel, he ceased to compose in Latin, and, imitating Dante, wrote a book in the vulgar tongue very graceful and pleasing, giving an account of the situation and history of the different parts of the world, including in the work a great deal of matter coming within the scope of cosmography, and much besides well worthy of being read on account of the elegance of the language. Moreover, it is excellent in this, too, that owing to the succinctness of

[1] Dino Compagni, quoted by Dean Church.

the style, the verses can easily be committed to memory. And as Dante, in his wanderings through the regions beyond the grave, took Virgil for his leader, so Fazio, when he set out to visit the different nations of the earth, made choice of Solinus as his guide [1]

Of Fazio's life there is very little known. Tiraboschi remarks that in one of his canzone the poet bitterly and despairingly complains of the straits to which poverty had reduced him, without, however, mentioning any particular circumstance. Some writers assert that he was solemnly crowned in Florence, but no proof is adduced; and certainly this does not seem likely to have happened, adds Tiraboschi, in a city where he had no permanent abode. Where he wrote his celebrated work, the Dittamondo, has not been ascertained, nor the precise period during which he was engaged in its composition. "Probably he began his poem about the middle of the fourteenth century, and was still at work on it in the year 1367, and it seems likely that he may have died soon after that date, leaving his task unfinished. One thing, however, is certain, namely, that he was one of the best poets of his age, especially in strength and energy of style." [2]

Dante Gabriel Rossetti supplies us with some corrections, and a few additional particulars of an interesting kind. Evidently he does not think it likely that Fazio suffered grievously from poverty. The high reputation enjoyed by the poet makes it probable that he did receive the laurel crown, as stated by various early writers, though it is not mentioned in what city that honour was conferred on him. Mr. Rossetti observes that there is much beauty in several of Fazio's lyrical poems. One of the canzone he particularly admires, and transfuses into English. It is the "portrait" of a lady of Verona, named Angiola, to whom the poet was attached, and as a love-song, the translator thinks it is not perhaps surpassed by any poem of its class in existence. "Its excellence is such," continues Mr. Rossetti, "as to have procured it the high honour of being attributed to Dante, so that it is to be found among most of the editions of the *Canzoniere*; and as far as poetic beauty is concerned, it must be allowed to hold even there an eminent place." Having remarked that

[1] Villani, *Vite degl' illustri Florentini.*

[2] [illegible]

Ut

Fazio, an exile by inheritance, seems to have acquired restless tastes, that he travelled over a great part of Europe in the latter years of his life, and composed in his old age the poem entitled *Il Dittamondo*,—the "Song of the World," or "Words of the World,"—the commentator thus enlarges on the theme: "This work, though by no means contemptible in point of execution, certainly falls far short of its conception, which is a grand one, the topics of which it treats in great measure—geography and natural history—rendering it in those days the native home of all credulities and monstrosities. In scheme it was intended as an earthly parallel to Dante's sacred poem, doing for this world what he did for the other. At Fazio's death it remained unfinished, but I should think by very little,—the plan of the work seeming in the main accomplished. The whole earth (or rather all that was then known of it) is traversed,—its surface and its history,—ending with the Holy Land, and thus bringing man's world as near as may be to God's; that is, to the point where Dante's office begins. No conception could well be nobler, or worthier even now of being dealt with by a great master. To the work of such a man, Fazio's work might afford such first materials as have usually been furnished beforehand to the greater poets by some unconscious steward."[1]

That Fazio visited the land of his ancestors, and even sojourned for a brief space in the city so beloved by her sons, can hardly be doubted after a careful perusal of the pages of the Dittamondo, in which Florence is described. The sketch is the work of an admiring eye and a loving hand, and the exile's heart beats proudly at the sight of the noble monuments and lovely surroundings of the city-republic. He found by experience how inextinguishable the love of country is, for neither eye nor heart grew weary in gazing at the scenes spread out before him—

> "Quivi provai com' è grande l'amore
> Della patria, perocchè di vederla
> Saziar non ne potea gli occhi nè il cuore."

Most of all, the Baptistry delighted him with its incomparable intaglios and marbles; and he observes that when the campanile shall have been finished, course after course,

[1] D. G. Rossetti, *Early Italian Poets* (Introduction).

as it was begun, nothing in all the world will surpass its beauty. Then the clear waters and the pure air, the charming women and the men who know so well on all occasions what to say and do, receive the tribute of the exile's praise. Swiftly sped the days he lingered in that pearl of cities; and as he passed out of the gates, with bowed head and downcast eyes, he felt that he had left his heart and his best self behind, and sadly questioned whether his eyes should ever again be gladdened with the fair vision of which he now took a tearful farewell—

> "Ahi lasso!
> Ritornerò più mai a rivedere
> Quest caro terren, che ora passo?"

A passage in another part of the poem leaves no doubt that the citizens of Florence pursued their animosity towards the Uberti from son to son, even to the fourth generation. Yet we do not find that a member of the family durst not set foot within the walls under any circumstances whatsoever—the penalty of being burned alive was not imposed, as in the case of Dante. The visit of one of the race to Florence is recorded by Dino Compagni. The Uberti were loved as they were hated, he says; and as an instance he mentions that when, under the protection of a cardinal, one of them visited the city, and the checkered blue and gold blazon of their house was, after an interval of half a century, again seen in the streets of Florence, many ancient Ghibelline men and women pressed to kiss the arms, and even the common people did him honour.[1]

Fazio married; but whether the Lady Angiola of Verona, immortalised in the canzone translated by Mr. Rossetti, became his wife, no one appears to know. It is certain, however, that the last years of his long life were spent in Verona, that he died there, and was buried in that city. A son of his, Leopardo by name, after his father's death settled in Venice, where "his descendants maintained an honourable rank for the space of two succeeding generations."[2]

Eminently calculated as the Dittamondo undoubtedly was to instruct and interest the author's contemporaries and the

[1] See Dean Church's *Essay on Dante*.
[2] D. G. Rossetti, *Early Italian Poets*.

next succeeding generations, the book, nevertheless, did not get a chance of accomplishing so great a good. Safe, but inaccessible withal, as far as the multitude were concerned, this, the earliest didactic poem in the Italian language, lay in manuscript for a hundred years in the libraries of the learned and the wealthy However, soon after the invention of printing, a folio edition was published at Vicenza (1474), but with such a multiplicity of errors as to render the perusal of the book a laborious and intolerable task. Venice produced a quarto edition in 1501, this also being disfigured with innumerable mistakes. These were the only editions of the Dittamondo given to the world between the fifteenth and the nineteenth centuries. Ranking among the *testi di lingua*, and highly esteemed by the Academia della Crusca for the purity of its style, the Dittamondo has had the honour of being quoted more than eight hundred times in the famous *Vocabularia*. As a proof of the richness of its historical matter, and its usefulness in illustrating Dante, it may be noted that the poem is many times quoted, and still more frequently referred to, in the notes to Cary's translation of the *Divina Commedia*.

In a famous bibliographical work, *Serie dei Testi di Lingua*, published in Venice, 1839, the author, Bartolomeo da Bassano, gives, under the heading of "Fazio degli Uberti," a minute description of the early editions of the Dittamondo. He styles the folio edition *rarissimo*, and mentions the sales at which copies were purchased. A story is told at the same time of an English gentleman who ordered a copy belonging to M. Floncel to be purchased for him, without, however, stating the price he was willing to pay. The bidding went up to eight hundred francs, and the lot was knocked down to the Englishman; but so provoked was he at having to pay so exorbitant a sum for his bargain, that as soon as he got the book into his hands he flung it into the fire.

The author cites a high authority in confirmation of the opinion that the two early editions are incorrect to an extraordinary degree; that, in fact, nothing could possibly be more disfigured or outlandish.

Lord Charlemont, the patriot-earl, spent, it will be remembered, several years of his early manhood in Italy, devoting himself to elegant pursuits, and cultivating assiduously the study of the language and literature of the country. In all probability it was at that time he became acquainted with the poems of Fazio degli Uberti, and obtained a copy of the Dittamondo. The passage which would seem to have most of all attracted his attention was the one containing a complimentary allusion to the woollen products of Ireland imported into Florence in the poet's day, that is to say, in the fourteenth century. On the foundation of the Royal Irish Academy, in 1786, Lord Charlemont was elected president. At one of the earliest meetings of that body, a paper on the "Antiquity of the Woollen Manufacture in Ireland," written by his lordship, was read; and in the first volume of the Transactions this essay was printed. The noble author adduces several instances in proof of the estimation in which Irish cloths were held at home and abroad many hundred years ago, and gives full weight to Fazio's testimony. A short notice of the poet and his book is very properly introduced, but no passages are quoted from the Dittamondo, except the one declaring Ireland worthy of renown on account of "the beautiful serges she sends us," and another dwelling on the perils attending the navigation of the Irish Sea. Lord Charlemont does not appear to have any doubt concerning Fazio's visit to Ireland. He remarks that the poet expressly says he had seen in Ireland "certain lakes of various natures." Furthermore, the writer of the essay is careful to state that the copy from which he quotes is of the very rare edition of 1474.[1]

[1] The Charlemont Library was sold in 1865, some of the rare books and manuscripts bringing very high prices, as may be seen on reference to the *Athenæum*, August 19, of the same year The following is a description of the copy above mentioned, taken from the catalogue prepared by Messrs Sotheby & Co.—"UBERTI (Fazio degli) DITTA MUNDI (in terza rima), first edition, excessively rare, very large copy, with the signatures (generally cut off) Vicenza, Leonardo da Basilia, 1474. This is probably the rarest of all the Italian poems, and may be regarded as a most interesting autobiography of the poet, who gives therein details of his various travels Like Dante, he not only gives the geography, but also the history of his own time. This poem, from internal evidence, is supposed to have been written about the year 1350, and contains a description of the British Empire, in which will be found mentioned a most remarkable fact, that Ireland was then already famous for her woollen manufactures. (See Lord Charlemont's MS. notes) Quadrino, Tiraboschi, and Gamba agree in styling this edition 'rarissima,' a fact fully borne ou[illegible]"

On reading Lord Charlemont's paper, the indication of an exportation of Irish seiges to the South of Europe in the fourteenth century was what particularly interested me at the moment in the account of the Dittamondo. However, the incidental mention of the "lakes of various natures" awakened my attention in no small degree, and I resolved to pursue inquiry in a new direction as soon as opportunity might serve for doing so.

As already said, I was much struck by the assertion that Fazio degli Uberti, in his travels in Ireland, "saw certain lakes of various natures." Assuredly, thought I, if the Florentine poet beheld any of the inland waters of Hibernia's isle, his eyes must have rested on

> "That dim lake
> Where sinful souls their farewell take
> Of this vain world, and half-way lie
> In Death's cold shadow, ere they die."

No traveller could pass through Ireland in those days without hearing such an account of Lough Derg as would make him deem all his labours worthless unless he should reach its mystic shore. Still less would it have been possible for a man of letters, especially an Italian *littérateur*, to be ignorant of a legend and unacquainted with a pilgrimage so renowned throughout Europe. Greater lakes no doubt there were, and lovelier sheets of water mirroring the Irish sky; but where in all the world was there a lake to compare in romantic and religious associations with that hid in the wilds of Tyrconnel, and bearing on its bosom the rocky isle and its wondrous cave, "where penitential man his soul in life may save."

Not one of the pious legendary beliefs (to quote a writer who has made this subject his special study) which attained a universal popularity among the people of Christendom, was ever so popular or so fearfully interesting as the legend of the Purgatory of Ireland's patron saint. "The Purgatory of St. Patrick," he continues, "was the grand mediæval wonder and glory of the Christian world Though Ireland had the fame of possessing such a place, the renown was not merely local—all Christendom were partakers in it as well. The renown of St Patrick's Purgatory resembled that acquired by a famous battlefield, on which the combined nations of Europe had fought and conquered; for each nation could speak of it with pride and exultation, each having furnished heroes for the adventure—that perilous adventure surpassing mere mortal strife, in which men encountered demons in the dread realms of the infernal regions. Whatever Ireland may have been famous for at any period of her history, there can be no doubt that it never was so famous for anything as it was at one time for St. Patrick's Purgatory."[1]

Now, the story of the penitential cave had its origin in the early days of Christianity in Ireland; and, like the equally fascinating Celtic legends of the visions of Tundale, St. Fursey's journey through the regions beyond the grave, and the voyage of St. Brendan, were known on the Continent wherever Irish missioners wandered or Irish schoolmen taught.[2]

In the twelfth century the fame of St Patrick's Purgatory received an extraordinary extension. Henry, a monk in the monastery of Saltry, in Huntingdonshire, fused the current legends into a consecutive narrative cast in Latin prose, and, in describing vividly and circumstantially the experiences of the knight Owen Miles, his vision of Hell, his passage through Purgatory, and his visit to the terrestrial Paradise, produced a pious romance and a tale of adventure than which nothing could have better fallen in with the religious enthusiasm and chivalric disposition of the age in which he lived. The work of the monk of Saltry was popularised by translation into the vulgar tongues. One English and three French metrical versions soon appeared; the Anglo-Norman poetess, Marie de France, the Sappho of her age, relating the story in a poem of three thousand verses.

And, as if nothing were to be left undone to spread the fascinating history into every corner of Christendom, religious writers accorded to it a prominent place in their works, and thus gave it a currency which no other mode of publication could have so effectually secured. Cæsarius of Heisterbach

[1] *Ulster Journal of Archæology*, vols. iv, v, to which Mr. William Pinkerton contributed articles of rare interest on the subject of St. Patrick's Purgatory.

[2] "La tradition du Purgatoire de saint Patrice se ratache aux premiers souvenirs du christianisme chez les Irlandais : la vision de Tundale, celle de saint Brendan, leur appartiennent aussi"—F. Ozanam, *Les Sources Poétiques d* "

directed attention in a very marked way to the mysterious island in Lough Derg, by recommending anyone who might have a misgiving as to the existence of Purgatory to go to Ireland and enter the cave of St. Patrick, where his doubts would be expelled.[1] Jacobus de Voragine, whose Golden Legend is said to have been more frequently transcribed than any book except the Bible, did still more by relating, in the fiftieth chapter of his work, the experiences in the world of shades of a pilgrim to the island in Lough Derg.[2]

Historians in their turn found it necessary not to pass over the Purgatory of St. Patrick in whatever account they gave of Ireland. Giraldus Cambrensis, in the twelfth century, mentions, though in a garbled sort of way, the mysterious occurrences which made an island, or, as he says, islands, in a certain lake in Ulster terrible and glorious Matthew Paris, in the succeeding century, relates the progress of a pilgrim through the purgatorial scenes, and penitential pains to which a voluntary imprisonment in the cave was the introduction. And in the fourteenth century, Froissart gives the story of the pilgrimage a prominent place in his Chronicles

St. Patrick's Purgatory is introduced with great effect by a Florentine writer of the same age in the famous and popular romance of *Guerrino il Meschino.* The hero of the tale, one of Charlemagne's knights, after going through extraordinary adventures in different parts of the world, is sent by the pope to do penance for his sins in St. Patrick's cave. There he undergoes still more wonderful experiences in the land of shades, and is permitted to advance as far as the threshold of the terrestrial Paradise, where he catches a glimpse of "the Emperor of heaven," surrounded by the full choir of angels.

Thus, wherever poetry was recited, or chronicles were perused, or sacred legends meditated, the story connected with that "insignificant islet in a dreary lake" was familiar as a

[1] Cæsarius of Heisterbach was a German religious of the Order of Citeaux. He became a monk in 1198, in the valley of St Peter, otherwise called Heisterbach, near the town of Bonn, in the diocese of Cologne, and did not die till nearly forty years afterwards He wrote lives of Saints" — D F MacCarthy, Notes to his translation of Calderon's Dramas.

[2] Jacobus de Voragine, Provincial of the Dominicans and Bishop of Genoa, was born about the year 1230.

household word. It was an enthralling tale to gentle and simple alike. However, the piety and romance of those days were not satisfied to be fed exclusively on charming recitals and quiescent musings The spirit of the age impelled to action. A pilgrimage to St. Patrick's Purgatory came to be regarded as an undertaking worthy of the ambition of the most valiant knight, a penitential ordeal creditable to the piety of the austerest devotee. Sin-laden mortals wended their way from distant lands to lay down their burden in the hallowed isle; gallant knights, with their warlike retinue, broke on the solitude of wood and hill with tramp of hoof and bugle-call; lowlier palmers wore a path along Tyrconnel's wilds; the cowled monk toiled towards the lake with the accoutred soldier and the wool-clad rustic.

There can be little doubt that at a very early period after the first promulgation of the legend, many devout and adventurous foreigners adopted the advice of Cæsar of Heisterbach,[1] and took their way to Lough Derg to perform the purgatorial exercises approved by the guardians of the sanctuary Remote as was the island of Hibernia in fact, and still more in idea, from the centres of European life, it was by no means inaccessible. French and Italian traders frequented its ports, and it is not improbable that oftentimes on board the merchant sail the pilgrims sped to Erin. Documentary evidence, however, cannot be cited in proof of the landing of these penitential visitants previous to the fourteenth century, the age of Fazio degli Uberti; but at that period, and thenceforth, such testimony is not wanting. About the middle of the century the arrival of a very distinguished pilgrim-prince from Italy is chronicled. The event is thus narrated in Mr Gilbert's *History of the Viceroys of Ireland*:—

"Among the archives of England are enrolled certificates, issued by Edward III during the viceroyalty of St Amand, declaring that Malatesta Ungaro of Rimini, and Nicolo de Beccaria of Ferrara, had performed pilgrimages to the famous Purgatory of St. Patrick, Lough Derg. Ungaro, Lord of Rimini, Fano, Pesano, and Fossombrone, was renowned in Italy for his warlike enterprises, his knowledge and piety. 'Whereas,' wrote the King of England, 'Malatesta Ungaro, of Rimini, a nobleman and knight, hath presented himself before

1 [illegible]

Ul

us, and declared that, travelling from his own country, he had, with many bodily toils, visited the Purgatory of St. Patrick, in our land of Ireland, and for the space of a day and a night, as is the custom, remained therein enclosed, and now earnestly beseeches us that, for the confirmation of the truth thereof, we should grant him our royal letters. we, therefore, considering the dangers and perils of his pilgrimage, and although the assertion of such a noble might on this suffice, yet we are further certified thereof by letters from our trusty and beloved Almaric de St. Amand, knight, justiciary of Ireland, and from the prior and convent of the said Purgatory, and others of great credit, as also by clear evidence, that the said nobleman had duly and courageously performed his pilgrimage, we have consequently thought worthy to give favourably unto him our royal authority concerning the same, to the end there may be no doubt made of the premised; and that the truth may more clearly appear, we have deemed proper to grant unto him these our letters, under our royal seal.'"[1]

In the *Ulster Journal of Archæology*, and in *Lough Derg and its Pilgrimages*,[2] we read of other strangers arriving from different parts of Europe about this time, with the object of visiting the famous shrine of penance in the north of Ireland. I pass on, however, to a somewhat later date in the century, in order to give at greater length an idea of the difficulties and dangers which valorous travellers had to encounter betimes on the expedition. The visit referred to is mentioned in all the accounts of the Lough Derg pilgrimage, notably in Mr. Wright's important work. However, I prefer availing myself once more

[1] Dr. Gilbert gives in a note (p. 543) a passage from Muratori's *Annals of Italy*, in which the last illness of the aged Malatesta, Lord of Rimini [A.D. 1364], is referred to, and a high testimony borne to the piety and good works by which such edification was given in his latter days.

The certificate given above is inscribed on the patent rolls in the Tower of London, under the year 1358.

[2] The author of this interesting monograph, the Rev. Daniel O'Connor, has collected an immense amount of information and traced the history of the pilgrimage from early times to our own day. This book will be found invaluable to those who desire to master the subject, and should be read in the same course with Mr. Wright's *St. Patrick's Purgatory*, and Mr. Pinkerton's papers in the *Ulster Journal of Archæology*. Readers of the *Irish Monthly* retain, no doubt, a very agreeable recollection of the Rev. John Healy's article on Lough Derg, which appeared in volume vi of the Magazine (1878).

of Mr. Gilbert's labours, and take the following narrative from his *History of the Viceroys*.

In the reign of Richard II., the Viceroy De Mortimer was waited on in Dublin by Ramon, Viscount de Perellos, Señor de la Baronia de Seret, Knight of Rhodes, and chamberlain to King Richard's father-in-law, Charles VI. of France. "This nobleman," continues the author, "arrived with letters from the King of England for safe conduct to visit the Purgatory of St. Patrick, with a retinue of twenty men and thirty horses. Ramon had been in the army of Charles V. of France, became Master of the Horse to Juan of Aragon, where his estates lay, and that king gave him command of three galleys which he sent to aid Clement VII. After the death of Clement, Ramon served Benedict VIII., until he determined, notwithstanding the papal dissuasion, to visit St. Patrick's Purgatory in Ireland, where he expected to learn intelligence of the fate of the soul of his beloved King Juan. He tells us that at Dublin he visited the Earl of March, King Richard's cousin, and Viceroy of Ireland, who, having perused the royal letters, received him very honourably, but endeavoured, with all his power, to dissuade him from persevering in an undertaking which he declared to be of the most perilous nature. As Ramon was not deterred by these representations, the viceroy despatched him to Drogheda, with letters to John de Colton, who, having distinguished himself in the service of England, had been promoted from the Deanery of St. Patrick's at Dublin to the Archbishopric of Armagh. De Colton also endeavoured to deter him from venturing into the territories of the northern Irish, who had made serious inroads upon the See lands of the English Archbishops of Armagh. Ramon, persevering in his resolution, passed safely, as a pilgrim, into Donegal, where, with many others on the same mission, he was, he records, loaded with gifts and escorted safely to his destination by the native chiefs, whose ancestors, according to their legends, had come to Erin from his native land of Spain."

As an example of the attraction to St. Patrick's Purgatory experienced by a class very different from that of princes, knights, and soldiers, I must cite an instance of a Carthusian monk's temptation to pass the cloistral bounds and make his way to the cave in Ireland. It would appear that a certain

Don John, of the Certosa at Rome, conceived an extraordinary desire to perform this pilgrimage, and, not obtaining the sanction of his superiors for the undertaking, fell into a state of despondency. The visitor informed St. Catherine of Siena, who had many friends and correspondents among the Carthusians, of this occurrence, and probably asked the holy woman to give Don John some prudent counsel calculated to restore his peace of mind. Anyhow, the saint wrote the troubled monk a long letter, in which the virtue of obedience and the practice of patience are insisted on, pious fancies rated at a low figure in comparison with a just notion of things, and the would-be pilgrim made to understand by implication that he need not proceed to a cave in Ireland seeking that divine grace which he is more certain to find in the cloister and in the study of himself. "My dear son,' says the saint in conclusion, "bow down your head in holy obedience, and remain in your cell embracing the tree of the most holy cross. Take good care (as you value the life of your soul and fear to displease Almighty God) that you do not follow your own will "[1]

From the various instances given above, it is easy to conclude that Ireland and her wondrous Purgatory were well known and much spoken of in Italy during the fourteenth century. The influence of Celtic legend and romance on the literati and poets of the south of Europe might likewise be divined from the same facts. However, in this connection still more striking proofs are at hand. The study of Dante and his immortal work by diligent and reverential commentators, has brought out in extraordinary relief the fact of the universal diffusion of the legends of which Erin was the nursing mother, and has revealed to the world of to-day the wealth and brilliance of that Celtic vein of romance which tinctured perceptibly the literature of Europe in its dawn, seized the imagination of the great Florentine, and formed the groundwork of passages in his deathless song. No one can suppose that it derogates from the originality of Dante's genius that he should utilise the material gathered in the course of his universal reading, and embody in a supreme achievement the poetic fancies with which the mediæval mind

[1] This letter is numbered 201 in the edition of the *Lettere di S. Catarina di Siena*, published at Florence in 1860

was nurtured and delighted.[1] Homer collected together the fragmentary treasures of song and story dispersed among the Greeks, and Shakespeare appropriated and immortalised the fugitive stores which lay scattered around him in oral and in written lore.

Dante's own countrymen, as far as I am aware, took the initiative in that branch of inquiry which led up to the Celtic sources of the Divine Comedy. About sixty years ago, Francesco Cancelliere published in Rome his observations on the Originality of the Divine Comedy. Twenty or thirty years later, French writers took up the theme: Frederic Ozanam treated the subject learnedly and charmingly in his work on Dante and the Catholic Philosophy of the thirteenth century, as well as in his interesting essay on the Poetic Sources of the Divine Comedy; and about the same time, M. Labitte published a treatise on the Divine Comedy *before* Dante. German scholars, it is needless to say, have worked the same mine with that ardour and perseverance which distinguish their literary labours. Not many years ago, this subject was brought in a striking way under the notice of Irish readers in an article published in the *Nation*, 30th October 1869; which article, judging from its scholarly tone and poetic feeling, as well as from the special knowledge it displays, can hardly have been written by any other than the lamented Denis Florence MacCarthy. The writer, having alluded to the Italian and Spanish accounts on which Calderon founded his drama of "The Purgatory of St. Patrick," thus continues:—

"This famous legend of St. Patrick's Purgatory had produced in Italy, at an earlier period, much more important fruit than had sprung from it even in Spain; for it is not too much to say that without it the *Divina Commedia* of Dante would never have taken the form it did. As an interesting

[1] "The *Divina Commedia* is of Dante's writing; yet in truth *it* belongs to the ten Christian Centuries; only the finishing of it is Dante's. So always. The craftsman there, the smith with that metal of his, with these tools, with these cunning methods—how little of all he does is properly *his* work! All past inventive men work there with him · as indeed with all of us in all things Dante is the spokesman of the Middle Ages; the Thought they lived by stands here, in everlasting music These sublime ideas of his, terrible and beautiful, are the fruit of the Christian Meditation of all the good men who had gone before him"—Thomas Carlyle's *Heroes and Hero-Worship*.

evidence of this we may mention that in 1865, when the fifth centenary of Dante's birthday was celebrated throughout Italy, one of the most remarkable contributions to the literature of the great poem that then appeared was a collection of the early legends that must have influenced Dante in the conception and treatment of the *Divina Commedia*. They were five in number; the three longest and most important being our Irish legends of St. Patrick's Purgatory, The Voyage of St. Brendan, and the Visions of Tundale. The title of this most interesting tract, of which but two hundred copies were printed, is as follows: *Antiche Leggende e Tradizioni che illustrano La Divina Commedia, precedute da alcune osservazioni di P. Villari, Pisa* 1865. Professor Villari, in his introductory remarks on Dante and Literature in Italy, refers thus to those three Irish legends: 'In questo periodo, l'Irlanda dimostra una singolare attività, producendo quelle che son forse le tre leggende più popolari del medio evo, e pigliano il nome appunto da tre Irlandesi S. Brandano, S. Patrizio, e Tundalo' After giving a copious analysis of the three legends, which he subsequently prints in full from old Italian versions, he corroborates the opinion we have expressed as to their effect upon the imagination of Dante in the following passages: 'Troviamo molte scene, molte pene e molti personaggi, che hanno qualche relazione con quelli, che ci veugono poi descritti da Dante. La descrizione di Lucifero, che inspira ed aspira le anime ridotte prima, sotto il martellare di fabbri infernali, in una pasta simile a ferro fuso, e poi in favelle, e che pure non passon morire, ha qualche cosa di veramente Dantesco.'"

Whatever Dante's indebtedness may have been to each of these legends respectively, one thing is certain: the great poet-theologian, as the Vicomte de Villemarque observes, was nurtured on the marrow of the Celtic legends[1] Poets of

[1] See *La Legende Celtique et la Poesie des Cloitres.* M. de Villemarque, speaking of the Voyage of St Brendan, quotes M. Renan's opinion that this legend may justly be considered one of the most astonishing creations of the human intelligence, and that it is the completest expression of the Celtic ideal. A version of the *Vision of Tundale* was published in Edinburgh in 1843, but the book is now so difficult to procure that it would be useless to refer readers to it. An abstract of the legendary narrative will be found in Mr. Wright's *St. Patrick's Purgatory* Tundale was a native of Cashel, and the history of his experiences in the regions beyond the

( )

lesser magnitude were not unaware, as we may well suppose, of the mine of precious ore embedded in the Celtic legends. At any rate, it would be difficult to believe that Fazio degli Uberti knew anything of Ireland and yet remained in ignorance of St. Patrick's Purgatory; or that, having set foot in this "kingdom of the zephyrs," he departed hence without visiting the famous cave by which many had entered the precincts of the invisible world, and round which a multitude of repentant sinners, less courageous or aspiring, had gone through the austere course prescribed, got rid of their remorse, and soothed their contrite pain.

But now the question was, how to get an opportunity of making acquaintance with the Dittamondo. No library in Dublin possesses the work except the library of Trinity College, where there is a copy, not so much preserved as actually buried alive, together with other sumptuously-bound first editions of Italian classics The conditions under which the precious tomes forming the Quin collection were bequeathed to the

grave is of an earlier date than that of the knight Owen's journey through Purgatory. Of a still more remote antiquity than that assigned to any one of the three legends referred to by Signor Villari is the story of the Vision of St. Fursey. This Vision is the earliest of all, for it belongs to the middle of the seventh century. It is undoubtedly of Irish origin. The Venerable Bede gives the life of the holy Abbot Fursey, who "was found worthy to behold the choirs of angels and to hear the praises which are sung in heaven" The earlier years of the saint were passed in a monastery on the island of Inchiquin in Lough Corrib, the latter were devoted to missionary work among the Franks. He is reverenced to this day as patron of Lagny and Peronne. The Rev. S. Baring-Gould, in his *Lives of the Saints*, records the incidents of St. Fursey's life, but has not space for an account of the Vision which, he says, appears to have been the original of Dante's *Divina Commedia*. The Rev. John O'Hanlon, in his *Lives of Irish Saints* (vol. i), relates the history of St Fursey in its various and interesting particulars, and gives the celebrated Vision in all its details. The author thinks there can scarcely be a doubt entertained that the Vision of St. Fursey furnished Dante in a great measure with the idea and plan of his divine poem, even various passages, he remarks, of the *Divina Commedia* seem drawn from St Fursey's Vision, for the coincidences are too striking to be fortuitous; and furthermore, he gives, to the great satisfaction of the reader, a number of these passages, sometimes in Cary's and sometimes in Longfellow's translation. The learned annotator of Cambrensis Eversus, the Rev. Matthew Kelly, does not indicate any one of these legends as more connected than the rest with Dante's glorious work, but he alludes in general terms to the great number of Visions originally published in Ireland, thence [illegible] the Continent, and [illegible] Dante [illegible]

University are very extraordinary. I shall only remark, that I could not dream of applying for permission, under existing circumstances, to pore over the four-hundred-years-old type, bristling with errors, in search of the pages relating to Ireland; nor could I ask anyone of my acquaintance, young or old, to do so for me. It would be easier to buy the book, even at an extravagant price. Quaritch's catalogues were therefore referred to, and it turned out, that although copies of the first editions and manuscripts on vellum, in various states of preservation, and at prices varying from twenty-five shillings to twenty-five pounds, were to be found in catalogues not many years old, the work had disappeared from later lists. Still, the poem had been reprinted twice in the nineteenth century—at Venice in 1820, and at Milan in 1826. Would it not be possible to find a copy of one or another of these modern issues? Old book-shops in Dublin were ransacked, foreign booksellers in London applied to, advertisements tried—all to no effect. A gleam of hope shone forth when Lord Charlemont, in the summer of 1882, presented to the Royal Irish Academy a number of manuscript volumes, containing original literary works of his illustrious grandfather, among them being "An Essay towards the History of Italian Poetry attempted in translated specimens of the more noted classical poets from Dante to Metastasio, inclusively." Surely, I thought, we shall find *Fazio degli Uberti on Ireland* done into English by the patriot-earl, who had owned a copy of the Dittamondo. Here again, however, hope lead on to disappointment only.

At length, a gentleman, setting out for Italy last autumn, kindly undertook to search Milan for a copy of the Dittamondo—"ridotto a buona lezione"—published there fifty-seven years ago. The first news I heard from the Lombard city was to the effect that the principal publishers had been applied to, but that they appeared to have no knowledge of the edition specified, or at best, knew just so much of it as to be quite certain that a copy could not be procured for love or money. Our traveller, remembering how Mr. Rooney and Mr. Traynor of Dublin can come to the aid of gentlemen in want of old books, bethought him of inquiring whether there might not be someone in Milan whose specialty lay in old books, and who might be willing to dispose of his treasures to the curious in such matters. In reply, he received the address of a collector answering to this description. Forthwith, following the clue he had obtained, he found himself in the street where stands the Ospedale Maggiore, with its sumptuously ornamented front—the glory of terra-cotta workmanship. Up and down he looked for some appearance of an old bookshop; but finding not the slightest indication of name, signboard, or establishment, he sought the assistance of a passer-by, who directed him to enter a mansion right opposite the hospital. Within he found no shop, certainly, but a spacious apartment like a chamber in an ancient palace, the floor encumbered with piles of books and manuscripts, and the walls lined with presses containing similar treasures. In the midst sat an old man, the monarch of all he surveyed. "Had he a copy of the Dittamondo?" "*Sicuro*—that he had; one that would enchant the signor—rare, precious, perfectly lovely!" And his eyes brightened as he proudly laid open a venerable volume before his visitor, and gave him to understand that for the insignificant sum of fifty lire he was at liberty to carry off the prize. "But," said the stranger from *l'Ultima Irlanda*, observing the old type of the "lovely volume," and remembering that unless the reading of the Dittamondo were "made easy" its perusal might be an impossibility. "But I do not want anything so valuable. What I am looking for is a copy of the poem printed in this city within the present century." The surprise and contempt expressed by the antiquary's attitude and countenance were inimitable. "I have not the book you require," said he; "it can be had for three or four lire" "Well, then," replied the traveller, "if you have the goodness to bring it to me to-morrow morning, I shall gladly pay five lire for the acquisition." Next day, just as our friend was preparing to set out for Verona, the old book-collector made his appearance with the new Dittamondo (now of a respectable age) in his hand, and was gratefully presented with the promised lire.

In due course the long-sought-for Dittamondo reached its destination. It is a large 16mo of 520 pages, excellently printed on paper not too fine, embellished with a portrait of the author, and enclosed in a paper cover the colour of brick-dust. The volume forms number 179 of the "Biblioteca Scelta di Opere Italiane antiche e moderne," was printed at the Tipografia Silvestri, Milan, and published on the 1st day of February 1826. To all appearance the copy had never been opened from the day it issued from the press. Without any difficulty—for a table of contents graces this edition—I discovered the part relating to Ireland. And there, to my satisfaction, I found St Patrick's Purgatory occupying ten out of the twenty-six verses devoted to our Land of the West The author having given more than three chapters to a description of England, with its inhabitants, its wonders, and its history, proceeds to Scotland, which region he dismisses in four verses of somewhat uncomplimentary epithets. Then he goes on to say.—

"In like manner we passed into Ireland, a country worthy of great fame amongst us for the beautiful serges that she sends us. Hibernia there awaits and invites us; and although the voyage is attended with danger, our desire to reach the shore vanquishes prudence. Winds from various points, bellowing and whistling, lash the waves upon the coast strewn with reefs and sandbanks.

"Though the inhabitants seem wild and the country is rugged with mountains, yet nevertheless it is a pleasant land to those who make acquaintance with it. Here are great pastures rich with grass, and the soil is so fruitful that Ceres holds none of her arts in reserve. A mild temperature prevails, as in springtime, refreshing the land with limpid springs and beautiful rivers.

"Here I saw lakes of various natures, one of which attracted me so much that my wistful eyes take delight in it still. They say that if a stick is thrust into it, the part in the ground speedily turns into iron, that in the water changes to stone, while the portion projecting above the wave suffers no alteration, but remains in its original condition Another lake I saw totally different—a wand of horn when stuck in it becomes an ash tree.

"Again, we came to a little island in which no one can die As soon as an inhabitant is about to pass away, he flings himself out of it. Moreover, there are remote caverns where no flesh corrupts, so tempered is the pervading air.

"I found that the people have flesh meat and various fruits for food, while for drink they have an unfailing supply of milk.

"Thus, exploring the distant parts of the country and making inquiries on the way, we got information concerning a certain very holy and devout monastery Thither we betook ourselves, and there were hospitably received. The good monks conducted us to the cave which makes the blessed Patrick so famous.

"'What shall we do?' said my beloved counsellor to me. 'Do you wish to pass within? You are so anxious to fathom the meaning of everything new and strange!'

"'No,' I replied, 'I will not enter without the advice of the monks, for it is terrible to me to think of penetrating to the very depths of hell.'

"Thereupon one of the monks answered: 'If you do not feel yourself pure and clean, resolute and full of faith, you cannot be sure of returning should you enter.'

"And I said: 'If you can satisfy me on this point: rumours are afloat through the world concerning many who have come back from those torments.'

"To which he replied: 'With regard to Patrick and Nicholas, there can be no doubt whatever that they went in and returned by this entrance. As for the others, I cannot venture to say that one in a hundred may not have the reputation of having made the descent. But I do not know one for certain.'

"Solinus broke in: 'Put away this idea and do not tempt your God. It would be a grievous thing if anyone were to perish here. It is enough for us to carry on our researches above ground.'

"'You are quite right,' said the monk. And then, departing, we bade farewell to the community whom we left behind.

"In this manner, traversing mountains, valleys, and grassy plains, we met those native tribes who love hunting beyond every other pursuit.

"Pearls, agates, and various metals are to be found in this country, and also assassagos which have this peculiar property, that when placed in the sun they form a rainbow.

"The island is about 120 miles in length, and takes its name from the Hibernian Ocean." (Lib. iv. cap. xxvi.)

It is pleasant to turn from the crude literalness of the above rendering to the easy flow of the fourteenth century verse.

"Similemente passammo in Irlanda,
  La qual fra noi è degna di gran fama
  Per le nobili saje che ci manda.
Ibernia ora qui ci aspetta e chiama,
  E benchè il navigar là sia con rischio,
  La ragion fu qui vinta dalla brama.

Diversi venti con mugghi e con fischio
  Soffiavan per quel mar, andando a piaggia,
  Lo qual di sassi e di gran scogli è mischio.
Questa gente benchè sembria selvaggia,
  E per gli monti la contrada acerba,
  Nondimeno ella è dolce a chi l'assaggia
Quivi son gran pasture piene d'erba,
  E la terre è sì buona, che Cerera
  Niente dell' arte sua mostrar si serba.
Quivi par sempre come in primavera
  Un aere temperato, che gli appaghi
  Con chiari fonti e con bella rivera.
Quivi di più nature vidi laghi,
  Uno fra gli altri è che sì mi contenta,
  Che ancor diletto n'han gli occhi miei vaghi.
Dico, se un legno vi ficchi, diventa
  In breve ferro quanto ne sta in terra,
  E pietra ciò che l'aqua bagna e tenta
La parte, che di sopra l'aere, serra,
  Dalla natura sua non cambia verso,
  Ma tal qual vi si mette se ne afferra.
Un altro v'è, che vidi assai diverso,
  Che qual vi pon di corno una verghetta,
  Frassino poi diventa, ed e converso.
Ancora vi trovammo un' isoletta
  Là dove l'uomo mai morir non puote,
  Ma quando in transir sta, fuor se ne getta.
E sonvi ancora caverne rimote,
  Dove alcun corpo non corrompe mai,
  Sì temperata l'aere vi percuote.
Carne e frutte diverse poi trovai,
  Ch'han per lo cibo, e latte hanno per poto,
  Del quale sanza fallo n'hanno assai.
Così cercando il paese remoto
  E domandando, ci fu dato indizio
  D'un monister molto santo e devoto.
Là ci traemmo, e là fu il nostro ospizio,
  Poi que' buon frati al pozzo ne menaro,
  Lo qual dà fama al beato Patrizio.
Quivi mi disse il mio consiglio caro.
  Che farem noi? Vuo' tu passr qui entro,
  Chè d'ogni novità cerchi esser chiaro?
Sanza il consiglio, rispos'io, non ci entro,
  Di questi frati; chè troppo m'è scuro
  Pensar cercar l'Inferno fino al centro.
E l'un rispose a me: Se netto e puro,
  Costante e pien di fede non ti senti,
  Se v' entri, del tornar non ti assecuro.
Ed io: Se puoi, qui fa che mi contenti;
  Fama di molti per lo mondo vola,
  Che [illegible]

Ed egli: Di Patrizio, e di Nicola
  E' manifesto, sanza dubbio alcuno,
  Che si calò e tornò per questa gola.
Degli altri ti so dir che di cento uno
  Che porti fama di ciò qui non passa;
  Ed io per certo non ne so niuno
Solino disse · Questo pensier lassa,
  E non volere il tuo Signor tentare;
  Tristo sarei, se alcum qui mai trapassa.
Basta a noi quel di sopra ricercare
  Tu dici ben, diss' egli: e qui dai frati
  Preso commiato, li lassammo stare
Così passando monti, valli e prati,
  Trovammo qui le genti, che vi stanno,
  Più che ad altro lavoro, al cacciar dati
Perle, gagate e assai metalli vi hanno,
  E assassagos, la cui natura è propria,
  Che posti al sole l'arco del ciel fanno.
L'Isola per lunghezza vi si copia
  Da cento venti miglia, e il nome ad essa,
  Quel d'Ibernio oceàno, vi si appropia."

And now, I may ask, does it occur to anyone to consider whether in all this there is a tittle of evidence that Fazio degli Uberti actually set foot on the Irish shore. I confess I have my doubts as to his having done more than pass through the island in the company of his guide and counsellor, Solinus, in the same sense that Dante traversed regions of the other world under the escort of Virgil. In the first place, he did not begin his wanderings until late in life, as Villani points out, and as he himself indicates in a passage of the Dittamondo, where he says (Lib. ii. cap. xxxi.)—

"E bench'il tempo è tardo,
Mosso mi son per veder peregrino
Del mondo quant'l Sol n'ha in suo riguardo."

He cannot possibly have visited all the countries he describes in his poem, and it is improbable that he attempted the isle lying at the farthest extremity of the world. Too far advanced in life to undertake a pilgrimage to the Purgatory of St. Patrick in the fashion of a hardy wayfarer, he certainly was not rich enough to journey to the wilds of Ulster with a troop of horses and attendants in the style affected by his noble compatriots. Moreover, there is, in his description of the country and its inhabita[illegible] which characterise a picture studied from the life, and which are not wanting in some other parts of the cosmography. All that he says of Ireland had already been said in books accessible to students of his time and nation, and certain to be consulted by so diligent a reader as the author of the Dittamondo.

Solinus,[1] for example, would inform him of the dangerous nature of the sea raging between Britain and Hibernia, "so very few days"; would describe for him the extreme fertility stormy and restless throughout the year as to be navigable on of the soil, "rich to such a degree that the cattle had from time to time to be driven off the pasture-lands lest they should be injured by overfeeding"; and would likewise support the assertion that the inhabitants were rude in their habits · which opinion, however, the Venerable Bede and other authorities would help to modify. Bede, moreover, would satisfy him of the salubrity of the climate and the abundant produce of milk, fish, fowl, and venison; while Giraldus Cambrensis would give him an idea of the copious water-supply of a country where "pools and lakes are to be found even on the summits of lofty and steep mountains."

As for the extraordinary properties of certain lakes, the story of the island where no one can die, and the places where no flesh corrupts, all these marvels were in wide circulation long before Fazio's time. He does no more than relate, in a cut-and-dry way, what earlier writers invested with ampler details and more picturesque colouring under the title of *The Wonders of Ireland*.[2] In what he says of the holy and devout monastery under whose guardianship the "Island of Purgatory" was placed, he closely adheres to the

[1] Caius Julius Solinus, a Roman geographer, flourished in the third century of the Christian era. His *Polyhistor* was translated into English by Arthur Golding in 1587.

[2] Speaking of the MIRABILIA URBIS ROMÆ, Ampère says: "Une classe nombreuse de livres portait ce nom (MIRABILIA) au moyen age: il y avait les *Merveilles de l'Orient*, les *Merveilles de l'Irlande*, les *Merveilles du Monde*." And Campion, writing in the sixteenth century, makes the following observation bearing on this point: "Every History of Ireland that I have seene, maketh one severall title, *De Mirabilibus Hiberniæ*, and therein with long processe treateth of severall Ilands, some full of Angels, some full of devils, some for male only, some for female, some where poore may live, some where none can dye. finally, such effects of waters, stones, trees, and trinkets, that a man would weene them to be but heedlesse and uncertain [illegible]"

written account of the pilgrimage. So far from being encouraged to penetrate into another world, penitents were exhorted not to attempt so much. Leave had to be obtained from the bishop of the diocese (or, as some say, from the "Archbishop of Ireland"), as well as from the prior, before anyone was permitted to enter the purgatorial cave. The Nicholas named with Patrick as having undoubtedly re-appeared after a visit to the other world, is evidently the pilgrim whose experiences are related in the Golden Legend.

However, though the author of the Dittamondo tells us nothing new about ourselves, his description of Ireland is extremely interesting, as showing what figure we made in the eyes of Europe five hundred years ago. And for my own part, I must say that if, on opening the old poem, I found no allusion to the famous cave in Donegal, I should have been disconcerted, amazed, and racked with historic doubts.

FRIENDS AT COURT

"*Tell me your company, and I'll tell you what you are,*" is merely a rough way of indicating the value which attaches to chosen and avowed friendships as a test of character. No doubt, accidental circumstances may lead to the formation of ties both intimate and enduring, and opportunity rather than election may establish relations which closely approach to "a noble and a true conceit of God-like amity." Still, no sooner have you learned who and what a man's dearest friends and constant companions are than you apply the discovery as a gauge of his judgment, a criterion of his taste, and a measure of his intrinsic worth.

For my own part, I confess that when anyone interests me particularly, I feel curious to know not only who are his friends and familiars in the daily intercourse of life, but what characters in history are his favourites, and which of all the saints in the calendar claims his homage of predilection. For it is not the eminently pious alone who are acquainted with the saints. Readers of history are not ignorant of the lives and characteristic qualities of the great and holy ones of Christendom who typify an epoch or personify a cause; they have their favourites among the canonised, and can discourse to you with intelligence of St Ambrose or St Gregory, of St. Edward of England or St. Louis of France, of the Angel of the Schools or the preacher of the Crusades Votaries of Fine Art have their preferences, too, for one or another of the white-robed army and the glorious company of the saints; and the frequenters of picture galleries, the students of Vasari, Rio, Mrs. Jameson, and the rest, will point out to you the objects of their admiration—arrow-pierced Sebastian or the mailed St. Maurice, rapt Cecilia or Dorothea flower-crowned, the seraphic St. Francis or the divine St. John

Nor is this predilection for one rather than another of the majestic and saintly personages portrayed in art simply a poetic or æsthetic fancy. There is, I think, something more in the attraction. The love for the pictured semblance betrays a deeper feeling; and I have oftentimes noticed the shy, half-conscious way in which the possessor of a good picture of a sacred subject descants on its merits; as if the subject were dearer to him than the artist's interpretation, and touched more nearly "the soul's secret springs" than he might be willing to acknowledge

Catholics, of course, relegate the poetry and æsthetics of the question to a secondary place. The saints are to us really and dearly companionable, and the pictures in which they are worthily portrayed are objects of affection as well as of devotion. The great body of the faithful are, I suppose, content with one heavenly protector, and invoke principally their name-saint, or the guardian saint of their country, or the patron of their parish, trade, order, or profession. But nevertheless there are many who, while paying honour to these their natural protectors, so to speak, feel still more specially and devoutly drawn to other blessed ones, on whom they rely for the discharge of offices of friendship—aid in the course of life's pilgrimage, and countenance before the heavenly throne. Oftentimes it is interesting to learn, or to surmise, how these celestial friendships began, when the sympathetic link was formed, and why this saint rather than another engaged the devout affection of a poor human soul sojourning afar from the eternal home.

Thus, when Cardinal Newman tells us that he loves St John Chrysostom as he loves David and St. Paul, who hears those words unmoved? who stays not to consider what the affinity may be between the great master of the English tongue and "John of the golden mouth"; between the illustrious convert of our day and the poet-king of Israel; between "Father Newman of the Oratory" and the Apostle of the Gentiles, in whom intellect and love were equal forces?

The [illegible] of St Stanislaus Kostka were presumably

Ignatius and Xavier. And yet it was not they who appeared to him in his dying hour, welcoming him to heaven. Close to the spot where he expired, the vision may be seen to this day, thanks to the painter's art, delineated on the wall in front of which lies the effigy of the saint sculptured in marble. The beholder recognises in the heavenly group the virgin martyrs, Agnes, Barbara, and Cecilia, together with the Immaculate Mother and a winged escort of the celestial host.

Of these three patrons, Barbara appears to have been the one most of all relied on by the youthful saint in seasons of trial and difficulty. In his boyhood he had himself enrolled as a member of a confraternity of the Blessed Virgin and St. Barbara; and it is recorded in the story of his life how, having fallen ill at Vienna in the house of a Lutheran, who would not allow a priest to enter the dwelling, Stanislaus, pining for the Bread of Life, turned to the beatified martyr whose festival he had kept a short time before with extraordinary devotion, and besought her to aid him in his utmost need. In answer to his prayer of faith, the Blessed Sacrament was brought to him by two angels in presence of St. Barbara.

Catherine Burton, whose life, under the title of *An English Carmelite*, forms an interesting volume of the Quarterly Series, brought out so punctually these many years under Father Coleridge's editorship, cherished a very special devotion to St. Francis Xavier, and was signally befriended by him in return. The Apostle of the Indies visited her in sickness, cured her, comforted her, and fulfilled in her regard all the offices of friendship Surely this is as strange an association of patron and client as could be named.

The late Most Rev. Dr. Dixon had an extraordinary devotion to St. Catherine of Siena. The primate did not choose as his friend of friends among the saints, Patrick or Malachy, or Francis de Sales, or Charles Boromeo, as one might expect. It is recorded of him that St. Catherine's works were daily in his hands; that he could hardly preach a sermon, or pay a visit, or say a few words, without mentioning her He used to say that St. Catherine did everything for him. By a strange coincidence, he died on the anniversary of the day when she passed to her reward: and not only on the same day of the month, but on the same day of the week, and at the same hour of the day. Some years before his death, he asked permission to be buried, when his time should come, in the little cemetery attached to the convent of the Sacred Heart, Mount St. Catherine, Armagh. After his death, this was found among the directions concerning his funeral, which he ordered to be as simple as possible: "Some kind friend will place a slab over my grave with the following inscription, and nothing more—

"Joseph, expectans resurrectionem carnis,
S. Catherina Senensis ora pro me."

In the ages of Faith, which were also the days of High Art, it was not unusual for the noble and rich to commission the great masters to paint votive pictures, in which the donors, their families, and their patron saints, should be represented as grouped round the enthroned Madonna and Infant Saviour. These pictures were intended for altar-pieces; generations prayed before them as they hung in the chapels of the great cathedrals and churches of Italy, Germany, and Flanders. In later times they are more likely to be found in public galleries or in private collections; but, wherever they are, they arrest attention as examples more than commonly interesting of the schools to which they belong. The association in these splendid panels of the human and the divine, of youth and age, of beauty, majesty, chivalry, and sanctity, forms a glorious vision, and one which cannot be contemplated even at this day without the deepest interest. In these pictures the saints are carefully individualised, and easily distinguishable by their characteristic expression and their attributes. The donors have left behind them, in some instances, not only these beautiful testimonies of their piety and munificence, but names that are enshrined in history, while in other cases, no record of their names is anywhere to be found, save, let us hope, in the Book of Life. Mrs. Jameson describes several pictures of this kind in her graceful, happy manner. Here is her account of one which she saw in the Museum of Rouen, attributed there to Van Eyck.—

"It is probably a fine work by a later master of the school, perhaps Hemmelinck. In the centre the Virgin is enthroned; the Child, seated on her knee, holds a bunch of grapes, symbol of the Eucharist. On the right of the Virgin is St Apollonia; then two lovely angels in white raiment with lutes in their hands; and then a female head, seen looking from behind, evidently a family portrait. More in front, St. Agnes, splendidly dressed in green and sable, her lamb at her feet, turns with a questioning air to St. Catherine, who, in queenly garb of crimson and ermine, seems to consult her book. Behind her, another member of the family, a man with a very fine face; and more in front, St. Dorothea, with a charming expression of modesty, looks down on her basket of roses. On the left of the Virgin is St. Agatha, then two angels in white with viols, then St. Cecilia, and near her a female head, another family portrait; next, St. Barbara, wearing a beautiful head-dress, in front of which is worked her tower, framed like an ornamental jewel in gold and pearls—she has a missal in her lap. St Lucia next appears, then another female portrait. All the heads are about one-fourth of the size of life. I stood in admiration before this picture—such miraculous finish in all the details, such life, such spirit, such delicacy in the heads and hands, such brilliant colour in the draperies! Of its history I could learn nothing, nor what family had thus introduced themselves into celestial companionship. The portraits seemed to me to represent a father, a mother, and two daughters."[1]

The Venetian painters were remarkable for the art with which they grouped the noble forms of earth and heaven into a splendid and suggestive scene; and many were the subjects of this class which they were commissioned to execute by their munificent patrons—the military commanders, the merchant princes, the guilds and religious confraternities, and the republic herself The guardian saints of Venice formed a numerous and a splendid host, and had the place of honour in the pageants and triumphs of the State. Besides the Apostle St. Mark, and the warrior-martyr Theodore, Venice counted among her protectors, St. George of Cappadocia, the patron of soldiers and patricians; St. Nicholas of Myra, the protector of seamen, merchants, and the citizens at large; St Catherine, the patroness of learning and the ecclesiastical Order; and St. Justina, whose name is associated with the great day of Lepanto In commemorative pictures, painted by command of the republic, contemporary celebrities are not always introduced; sometimes the guardian saints alone appear in presence

[1] *Legends of the Madonna.*

of the Madonna, sometimes Venice herself is the only figure divested of the aureole of sanctity which is seen in heavenly company. Thus St. Justina is often placed on one side of the Madonna, accompanied by St. Mark or St. Catherine; or with St. Mark she presents Venice (under the form of a beautiful woman, crowned and sumptuously attired) to the Virgin, as in "a grand, scenic, votive picture, painted for the State by Paul Veronese"[1]

Perhaps the last place in which one would expect to meet this same beautiful St. Justina, bearing the sword of martyrdom, is the arsenal. Yet there she is: within, pictured as interceding in heaven for the Venetians; and without, a noble sculptured form elevated on the pediment of the great gateway. But the arsenal of Venice was no ordinary storehouse of the munitions of war. It included the shipbuilder's yard and the artillery school. It was the pride and strength of the republic, the envy and terror of her foes, the very heart of Venice. If the arsenal were endangered, then might the Queen of the Adriatic tremble. One night—it was the 13th of September 1569—the city did in truth tremble in all her hundred isles. The inhabitants, roused from their sleep by an awful noise and the shaking of the houses, rushed wildly out; the nobles ran to arms; all was confusion and uncertainty, until the light of a conflagration revealed the nature and extent of the disaster The powder magazine had exploded, and the walls and turrets of the arsenal were blown into the air. At thirty miles' distance the explosion was heard. Report magnified the extent of the devastation; it was believed that all the naval stores of Venice were destroyed; and at Constantinople, the implacable, deadly foe of Venice and of Christendom rejoiced that the strength and prestige of the great maritime power of the West were gone for ever.[2] But when the Venetians came to compute their losses, it was found that comparatively little injury was done. Few lives had been lost, and only four galleys destroyed. Once more the arsenal became the centre of energy and movement; the towers and walls were rebuilt, and the artillery was remounted; and in the following year Venice was ready with an effective maritime force to join the League which Pope Pius v. was organising for the defence of Christendom against the overwhelming

[1] *Sacr*[illegible] [2] Daru *Hi*[illegible] *V*[illegible], t. 5.

power of the Turks. At Lepanto, the Venetian galleys, mounted with heavy ordnance, served by the renowned bombardieri of the republic, and navigated by rowers ready at a moment's notice to join the men-at-arms in a hand-to-hand struggle, contributed in an eminent degree to the catastrophe in which the maritime glory of the Crescent set for ever.[1]

The victory of Lepanto, a "victory so glorious, complete, and decisive as had never before been achieved by Christendom,"[2] was gained on the 7th of October, which, in the year 1571, fell on a Sunday. It was the feast of St. Justina of Padua, who, since the surrender to Venice of that and other cities of the mainland in which she was honoured, had been held in particular veneration by the republic. The tidings of the defeat of the Turks had been sent after the battle to the pope, but owing to contrary winds the envoys did not reach Rome until messengers from Venice had already brought the intelligence to his Holiness. Through the same medium, likewise, Philip II received the earliest tidings of the victory. Venice, in fact, was the first to be gladdened with the glorious news, the gonfalonnier Giustiniani having received orders to proceed at once in his galley from the bloodstained waters of the gulf and carry home the intelligence.

On the evening of the 17th of October, the galley, with the banner of the angel Gabriel floating from the mast, sailed past the lagoon, her crew and men-at-arms rending the air with shouts of victory. As the vessel entered the Canal of St. Martin, the salvos of her guns re-echoed through the city. In the campanili, the brazen tongues caught up the signal; and the populace, wild with joy, ran out upon the quays and open places, joining the roar of their voices to the thunder of the artillery and the clangour of the bells. Presently the galley neared the shore; and a strange apparition she presented, looming in the dusk. All the soldiers on board carried Turkish banners, and the rowers were dressed out in the spoils

[1] The contingent of Venice to the forces of the League far exceeded that which the King of Spain contributed, or that which the rest of Italy supplied. Of the 243 ships of war and other vessels brought into action, 121 carried the standard of the republic Her soldiers, navymen, and rowers amounted to 41,000 in a total of 86,400. See the computation of the allied forces in Guglielmotti's *Marcantonio Colonna alla Battaglia di Lepanto*, lib. ii. cap. xiv.

[2] Ranke.

of the enemy. Giustiniani stepped ashore at the piazza of St. Mark, and was carried by the people to the Ducal Palace, where he was introduced to the Council. Having heard the intelligence of the triumph of the Christian arms, the Doge and the Signory proceeded to the Church of St. Mark to return thanks to Almighty God, and notwithstanding the lateness of the hour, they had a solemn Mass celebrated by a foreign priest who happened to be on the spot. By this time the papal legate and the ambassadors had in their turn appeared on the scene. The entire population were in the piazza; and the vast multitude, with one accord raising their voices, sang the *Te Deum*.[1]

Venice had her full share in the losses, as well as in the glory, of Lepanto. Barberigo, their noble provveditore, was mortally wounded in the fight, yet survived long enough to learn that the Turks were routed, and to give God thanks that he had lived to see that hour. Thirty-seven captains of galleys were killed or wounded. The bombardieri, the soldiers, rowers, pilots, all suffered severely. Out of 15,440 of the allied forces placed *hors de combat* on that day, between 9000 and 10,000 were in the Venetian ranks.[2] But none should mourn for those who fell so gloriously. It was the duty of all to rejoice for the deliverance of Christendom, and by a public decree the 7th of October was set apart to be observed for ever as a national festival.

To the arsenal were borne the red and yellow standards taken from the Turks, and there, even to this day, they hang in limp and tattered folds. Girolamo Campagna was com-

[1] See an account of the rejoicings at Venice, quoted from an inedited document by M. Yriarte in his *Vie d'un Patricien de Venise au seizième siècle*.

[2] See the interesting and valuable work already quoted, *Marcantonio Colonna*, etc. The author takes trouble to show how important a part the Venetians played in the heroic drama of that day. He gives a picturesque description of the battle,—not more so, however, than Prescott does, in his style of easy elegance,—and he adds some characteristic touches which I do not remember to have noticed in other pictures of the momentous scene. When the combined fleets were drawn up in line of battle, Don John of Austria displayed the great standard of the League which the pope had blessed and sent to him, that he might unfurl it on the day of conflict. At sight of the crimson banner, embroidered with the image of the crucified Redeemer, all the men on board the galleys, from the captain-[illegible] their

missioned to execute a figure of St. Justina to surmount the gateway, as a testimonial of the triumph and gratitude of the republic. This memorial, too, survives, and still meets the gaze of the traveller when, having come to the arsenal to see the lions of the Piræus standing at the entrance, he lifts his eyes perchance, and wonderingly inquires what heroine of earth or saint of heaven has thus been raised on high. After the victory of Lepanto, St. Justina was formally ranked among the patrons of the republic, and a coin was struck, having on the reverse a standing figure of the saint, with this legend inscribed around. *Memor Ero Tui, Justina Virgo.*

As time rolled on, the Queen of the Adriatic lost her splendour. her military glory waned, her maritime supremacy was lost, her artists left no successors. Still, as long as she retained the semblance of an independent existence, the festival of St. Justina was celebrated with magnificence in Venice. Goethe, who visited that city in October 1786, tells us how picturesque and impressive was the scene on the day of commemoration. Thus he describes the spectacle:—

"This morning I was present at High Mass, which annually on this day the Doge must attend, in the Church of St Justina, to commemorate an old victory over the Turks When the gilded barques, which carry the princes and a portion of the nobility, approach the little square, when the boatmen, in their rare liveries, are plying their red-painted oars, when, on the shore, the clergy and the religious fraternities are standing, pushing, and moving about, and waiting with their lighted torches fixed upon poles and portable silver chandeliers; then, when the gangways, covered with carpet, are placed from the vessels to the shore, and first the full violet dresses

knee and confessed their sins, while the priests on board of each galley pronounced the words of sacramental absolution, and, in the name of the Sovereign Pontiff, granted a plenary indulgence to all. Good food with generous wine was distributed, so that all might be strengthened for the approaching contest. Don John, the generalissimo of the Christian armada, and Colonna, the captain-general of the pope, sailed round in light vessels, animating to the heroic point the courage of those now called upon to fight joyfully to the death for their faith and their country. Don John then returned to his galley; and, fired with the enthusiasm of youth and animated with an intense desire that all should be filled with the noble frenzy of the strife, commanded the trumpets to sound, and danced the gagliarda with two cavalier on the quarter-deck (piazza d'arme) in the sight of the whole fleet"

of the savii, next the ample red robes of the senators, are unfolded upon the pavement, and lastly, when the old Doge, adorned with his golden Phrygian cap, in his long golden *talar* and his ermine cloak, steps out of the vessel—when all this, I say, takes place in a little square before the portal of a church, one feels as if one were looking at an old worked tapestry, exceedingly well designed and coloured. To me, northern fugitive as I am, this ceremony gave a great deal of pleasure. . . . The Doge is a well-grown and well-shaped man, who perhaps suffers from ill-health, but, for dignity's sake, bears himself upright under his heavy robe. . . . About fifty *nobili*, with long, dark-red trains, were with him. For the most part they were handsome men, and there was not an uncouth figure among them. . . . When all had taken their places in the church, and Mass began, the fraternities entered by the chief door, and went out by the side door to the right, after they had received holy water in couples, and made their obeisance to the high altar, to the Doge, and the nobility."[1]

How the Church of St. Justina looks in the nineteenth century, and whether any picturesque procession ever crosses the little court once swept by the red trains of the *nobili*, I am not able to say. I never saw the church; nor should I, if I found myself again in Venice, know which side to turn in search of it.

[1] *Letters from Italy*. Translated by the Rev. A. J. W. Morrison.

THE LADY DERVORGILLA

FACTS are stubborn things, they say; but so, for that matter, are fictions. One of the most obstinate of our historic inventions is that which attributes the Anglo-Norman invasion and all its woes to the light conduct of the Lady Dervorgilla, wife of Tiernan O'Ruark, Prince of Breffny. The legend holds its own to the present hour, although competent authorities have shown that the abduction of this "degenerate daughter of Erin," by Dermod Mac Murrough, King of Leinster, was deficient in all the elements of romance; would not have been, in that age of the world, a sufficient cause for the catastrophes that followed; had nothing whatever to do with the landing of foreign adventurers on our shores; and was altogether a thing of the past when the perpetrator of the outrage, expelled from his dominions by a host of confederate foes, crossed the sea in the hope of obtaining such military aid as would enable him to chase his enemies beyond the frontiers of Leinster and reseat himself on the provincial throne.

Moore, in the character of historian, related the occurrence in language of becoming sobriety, while he animadverted with a fine irony, which the Bard of Erin must have himself appreciated, on the "strong tendency to prefer showy and agreeable fiction to truth, which enables romance to encroach upon, and even sometimes supersede, history." But Moore, the poet, had already heightened sensational interest of the story, and had done his best to perpetuate the imaginative version which, it must be allowed, Geoffry Keating's prose had long before coloured to a glow that would do credit to the most florid verse.

O'Ruark, if romance delight us, set forth on a pilgrimage to St. Patrick's Purgatory, leaving his wife, the daughter of O'Melachlin, King of Meath, safely secluded in the wild fastnesses of Breffny. King Dermod, a former suitor of "this fair and lovely lady," seizing the opportunity thus afforded, galloped across the country to Connaught, attended by a party of horse, seized the princess, and carried her off in all haste to his capital city, Ferns. Breffny's lord, his vows fulfilled and penance performed, left the shores of the dim lake and sought the home of his affections. As he drew nigh to his castle at Dromahaire, a strange presentiment clouded his spirit. The valley, indeed, lay smiling before him, but no lamp from the battlements burned, no sign of expectancy or welcome greeted the devoted husband on his return. Within the castle all was changed. Silence reigned in the festive hall, the lute lay unstrung; the young false one, in a word, had fled! Like wildfire spread the news over the land of Erin. The virtuous princes, O'Ruark's compeers,—the King of Meath, the Ard-righ himself,—animated with righteous indignation, mustered their forces, swooped down on Leinster, and forthwith hurled from his throne the perfidious Mac Murrough, who, flying to England, sold his country to Henry Fitz-Empress, and then immediately returned at the head of an army of proud invaders, and began the battle not yet ended—Virtue and Erin on one side, the Saxon and Guilt on the other!

But there is a different reading of the tale. O'Ruark and Mac Murrough, it appears, had long entertained a bitter animosity towards one another. The latter, in concert with the Ard-righ, or supreme monarch of Ireland, Turloch O'Conor, had entered Tiernan's patrimony, committed great ravages in Breffny O'Rourk, and forcibly expelled the chief. The pious pilgrim (of the poetic version) was engaged, not at Lough Derg, but on a military expedition in a distant part of the country, "in pursuit of kerne, thieves, and outlaws that had mightily annoyed his people," when the Lady Dervorgilla, who had been maltreated by her husband and was residing in an island in the kingdom of Meath, was carried off by the King of Leinster, probably with her own consent, and certainly with the approval of her brother, Melachlin O'Melachlin, the recently appointed lord of East Meath.[1] The journey can

[1] Referen [illegible] *and Conquest of* [illegible] en a

hardly have resembled a flight, for the princess took with her to Ferns her cattle, her furniture, and the valuables which constituted her dowry, altogether an amount of heavy baggage totally inconsistent with the circumstances usually associated with an elopement.[1] So prudent an arrangement was not out of keeping with her time of life, for this "Helen of Ireland" was forty-four years of age when she removed with her belongings to Leinster. Nor can her companion be described as a youthful gallant. King Dermod was, by nearly twenty years, the senior of the daughter of the princely house of O'Melachlin. This unfortunate abduction, elopement, or what you will, took place fourteen years earlier than the momentous flight of Leinster's lord across the sea. Moreover, the Prince of Breffny's honour had been satisfied by a monetary *amende* of no mean value a considerable time before the fugitive king entered into an alliance with the spendthrift lords and adventurous knights of Southern Wales.[2]

Discrepancies must again be encountered if we would enter into the question of the later life of Dervorgilla,[3] who was obliged to quit Leinster with her goods and chattels the year after her removal thither. According to the Four Masters, she returned to her husband; other historians say she was brought back to her relatives in Meath; while Meredith Hanmer cuts

common usage of war in Ireland to carry off noble women, and hold them to ransom again. A castle on an islet of Lough Ree has been named as the place of Dervorgilla's temporary residence.

[1] The Brehon laws, by which Ireland was then governed, secured to married women the control over their own property. When the husband and wife had each property of their own, the wife was called "the wife of equal fortune." She was in all respects recognised as equal to her husband, and neither party could contract without the consent of the other.—Walpole's *Kingdom of Ireland*.

[2] Four years before the invasion of the English, O'Ruark agreed to receive 100 ounces of gold (nearly £4000 of modern currency) as *eineach* or compensation (modern "damages") for the injury inflicted on him by Mac Murrough.—*Historical Memoirs of the O'Briens*.

[3] Miss Charlotte M. Yonge, in her *History of Christian Names*, observes that this name, properly Dearbhforghal, was a very tough one for the genealogists And they had a good deal of it, she adds, "for it was very fashionable in the twelfth century both in Scotland and Ireland, and was turned into Dervorgilla and Dornadilla by the much-tormented chroniclers." I have seen it spelled *Dearbhfhorguill*, according to a practice, prevalent in ancient Erin, of scattering vowels with a lavish hand and shovelling in consonants [illegible]

short the discussion on her subsequent career by lightly suggesting that she may have made away with herself. "Belike," says he, "shee hanged her selfe when shee had set all the country in uprore." On the whole, the evidence seems to be in favour of the return to Meath. Nor would this necessarily imply that she was not received by her husband O'Ruark, in fact, had obtained not long before this date a territory lying about Athboy and the Hill of Ward, in exchange for a tract in his own patrimony, and he became thenceforth so involved in the commotions of that focus of disorder, Royal Meath, that it seems highly probable his residence and head-quarters were transferred from the wild woods and bogs of Breffny O'Ruark to the region of golden harvest and rich pastures watered by the Boyne and its tributaries.[1] Anyhow, there can be no doubt whatever that Tiernan's wife was residing in Meath, or thereabout, in the enjoyment of liberty, wealth, and honour, a few years after the unfortunate expedition into Leinster.[2] In 1157 her name figures with great distinction (as does the Prince of Breffny's also) in connection with a singularly auspicious and interesting event—the consecration of the Abbey Church at Mellifont.

The mention of Mellifont, the first home of the Cistercians in Ireland, awakens so many sacred and touching memories, and withdraws the mind with so gentle a fascination from the strifes and nameless confusions which make up the history of those days, that leave may be taken to brighten a page or two of this narrative with a sketch of the incidents attending its foundation, and connecting in indissoluble association the names of St. Bernard of Clairvaux and St. Malachy O'Morgair.

Some eighteen years before the period we are concerned with, that is to say, in the year 1139, Malachy, Bishop of

[1] The kingdom of Meath extended from the Shannon eastward to the sea. It included the present counties of Eastmeath and Westmeath, together with parts of Dublin, Kildare, King's County, and Longford The northern boundaries were Oriel (Louth) and Breffny. Breffny was divided into two principalities That of Breffny O'Ruark included Leitrim and a part of Longford.

[2] Antiquaries of the highest authority decline to indorse the vulgar reading of Dervorgilla's story. Dr. O'Donovan, I understand, believed that a conclusion more favourable to the lady was the right one to arrive at; and I know that Professor O'Curry purposed, had time been allowed him, to put the matter in a truer and more creditable light.

Down, undertook a journey to Rome to visit the holy places, obtain from the Sovereign Pontiff the confirmation of certain reforms he had carried out in ecclesiastical matters, and solicit the pallium for the episcopal Sees of Armagh and Cashel. A very determined opposition had been made to the prelate's departure by his flock, for they dreaded the dangers to which he must be exposed on so tedious and difficult a journey, and could not content themselves to be deprived for so long a time of the presence of a pastor who, gentle as an angel in his ways, knew nevertheless how to defend the helpless and fight the battles of the poor of Christ. But in the end all opposition had been overcome, and Malachy, taking with him five priests, some other clerics and the necessary attendants, set forth in the style of humble pilgrimage which he invariably adopted in his journeys

On the way through France, the bishop and his companions left the main road and diverged into the solitudes of Champeigne to visit the monastery of Clairvaux, situated in a deep gorge once called the Valley of Wormwood, from being the resort of wild animals and the hiding-place of robbers and outlaws, but now the peaceful home of saintly men, beautified by the labour of their hands and fitly named the Happy or Bright Valley—Clarivallis Abbot Bernard governed the Cistercian colony there established, and his fame had gone forth to the uttermost extremity of the known world, even to the land of Malachy's birth and love. The pilgrim strangers received a brotherly welcome, and the visit was felt to be one of no common interest. Great was the edification which the pious guests received in witnessing the holy and laborious life of Bernard's spiritual sons, while the monks, on their part, regarded it as a heavenly dispensation that the saintly bishop from the Western isle tarried with them for a while, and blessed them with effusion as he said farewell and set his face once more towards Rome. This meeting of Bernard and Malachy was the beginning of one of those exquisitely holy and tender friendships that we read of not unfrequently in the lives of saints "To me also in this life was it given to see this man," says Bernard. "In his look and word I was restored, and rejoiced in all manner of riches. And sinner as I was, I found grace in his sight from that time forth even to his death." Of Malachy it is not too much to say that he left his heart in that Happy Valley. And as he neared the Alps, and climbed the mountain barriers, and passed on his weary way across the Lombard plains, a longing to return to the Cistercians grew more and more intense within him. He prayed God that this might come to pass, and he resolved to ask the Father of the Faithful, as a favour which was very near his heart, that he might be allowed to resign his episcopal charge, and, with the permission and blessing of his Holiness, live and die at Clairvaux.

Innocent II., who then sat in the chair of Peter, received the Irish prelate with every mark of favour and consideration. After many interviews and conferences with the pope, in which affairs of great importance were arranged in regard to the Church in Ireland, and Malachy's petition that he might end his days in Bernard's monastery was not forgotten, the bishop prepared to depart. In the last audience, the pope took the mitre from his own head and placed it on Malachy's, bestowed on him the stole and maniple which he was himself accustomed to use in celebrating the Holy Sacrifice, gave him the kiss of peace, and with the apostolic benediction sent him back—not to Bernard and Clairvaux, but to his distracted native country in the capacity of papal legate.

Returning by the same route to his distant See, Bishop Malachy visited Clairvaux once more, and confided to Bernard's capacious heart the story of his mission to the Holy Father, the hopes and fears excited by the prospect that lay before him in the troubled land to which he was hastening, the pang he must endure in bidding a long farewell to the Bright Valley, the Cistercian brotherhood, his God-given friend the abbot. Bernard, we may be sure, knew what to say. He could arouse Christendom to the passion of the Crusades, he could "stay up the weary with a word," he could let his speech fall like a shower of soft tears on the heart of the sorrow-stricken. True, Malachy must depart, he must ride the storm in the sea-girt land, he must do the pope's behests. But then, are there no dark defiles, no desert vales in Erin? Are there no men among the Gael willing to withdraw from the turbulent scenes of life, practise penance, and awaken a vainglorious, war-distraught generation to a sense of the necessity and dignity of labour? Would it not be possible, in a word, to found another Clairvaux in Malachy's native land? This, indeed, was something for the holy men to put their heads together over, to plan and to accomplish. Saints do not usually suffer happy inspirations to fade away like sunset clouds; and so, without letting the grass grow under their feet, the bishop and the abbot took the first step towards the realisation of their pious design. It was settled that four of Malachy's companions should stay with Bernard to learn the discipline of the monastery, take the Cistercian habit in due course, and await the moment when the brethren might be able to establish a colony in the Western isle.

Not long after his return to Ireland, Malachy sent to Clairvaux two more postulants with a letter to Bernard, and a staff (stout Irish oak, we may be sure) which he requested the abbot to use as a support in his declining years. In his reply, after acknowledging the consolation which the bishop's letter, the gift, and the arrival of "the brothers come from a distant land to serve the Lord," had given him, the abbot goes on to recommend that a place should be selected and prepared for the reception of the monks, when the time should come for sending them back to Ireland,—a place secluded from the tumults of the world, and after the model of those localities which his friend had seen when with the Cistercians in France. Meanwhile, a site in every way suitable for the purpose was given to Malachy by Donough O'Carroll, Prince of Oriel, who, to the territory required for the monastery and its precincts, added other endowments "for the prosperity of his soul and in honour of Paul and Peter."[1] Hid away in a gentle vale surrounded by low hills and watered by a rapid stream, with Tredagh (Drogheda) and the sea four or five miles to the east, and the Boyne flowing at less than half that distance on the south, lay the tract which the brethren were to clear and cultivate, beautify and sanctify. After two years' novitiate, the Irishmen made their profession at Clairvaux. A certain number of French monks were chosen as assistants for them in the new foundation; among them, Brother Robert, a truly obedient son, whom Bernard spoke of as able to promote the interests of the religious family both in building and in all other necessary works. As superior of the little colony, the

[1] The ancient Irish did not use the prefix "saint" when naming personages of eminent holiness. It would have been considered disrespectful to call children after the great servants of God. A compound name was adopted, signifying the servant or devotee of Patrick or Brigid, etc.)

abbot named Christian O'Conaichy—"your dearly beloved son," he said to Malachy, "and ours."

In 1142 the Cistercians arrived in Ireland, were put in possession of the land which the bishop and the prince had assigned to them, and began at once to make a clearing in the woods and lay the foundation of the monastic buildings There can be no doubt that while the structures slowly rose, the laborious monks lay encamped around, just as Bernard and his first companions had done in the more savage scene of the Valley of Wormwood, with wattle huts for a shelter, dried leaves or chaff for a bed, and a rough log for a pillow; while their simple fare was supplied by the rapid growth of their garden, the produce of the surrounding woods, and the yield of the gentle stream. Even at this stage the community increased, and Bernard rejoiced to hear that, in a temporal as well as a spiritual sense, the settlement at Mellifont made good progress. In five or six years, if some branches were not actually established in other parts of the island, there was every prospect of this being done before long; for princes and people were alike delighted with the Cistercian family, and foundations were projected by the rulers of Meath, Leinster, and Connaught.

Meanwhile, Providence was preparing another and a final joy for Malachy. Just at the moment when circumstances rendered it imperatively necessary that the papal legate should confer with the head of the Church on important matters, word was brought to him that Pope Eugenius III., who was then in France, was about to visit Clairvaux, the home of his early religious life. Taking the resolution, therefore, of seeking the pope in Bernard's monastery, Malachy, with the consent of the bishops whom he had convoked in Synod, and who the more readily acquiesced in the project since the visit to Clairvaux would be more easily accomplished than a journey to Rome, set out (1148) for Scotland, intending to pass rapidly through England to France. Delays occurred on the way, through the hostility of King Stephen, and when the legate arrived in the Bright Valley, the pope had left, and was already on his way to Rome. But Bernard was there—the same Bernard that his friend of "the pure heart and dove-like eyes" had known nine years before, though he had suffered much since then in sharp conflicts with the heresies of the day, and with the spirit of wickedness seated in high places. Great was the joy when the Irish wayfarers were signalled at the abbey gates, and Bishop Malachy stood within the sacred precincts. "He arrived amongst us," says his friend, "like an angel sent by God, and we received him with the reverence due to his sanctity. Though he came from the West, he was truly the dayspring from on high which visited us." Several abbots happened to be at the monastery just then, and a bright holiday shone upon all.[1] After a few days, however, there supervened a change Bishop Malachy fell ill, and presently, to the grief of the Cistercians and the consternation of the clerics of his company, it became evident that his earthly career was drawing to a close. He himself knew it, and rejoiced that the Lord in His mercy had led him to the place he sought; that he was to die where fain he would have lived Bernard and the brethren, and the abbots who had come from afar, hastened to the upper chamber where the bishop lay dying, and, standing round his bed, poured forth their souls in prayer. "With psalms and hymns and spiritual songs," says Bernard, "we followed our friend on his homeward journey. Such grace was in his body, such glory in his face, as even the hand of death could not wipe away. Truly he fell asleep. All eyes were fixed upon him, yet none could say when the spirit left him The same brightness and serenity were ever visible. He was not changed, but we."

On the shoulders of abbots the body of the saint was borne to the church, Bernard offered the Holy Sacrifice for the departed; and when the sacred functions had been brought to a conclusion, the Cistercians buried their beloved guest in a favourite place in the oratory of the Blessed Virgin, where, five years later (1153), they laid their abbot and founder beside him.[2]

[1] Among the holy company was St. Gilbert of Sempringham. For an account of the meeting of the saints at Clairvaux, see the beautiful *Life of St. Gilbert*, by Father Dalgairns.

[2] This account of St. Malachy at Clairvaux is taken in substance from Cotter Morrison's charming book, *The Life and Times of St. Bernard*; and from Canon O'Hanlon's exhaustive *Life of St Malachy O'Morgair*. The latter work, long out of print, contains in full the letters addressed by "Brother Bernard, Abbot of Clairvaux, to his most beloved father and reverend lord, Malachy, by the grace of God Bishop and Legate of the Holy and Apostolic See"; and also (for the first time translated into English) St. Bernard's two discourses on the life, labours, and virtues of St. Malachy.

Before St. Bernard's death, Mellifont had already sent out four important colonies. The abbey of Bective, on the Boyne, was founded by the King of Meath Baltinglass, on the Slaney, was endowed by Dermod Mac Murrough; one of the O'Ferralls was the first benefactor of Shreul; and Nenay, in the county of Limerick, owed its origin to the munificence of Turloch O'Brien Other abbeys (for the Cistercian houses were all abbeys) arose in quick succession, and Mellifont was the parent of a numerous offspring even before the community had accomplished their task in their own secluded vale, and brought their abbey-church to completion At length, however, in 1157, the sacred edifice was ready for consecration. The event was one that called forth the generosity of the princes ruling the circumjacent territories, and excited the liveliest interest among the people at large. To add to the solemnity of the occasion, a Synod was convoked for the same date, and prelates and princes were invited to the abbey to deliberate on matters affecting the general welfare of Erin. Thither came Gelasius, the learned and holy Archbishop of Armagh, and Christian O'Conarchy, the first abbot of Mellifont, now head of all the Cistercians in Ireland, Bishop of Lismore, and Legate of the Holy See. Seventeen other bishops responded to the summons, attended by a large following of the clergy of inferior ranks. O'Loughlin, Monarch of Ireland, provincial kings, princes of high standing, chieftains of the Gael, all with their splendid retinue, their military escort, their clansmen and retainers, did honour to the auspicious day, and filled the Cistercian valley with the pomp of royalty, the flash of spears, the joyous movement of a festive crowd. Even the cattle had their place in the processions that advanced towards the abbey, as the donors' herdsmen drove them through the defile, and set them at large to pasture on the well-farmed uplands. As an offering for his soul to God and the monks of Mellifont, the Ard-righ presented on this occasion one hundred and forty oxen, sixty ounces of gold (between two and three thousand pounds of our currency), and a townland near Drogheda. Dermod O'Melachlin, King of Meath; O'Eochy, King of Down, Tiernan O'Ruark, Prince of Breffny, each made an offering of sixty ounces of gold; and the Lady Dervorgilla, with a munificence hardly inferior to that of the monarch himself, bestowed the same amount in gold, presented a gold chalice for the altar of the Virgin, together with chalices, sacred furniture, and vestments for the nine other altars erected in the church.

Dervorgilla's resources were not exhausted by this bestowal, nor was her generous hand thereafter stayed. As a benefactor her name is associated with another great religious establishment, namely, that of the Seven Churches at Clonmacnoise. Among the striking group of ecclesiastical ruins overlooking the wide expanse of the Shannon, antiquaries distinguish, as the most beautiful relic of all, the doorway of the Gothic chapel which the Princess of Breffny built for the community of nuns who had their habitation within the sacred enclosure. The monuments of early days, massed on the riverside, preserve the memory of her race. One of the churches is called the "Church of the Kings," for it was built by the O'Melachlins and chosen as their burial-place. Among the crosses is one named after them; and a heap of tumbled fortress-work is pointed out as the site of their castle. Her husband's family, if popular nomenclature may be relied on, appear to have had some connection with Clonmacnoise, which, indeed, was the favourite burial-place of the kings, princes, and chieftains of the country. The great round tower is styled O'Ruark's.

Turning to the *Annals of the Four Masters* for the record of Dervorgilla's death, we find the following brief entry, under the date A.D. 1193: Derforghaill, wife of Tiarnan O'Rourke, and daughter of Murchadh O'Maoileachlainn, died in the monastery of Droicheat Atha, in the eighty-fifth year of her age. There can be no doubt that the "Monastery of Drogheda" signifies the abbey at Mellifont. Later compilers of history, supplementing this bald statement, hazarded the incredible conjecture that Dervorgilla spent the last years of her life in cloistral seclusion and penitential atonement for her sins in the Cistercian house; while inquirers of a still more venturous turn improved the occasion by indicating some dungeon-like excavations, discovered among the monastic ruins, as the probable scene of her expiatory austerities. The idea of the Lady Dervorgilla, or any other woman, taking up her abode within the Cistercian precincts was simply absurd, especially as religious retreats for women abounded in Ireland,

and there would have been no need in that age of the world to seek a cell on the monks' premises. Still, the Four Masters had set down in all soberness a very strange thing, and no explanation was forthcoming. Meanwhile, however, new sources of historic lore turned up. *The Annals of Lough Cé*, lately rendered accessible to other besides Celtic scholars, while leaving the record of the Four Masters undisturbed in its solid truth, light up the mystery in a phrase. Thus writes the ancient chronicler. *Derbhorcaill, daughter of Murchadh O'Maelsechlainn mortua est in pilgrimage in the Monastery of Droichet-atha.* Furthermore, continuing our search in a retrograde direction through the same body of annals, we find that this pious expedition to Mellifont was not the only one undertaken to the same sanctuary by the Princess of Breffny. It appears that she had also made a pilgrimage to the abbey in the year 1189.[1]

From what quarter of Erin did this aged pilgrim set forth on her last journey through the land? Not, I should say, from any part of the already extinct kingdom of Meath O'Melachlin's regal sway had ended in a dire convulsion. The fair wide territory ruled by her father, her brother, and her kinsmen of a more remote degree, had been given by Henry Fitz-Empress to his liegeman, Hugh de Lacy. Mail-clad foreigners rode rough-shod across the plains, held the strong places, and fed on the fat of the land. From the Shannon to the sea, the Lord Palatine's castles bristled on the land, and bade defiance to every assertion of primeval right. No doubt the pilgrim's equipment would then, as in other evil days, pass the devotee throughout a hostile territory; and Dervorgilla with her attendants may have traversed Meath without encountering molestation But it seems highly improbable that her place of residence was in those parts.

Breffny, on the contrary, remained intact. Dermod Mac Murrough, fired with the old passion of hatred and revenge, had invaded the principality in conjunction with the foreigners; but the clan O'Ruark had twice routed the intruders, and a chief of the name ruled the wild region without dispute. We

[1] *The Annals of Lough Cé*, edited, with a translation, by William M. Hennessy, M.R.I.A. Published by the authority of the Lords Commissioners of Her Majesty's Treasury, under the direction of the Master of the Rolls.

may safely assume, therefore, that in the well-defended territory lying about Dromahaire, the Lady Dervorgilla had her home.

Though she had already passed the term of middle age when the Anglo-Norman invaders, with swift destructive onslaught, seized the rich patrimonies of the Gaelic chiefs and demolished the ancient State, she still lived on until all the prime agents in that catastrophe had vanished in their turn through the gates of death—King Dermod and Earl Strongbow, Fitz-Stephen and De Lacy, Henry Fitz-Empress himself. Those, too, among the native princes who had striven to arrest the torrent of destruction had likewise disappeared. Her husband had been cut down at the Hill of Ward by the new lords of Meath His head, "a woeful spectacle to the Irish,"[1] was spiked over the northern gate of Dublin, "exposed on that side of the stronghold of the stranger which looks towards the pleasant plains of Meath and the verdant uplands of Cavan."[2]

Fortunate in the circumstances of her death, the Lady Dervorgilla's last journey to the Cistercian valley brought to a close the pilgrimage of her earthly life. What were the last objects that greeted those failing eyes? The gently receding hills guarding the vale of rest, the stately monastery, raised stone upon stone by the sons of Malachy and Bernard, the abbey church, upon whose several altars she had laid her gifts! And what were the last echoes that fell on those life-wearied ears? The peaceful sounds of labour in the fields, the chants of the choral service borne upon the breeze, the heaven-appealing clangour of the bells!

The honourable sepulture due to a friend and benefactor was gratefully given to her by the monks. With a strong-voiced *Miserere* and a whispered *Requiescat*, they laid her in the consecrated soil, there to mingle dust with dust, there to await "the morning of the Resurrection"

[1] *Annals of the Four Masters.* [2] M'Ghee's *History of Ireland.*

DERMOD OF THE FOREIGNERS

ALTHOUGH the abduction of the Lady Dervorgilla was not the cause of the irruption of a host of military adventurers and the dissolution of the ancient order in the Island of the Gael, the audacity of the outrage, nevertheless, spread east and west a sinister impression, and drew down on the perpetrator a heavy chastisement. Insult being added by this act to the injuries already inflicted on the Prince of Breffny by the potentate of Leinster, O'Ruark's vindictive passions were naturally aroused to the maddening point. Distinguished as a military chief, and supported, as a matter of course, by his father-in-law the King of Meath, he yet could have little hope of making Dermod Mac Murrough feel the weight of his avenging arm as long as Turlough O'Conor, King of Connaught and Monarch of Ireland, remained indifferent to his cause or stood in array against him.

O'Conor had now for more than forty years occupied the position of reigning sovereign of the western province; and during the last seventeen years he had been, sometimes with and sometimes without opposition, paramount lord of all Ireland. He and Mac Murrough had maintained a close alliance, cementing their friendship in kingly fashion As brothers they had striven together in cruel foray and in unrighteous aggression. Partaking of one another's crimes, they had shared the plunder which their red hands had seized. In dismembering Munster, in dividing Meath, in threatening Ulster, the Ard-righ had had the assistance, or the countenance, of the King of Leinster. About two years before this time they had marched side by side at the head of a powerful armament, to desolate the southern province; and at the battle of Maonmore, Dermod Mac Murrough bore a conspicuous part in routing King O'Brien, and slaughtering the brave Dalcassians who, according to their wont, would neither fly from the field nor ask for quarter.[1] Still later, these sceptred raiders had made a hostile incursion into O'Ruark's territory, defeated the chief, and wrested from him a part of his inheritance.

Under these circumstances it might seem a hopeless task to endeavour to detach the Ard-righ from the Leinster alliance, and induce him to espouse the cause of a prince whom he had himself so recently assailed. However, O'Ruark was no mean hand at intrigue, as the event proved. He had the address to persuade O'Conor that Mac Murrough secretly favoured the pretensions of the Princes of Aileach to the sovereign authority, and that when the next contest for supremacy should convulse the island, King Dermod, if not sufficiently humbled meanwhile, would support the northern dynast, O'Loughlin, and thus throw a considerable weight into the scale in opposition to the Connaught claims. Turlough, though already on the brink of the grave, had lost none of the ambition of his earlier days. That which he could not expect to enjoy much longer himself, he yet hoped to secure for his dynasty. To weaken O'Loughlin, Prince of Aileach, would certainly be desirable. To humble, and if possible subdue, Mac Murrough would seem at this juncture to be a stroke of good policy. Moreover, the King of Leinster had given cause of umbrage to the monarch by undertaking, on his own account solely, this latest attack on the Prince of Breffny. He had not only carried away O'Ruark's wife, but he had wasted and spoiled O'Ruark's territory with a thoroughness that showed how little romance had to do with the expedition.

And so it turned out that when Dervorgilla's enraged father, and her injured husband, appealed to the supreme authority for vengeance on the abductor, the Ard-righ, "moved with honour and compassion," undertook to redress the wrongs of the claimants, made no account of his late companion in arms, and called out an army to invade Leinster in conjunction with O'Ruark.

[1] In this battle the army of the south lost 7000 men. Every leading house in North Munster mourned the loss of either its chief or its tanist; some great families lost three, five, or seven brothers on that sanguinary day. The household of Kinkora (royal residence of the O'Briens) was left without an heir, and many a near kinsman's seat was vacant in its hospitable hall.—M'Gee's *History of Ireland*

Dermod, enthroned in his capital city, "Ferns the stately," and lording it over an "extensive land of wealthy warriors," might probably have defied the O'Conors and O'Ruarks in coalition had he been wise enough to have secured the allegiance of the subordinate princes and tributary chiefs of the province. But his barbarous treatment of some, and his tyrannical oppression of all, had so alienated his natural supporters that they were disposed to withdraw from him in his season of distress, and make common cause with his enemies. He had laid a heavy hand on the Danes of Dublin in revenge of their treacherous slaying of his father, and had continued to grind them with excessive imposts. O'Moore, Lord of Leix, with whom he was closely connected by marriage, he had loaded with fetters and blinded, "against the guarantee of the laiety and clergy." The Lord of Hy-Faelain (O'Byrne's country), and Murrough, a chief of the O'Tooles, he had killed; and by treachery or force he had got into his power the Lord of Feara Cualann (Wicklow) and a number of other chieftains, all of whom he deprived of life or sight. Between him and the most powerful of his tributaries, the King of Ossory, a feud of the deadliest character had long existed. When, therefore, the Ard-righ sent messengers to the Leinster chiefs and princes, his envoys met with a favourable reception. Mac Turkill, King of Dublin and Fingall; Mac Gillopadrigh, King of Ossory, and the powerful septs of the O'Byrnes of Wicklow, falling in with O'Conor's plans, forthwith "turned heads upon their lord, King Dermod" In the following year (1154) a strong force was led into Leinster, O'Ruark took his revenge, plundering both churches and territories, and the Lady Dervorgilla, with her stock and valuables, was conveyed back to Meath. Fearing that his stronghold at Ferns might fall into the hands of his enemies, Dermod fired the city, and, in so doing, caused the destruction of the abbey founded by St. Aidan six hundred years before Deserted and defeated, the King of Leinster had a hard time to pass for about two years.

But then there came a change in the condition of things. In 1156 Turlough O'Conor was gathered to his forefathers, and laid to rest near the high altar in the cathedral of Clonmacnoise.[1]

[1] His father, Roderick O'Conor, died in the monastery of Clonmacnoise, where he resided after he had been blinded by the O'Flahertys, a powerful sept of the [illegible] nois.

The historians of his principality styled him Great, eulogised his kingly qualities, and enumerated the magnificent bequests which he made to different churches: gold and silver, steeds and cattle, chessboards and arms, robes and cups, and precious stones. Nevertheless, he was vainglorious, unscrupulous, and on occasions treacherous. His long reign was spent in strife, in sowing dissensions, and in molesting his fellow-princes. In vain the Primate Gelasius and other prelates of the Church exerted their influence in behalf of Murrough O'Melachlin, King of Meath, whom O'Conor seized in spite of solemn guarantees, and robbed of his inheritance. One of his own sons was blinded by his orders; and another, Roderick, whom he put in fetters more than once, was not released from his last incarceration until the prelates, clergy, and chieftains of Connaught had held a public fast at the Rath of St. Brendan, and besought heaven to mollify the inexorable father's heart. No idea of enlightened patriotism seems ever to have crossed King Turlough's mind, nor would it appear that even the mistaken notion that his crimes might benefit the nation, was at any time harboured in his breast. The slaying, the spoiling, the dividing, were all for the aggrandisement of the O'Conors.

And yet the policy so unscrupulously sustained proved unsuccessful. High rose the sun at Aileach when O'Conor's funeral rites were ended. With less bloodshed and contention than was usual on the accession of a new monarch to the throne of Ireland, the supreme power passed into O'Loughlin's hands, and the O'Conors were obliged to decline for a time into a provincial rank. Roderick succeeded his father as King of Connaught. To make his throne secure, he began his reign by imprisoning three of his brothers, one of whom he blinded; and as he did not relinquish the hope of ultimately acquiring the pre-eminent position which his father had enjoyed, he endeavoured by treaties, intrigues, and coalitions to strengthen the O'Conor interests There was a pacific meeting, as the annalists record, between Roderick O'Conor and Tiernan O'Ruark, and they took mutual oaths to support one another before sureties and relics. There were hostile meetings, too, between the forces of these allies and O'Loughlin's troops For a time the west and north were in strife, but the Connaceans got the worst of the encounter. O'Ruark in the end made peace with the conquerors, "so that his own land was left to him"; and Roderick was obliged to deliver up hostages to the Ard-righ. That he did not, therefore, sheath his sword, he plainly showed by proceeding to throw a bridge across the Shannon at Athlone, "that he might have a passage to take the spoils of Meath." After a battle with the forces of Meath, marched to the spot to prevent the execution of his project, he succeeded in spanning the strong current of the stream[1] From his vast stronghold at the head of Lough Swilly, the Monarch O'Loughlin held the petty princes in awe, and domineered over the provincial kings. In the later years of his reign he had, it is said, the hostages of all Ireland in his hands.

Among the first of the provincial princes who delivered up hostages and acknowledged the supremacy of O'Loughlin, was the harassed King of Leinster. His timely submission was well received and promptly rewarded. An army was sent to his assistance, and in a short time he found himself restored to his rightful position. Together the monarch and Mac Murrough made an incursion into Ossory and Leix, burning up all before them, and obliging the O'Moores and Killpatricks to fly across the Shannon into Connaught. Through their united efforts they succeeded in expelling from Leinster the son of Mac Phealain, who had been established there by O'Conor and O'Ruark. Later on, the Danes of Dublin were brought to their knees, forced to give Dermod a tribute of 1200 cows, and compelled to acknowledge him as lord paramount. Thus reinstated and supported by the highest authority in the land, the King of Leinster might very well have exercised some regal wisdom in conciliating his disaffected subordinates, and obliterating in a degree the memory of his earlier oppressions. At anyrate, he might have established a politic peace with the neighbouring rulers. But he was deficient in tact, temper, prudence; predatory expeditions continued to be his delight, and tyranny his practice.

In this our "Age of Whitewash" more difficult things have

[1] Roderick's father had likewise made a passage over this part of the Shannon, and for a like purpose. These structures, according to the best authorities, consisted of a rude crossing of hurdles and stems of trees carried over piles of stones laid in a fordable pass of the river, and covered with clay and gravel. They could easily be destroyed by a hostile party, and were some[illegible] the causeway.

perhaps been attempted than the clearing of Dermod Mac Murrough's character from sundry of the aspersions cast by common consent upon it. I have no fancy to attempt such an undertaking. However, I must say that I think it would be no easy matter to prove that he was much worse than his contemporaries In cold-blooded treachery he was outdone by O'Loughlin. In profligacy he had more than a match in Roderick O'Conor. Assuredly, he was guilty of a sacrilegious and unheard-of deed when, in 1135, he forcibly took the Abbess of Kildare out of her cloister, compelled her to marry one of his own people, and killed 170 of the inhabitants of the town and monastery who rose in defence of their abbess.[1] But we have a pendant for this atrocity in Tiernan O'Ruark's outrage in 1128 on the Archbishop of Armagh—"an ugly, ruthless, unprecedented deed, which earned the malediction of the men of Erin, both lay and clerical."[2] The barbarous practice of blinding was not indulged in by Dermod alone. It was in those days a usual way of incapacitating a rival from reigning, unfitting an opponent to command, or injuring an enemy of any kind. It was common in Ireland, had prevailed in England from an earlier period, and was so usual among the Normans that some writers have hazarded the suggestion that it was probably an invention of that chivalrous race. However this may be, the princes of the Norman and Plantagenet lines were experts in its use. Henry I., as everyone will remember, disposed of his eldest brother's claims to the throne of England by imprisoning him for life, and causing his eyes to be put out. Death or blindness, says Lingard, or perpetual imprisonment, were the usual portion of those who offended Beauclerc; and it is on record that he extinguished the sight of a poet who had satirised him, in order that other versifiers might learn what they must expect if they displeased the King of England[3] Henry II, to punish the Cambrians who had risen up against him, treated his numerous hostages, the children of the noblest families in Wales, with shocking barbarity, causing the eyes of all the males to be rooted out, "satiating himself with blood, and covering himself with infamy."[4] William the Conqueror doomed his fellow-creatures to blindness for lesser offences and on slighter provocation. In his kingly solicitude for the pre-

[1] *Annals of Clonmacnoise.*
[2] *Annals of Lough Cé*
[3] *History of England*
[4] *History of England*

servation of the game in the large forests for the deer which he made, he enacted that "whoever killed a hart or a hind should be blinded."[1] The invaders of Ireland did not relinquish the practice in the country they overran. A notable instance occurred in 1250, when "The hostages of Connaught were blinded by the English at Athlone."[2]

In point of fact, King Dermod of Leinster bore a family resemblance to the princes of his nation, and to those of the world at large, in his day. Seeing that he was so quarrelsome with his fellow-magnates, and so ferocious in his enmities, one cannot, perhaps, help fancying that when he was left undisturbed in his own territory, his immediate subjects must have passed a terrible time under his personal sway. Not quite so, however. On closer inquiry, it appears that while he exasperated the tributary chieftains by his rapacious levies, he was generous in his benefactions to the poor, and favoured the commonalty in an unusual degree. The mass of the people seem to have been attracted rather than repelled by the attitude of barbaric strength which he maintained. His towering stature, his stentorian voice, hoarse from shouting in battle, his valour, and his capacity for command in war, impressed them favourably, and they observed with satisfaction that he was not one of those princes who from preference victimise the meaner sort of men. It must be remembered that in the Ireland of that day, as in far earlier times, the people had safeguards which protected them in a considerable degree from the violence and caprice of despots; else, indeed, how would it have been possible for them to live in the midst of the incessant commotion kept up by the sanguinary feuds of contentious rulers, and under a political condition bordering on anarchy? The feudal system of serfdom and vassalage had not yet superseded the patriarchal state of society. The land belonged not to the chief, but to the sept; neither petty prince nor superior king had any power to oust a clansman from his home or starve him in his cabin Justice between man and man was administered according to the Brehon code, by judges who had undergone a long and hard course of study, who were not

[1] See the Anglo-Saxon Chronicle. "He loved the tall stags" says the annalist, "as if he were their father, and also appointed concerning the hares that they should go free"

[2] *Annals* [illegible]

appointed by the will of the prince, and who could not be removed at his pleasure. Again, the learned bodies—the ollaves or poet-philosophers, the historians and antiquaries, the bards, grouped in families and occupying an elevated and independent position—wielded a very strong power, and while enjoying a well-established immunity from legal imposts, and from disturbance even in periods of civil strife, were in a position to extend protection to the lowly and defenceless, who, when pursued by an enemy, might claim sanctuary within the demesne lands set apart for the maintenance of the literary classes. Dermod of Leinster, even in his most ungovernable moods, never would have dared to put out the eyes of a poet of the Gael. Lastly, the religious establishments conferred the greatest benefits on the people tenanting their lands, as well as those living in their vicinity; they stood, someone has well said, as a rampart between the oppressed and the oppressor, their precincts were held sacred by the princes who were the donors of them, and even by hostile armaments invading the circumjacent territory. Schools were kept open in the monasteries, to which all were welcome,—the lowly and the high-born standing in the same class, and singing in the same choir. In seasons of scarcity, there was corn in the granaries to feed the distressed. In days of warfare, an inviolable peace reigned within the termons, as the demesnes of church and monastery were called. The tenants on such lands enjoyed the benefit of sanctuary in whatever part of the property they dwelt, while all, without distinction, even those who were not tenants on the termon lands, were admitted to sanctuary within the ground immediately surrounding the sacred edifice, and were allowed, on the approach of danger, to store provisions and other property on the premises. Furthermore, ecclesiastics enjoyed the privilege of personal sanctuary even outside the precincts of their churches and monasteries. No bloodthirsty chief or fiery kerne would venture to strike down a fugitive in the arms of a priest or monk.

Dermod's favourite residence was at Ferns, the seat of government of the Mac Murroughs of Hy-Kinselagh.[1] On an

[1] Hy-Kinselagh contained a great part of the county of Wexford, and some adjoining parts of Carlow, Wicklow, Kilkenny, and Queen's County. It was the patrimony of Dermod's family. His full title would run thus: Dermod Mac Murrough O'Cavanagh, Prince of Hy-Kinselagh, King of Leinster and the Danes.

eminence stood the royal fortress, with its formidable earthworks, and its dun-like aspect. Close by rose the abbey, which in 1161 he erected in the place of the ancient edifice destroyed in the conflagration already referred to. A community of canons regular of St. Augustine were in possession of the new monastery, and their maintenance was provided for by an endowment of six extensive townlands. In the lower ground rose the city, properly so-called, an assemblage of wattle structures, easily consumed by fire, but also easily rebuilt. Far beyond the boundaries of Leinster, Ferns was regarded with religious veneration on account of its holy well, its sacred shrines, and its intimate association with saints of the olden time. Here St. Aiden (or Maidoc) formed his monastic establishment in the sixth century, and here he fixed the seat of his bishopric. This, too, was his burial-place, and that of his successor, St Molin.[1] St. David of Menevia received special honour in Ferns, as the teacher and beloved friend of St. Aiden; and constant intercourse had been kept up throughout the ages between the holy men of Wales and those of Ferns, in pious memory of the friendship that united the patron saint of Cambria and the founder of the Metropolitan See of Leinster. At one time, it is said, fifty bishops came from Wales on a pilgrimage to Ferns; and we are not surprised to learn that Lagenian devotees crossed over in crowds to pay their vows at St David's shrine.

Naturally, the Augustinians regarded King Dermod with kindly feelings, and the grateful consideration due to a generous benefactor. Later on, the canons of Ferns Abbey, and members of the ancient Order in another land, had it in their power to do him good service, and did not suffer the opportunity to slip by unutilised. But the Augustinians were not the only religious body that considered it a duty to pray for Mac Murrough when the great oblation was offered on their altars for the living and the dead. The Cistercians were indebted to him for one of the first foundations planted from Mellifont, that of the Abbey de Valle Salutis, situated on the banks of the Slaney at Baltinglass. The introduction into a territory of a colony of "grey monks of the Order of the

[1] Among the treasures of the Royal Irish Academy are the shrine and the bell of St. Aiden. In the Library of Trinity College is preserved the Evangelistarium of St. Molin, with its ancient box.

Desert," as an ancient chronicler styles the Cistercian family, might well be regarded as an act worthy of a statesman,—for these men who sat down in waste places and beautified the wilderness by their skilful toil were bright exemplars to rich and poor. "Agriculture," says D'Arcy M'Gee, "seems first to have been lifted into respectability by the Cistercian monks."[1]

Whether the nunnery of St. Mary of Hoges, so-called from an adjoining village, owed its establishment directly to Dermod Mac Murrough, or was simply indebted to him for considerable endowments, I cannot say. Probably one of his immediate predecessors in the sovereignty was the actual founder. The nunnery grounds, the gift of the kings of Leinster, lay near the Danish city of Dublin, covering the area between the present College Green and St. Stephen's Green, and running eastward alongside of our College Park. Near the site now covered by the Protestant Church of St. Andrew stood the buildings occupied by the nuns, canonesses of the Order of St. Augustine, who formed a community composed "not of the younger sort, but of elderlike persons who desired to live single after the death or separation of their husbands"[2] As a dependent cell to St. Mary's, Dermod Mac Murrough founded, in 1151, the nunnery, sometimes called De Bello Portu, on the west side of the river Suir, opposite the King's Tower in Waterford. Another dependency of the same establishment, situated in the county of Carlow, is also named as having been founded by him about the same time.

But the religious house with which the King of Leinster's name is more frequently associated, and the one that was the last to receive a founder's endowments from him, was the priory of All-Hallows, situated near Dublin, and in the same quarter as the nunnery of St. Mary. According to the Annals of Leinster, Dermod Mac Murrough having become ill during a visit to Dublin in 1166, called all his priests about him and made a

[1] *Life of Art Mac Murrough.*

[2] See Haliday's *Scandinavian Kingdom of Dublin*, edited by John P. Prendergast. The author remarks that the statement quoted above, from a manuscript in the British Museum, "respecting the class of females inhabiting the nunnery, is supported by the fact that the ground on which the nunnery stood is called 'Mynechens Mantle,' and its possessions Munchens fields, thereby making it the residence not of young nuns, but of those elderly nuns of the superior class, termed Mynechens by Du Cange."

vow, if he recovered, to build a religious house on the spot where he lay sick.[1] The king recovered; and soon after, having succeeded in taking hostages from O'Carroll, Prince of Uriel (Louth), he endowed a monastery on the specified site for canons of St. Augustine brought thither from some part of O'Carroll's territory. The monastic buildings were erected on the place where Trinity College now stands. The grounds extended to the Anna Liffey, and ran eastward between the river and the demesne of St. Mary's nunnery. By the foundation charter,[2] the King of Leinster, for the love of God and his soul's salvation, "grants to his spiritual father and confessor, Edan, Bishop of Louth," for the use of the canons, the lands of Baldoyle, with their serfs and descendants, their issue and offspring, present and future; and commands all Leinster and Dublin men quietly to secure to the same bishop and his canons, and their successors, the aforesaid lands, to be held and possessed for ever, etc. Among the witnesses to this charter were St. Laurence O'Toole (Laurentio Dublin); the Abbot of Glendalough (Benigno Abbate de Glendolachâ), and the king's son (Ennâ figlio meo) Additional grants were soon after conferred on the priory of All-Hallows, including the townlands of Clonturk (Drumcondra) and Donnycarney near Dublin, and other more remotely situated possessions,—towns and granges, with their oblations, tithes in woods, pastures, wells, waters, fisheries, and so forth. The bishop, whom Dermot in his charter styles his spiritual father and confessor, was Edan O'Kelly, a very distinguished ecclesiastic, the successor in the See of Louth (Clogher) of Christian O'Morgair, the brother of St. Malachy. He was consecrated in 1139, by the saint whose scholar he had been. The Four Masters, in recording the death of Bishop Edan, under the date 1182, call him the Chief Canon of Ireland. From this, and from the fact that the new religious house of All-Hallows was given to him, we must suppose that he was head of the Augustinians in Ireland.[3]

[1] Quoted by Haliday

[2] See Dugdale's *Monasticon Anglicanum*, vol vi.

[3] King Henry II. confirmed the grants made by Dermod Mac Murrough to the priory of All-Hallows. At the dissolution of monasteries in the reign of Henry VIII., these possessions were handed over to the Mayor and citizens of Dublin in compensation for the losses sustained in the rebellion of Lord Thomas Fitzgerald. Later, Adam Loftus, by the grace of Queen

Thus, bountiful to people of low degree, and munificent in his gifts to religious establishments, Dermod Mac Murrough had secured the goodwill of two powerful bodies in the State—the mass of the population and the ecclesiastical fraternity. There remained another extremely influential party, namely, the Bardic order, including the professors in each branch of learning, and the king had won over this important class, we must conclude, by an enlightened patronage, for no trace can be discovered of his having provoked the enmity of the poet-satirists, or incurred the displeasure of the savans of his day. A most interesting example of the literary work of that period, and a memorial of Dermod's appreciation of the labours of the learned, has come down to us in the Book of Leinster, one of the treasures in the rich store of Irish literature preserved in Trinity College. This precious volume is not one of "the countless hosts of the illuminated books of Erin." It is an unadorned compilation of historical and topographical tracts, genealogies, calendars of saints, and Irish versions of mediæval writings. It contains poems in great number, amongst them compositions of every date, from Duvach, royal poet of the Monarch of Ireland and St. Patrick's first convert at Tara, down to O'Dunn, chief poet of Leinster in Dermod's reign. Altogether, this "heirloom of history" forms, according to the highest authority, "the largest and perhaps the most valuable collection surviving, both in prose and verse, of ancient Gaelic literature." [1]

The Book of Leinster was compiled for Dermod Mac Murrough under the superintendence of his tutor, Hugh Mac Crimthan, the chief historian of Leinster, by Finn Mac Gorman, afterwards Bishop of Kildare. On the top margin of one of the pages is a memorandum written in a strange but ancient hand

Elizabeth Archbishop of Dublin, prevailed on the Corporation to bestow the monastery of All-Hallows and all its precincts on the College of the Holy and Undivided Trinity founded by Her Majesty. The Corporation are still the chief proprietors of the fee of the parishes of Baldoyle, Donnycarney, and Clonturk or Drumcondra. The great Missionary College of All-Hallows links the apostolic work of Catholic Ireland in our own day with the religious foundation of the twelfth century. The institution stands on ground given to the priory by Dermod Mac Murrough; and this ground was obtained on lease from the Corporation, through the influence of Daniel O'Connell, the first Catholic Lord Mayor of Dublin after Emancipation.

[1] Dr. J. T. Gilbert's *F[illegible]*

—an apostrophe addressed to the Virgin Mary concerning "a great deed that has been done in Erin this day, the kalends of August": Dermod, King of Leinster and of the Danes, "has been banished over the sea eastwards by the men of Erin."[1] About three years ago the poetic contents of this "time-blackened volume" were brought under the notice of students in a striking way. Professor Atkinson, in the course of a Lecture on the Metrical Laws of Irish Poetry, the first of a course on Celtic Philology delivered in Trinity College, declared it to be his belief that Irish verse was the most perfectly harmonious combination of sound the world has ever known,—that, in fact, he knew nothing in the world's literature like it; and having gone on to show what was the Irish equivalent for rhyme,—"Something infinitely more varied, that lends itself to a far richer series of harmonies than mere rhyme can present," —proceeded to delight his audience with alliteration, assonance, and versification taken from poems preserved in the Book of Leinster.

Little, comparatively speaking, is known of Dermod Mac Murrough's domestic relations. Authorities agree that his first wife was Cacht, the daughter of O'Moore, Prince of Leix. It would appear that he married, secondly, Mor O'Toole, whose father, Murchertach, chief of Hy-Murray, the southern half of Kildare, was married to a daughter of O'Byrne, a neighbouring chieftain. The Lady Mor's brother, Lorchan (or Laurence), the distinguished Abbot of Glendalough, who at a later period was taken from his monastic seclusion in the Wicklow mountains and installed, as the old writers have it, "Archbishop of the Danes and of Leinster," had suffered much in his youth from Dermod; for the king having got the chieftain's son into his hands, treated the boy with great cruelty, sending him to dwell in a desert place, where he was half-starved and ill-clothed during a captivity of two years. If the Lady Mor resembled her brother, St. Laurence, in manner and in person, she must have been sweet and gracious, dignified and handsome. However, her married life was not happy. Dermod, it is said, deserted her, and proceeded to negotiate a marriage with the daughter of O'Carroll, Prince of Oriel. Under these circumstances she disappeared one night; and it was not known where she lay concealed until many years later, when, on coming out of the

[1] O'Cur [illegible]

nunnery of St. Mary to attend a Requiem Office for her brother the archbishop, who had closed his earthly pilgrimage some time before at Eu in Normandy, she was seen and recognised.[1]

Dermod Mac Murrough had several sons whom he recognised Enna, Conor, Art, and Donald Cavanagh are mentioned. According to Dr. O'Donovan, Conor was the only son born in wedlock, while other authorities claim this distinction for Enna, the ancestor of the Kinsellas and some branches of the Mac Kennas. This prince was elected tanist, or heir-apparent to the throne of Leinster, and continued to occupy that rank until he was blinded by Mac Gillopadrigh, King of Ossory, in 1166 Art is named by certain historians as having been among the hostages of Leinster slain at Athlone in 1170 by Roderick O'Conor. Undoubtedly, the most distinguished of the above-named princes was Donald Cavanagh, sometimes surnamed the Handsome. He was a gallant warrior and a trusty lieutenant of the king,—standing faithfully by his father in seasons of trouble, and fighting manfully by his side or in his cause when armies were in the field. From him directly descend the Kavanaghs of Leinster—Arthur Mac Murrough Kavanagh of Borris being now chief of the name.

The only daughter of King Dermod was Aife or Eva, the

[1] Haliday, *Scandinavian Kingdom of Dublin* The ancient authority quoted in this work says that Mor O'Toole had taken with her in her flight a quantity of valuable property. The insinuation is, that the property was the king's. We should rather suppose that in this case, as in that of the Lady Dervorgilla, the fugitive took only what was her own by the law of the Brehons. The Requiem Office which the nun of St Mary's came out to attend, took place no doubt either in the priory of All-Hallows, close to the nunnery, or in the cathedral church of the Holy Trinity (now Christ Church), within the walls of Dublin. Wherever performed, the celebration must have been of the most solemn and affecting character; for the choral service in the cathedral and in the priory had been greatly improved by St. Laurence, who, "being a pious and devout man, constant in divine offices, and a lover of beauty in God's house," had left nothing undone to give dignity to the celebrations. We are told that "he caused Regulars to stand as singers around the altar to praise the name of the Lord," and would have "melodious modes to be used in the choir-singing." For these particulars and others in connection with the discipline introduced by St. Laurence O'Toole, see an interesting series of articles on "The Priory of All-Saints, or All-Hallows, Dublin, contributed to the *Irish Ecclesiastical Gazette*, in [illegible] by the Rev. J. Stubbert.

child of his first wife, Cacht O'Moore, of Leix, and the destined bride of Strongbow, Earl of Pembroke. Her five granddaughters were given in marriage to scions of the noblest houses in England, and had for their dowry respectively, the counties of Carlow, Wexford, Kilkenny, Kildare, and Dunamase, comprising the greater part of Leix, now Queen's County. The Lady Eva's descendants form a long line, in which appears at our day no less conspicuous a personage than VICTORIA, Queen regnant in these realms.

OLD HOUSES RE-STORIED

THE lordly mansions which, in the streets of Dublin, raise a proud front amidst more humble structures, not unfrequently rivet the astonished gaze of the stranger, who, in the one breath, is told the historic names by which these dwellings once were designated, and the uses to which they are in latter days designed. Various, indeed, has been the fortune of stately houses, the home of the brilliant or the powerful, and the resort of all that was distinguished in the political and social life of Ireland before the Union was carried and the imperial standard hoisted on Dublin Castle. In some instances their altered destiny simply marks the descent from pre-eminence to a low estate, and typifies the changed condition of a dismantled capital; while, in other cases, the way in which the halls, deserted by their princely owners, are turned to account, has oftentimes a strange significance.

Fortune was hardly pitiful in transforming the good Lord Moira's once brilliant residence into a refuge for mendicants; or in converting the edifice so intimately associated with the memory of the noble earl who headed the volunteers, into a range of offices for Civil Service clerks; or, again, in turning the corridors and reception-rooms of Lord Powerscourt's town mansion into the goods stores of wholesale warehousemen. One cannot say that Leinster House was appropriated to any ignoble use when assigned for the location of the society incorporated for the improvement of husbandry and other useful arts in Ireland; and yet the sights and sounds attendant on cattle shows and agricultural exhibitions are not precisely those that fall in best with the remembrance of *these Geraldines! these Geraldines!*

But there is something of the irony of fate, if not of the spirit of retribution, in the destiny that has in two or three instances overtaken the mansions of such aristocrats as the Brabazons, the De la Poers, the Beresfords. In the Earl of Meath's luxurious dwelling, the Sisters of Charity now keep house for the sick and hurt, who are carried up the elegant staircase, laid beneath the richly-stuccoed ceilings, and made as much of as if they were the very heirs of the vanished lords. Tyrone House is the central office of commissioners whose business it is to allocate some five or six hundred thousand a year for the education of the people whose religion the former residents traduced, and whose existence they did their best to ignore. A certain high and wide red house, the scene in bygone times of splendid hospitalities, is now a hospital for children—for the children, in the fourth generation, of the Croppies whom the munificent host had in the days of '98 tortured with pitch-caps, hung up at triangles, and scourged in the riding-school.

So striking a vicissitude in the destiny of historic houses does not pass unnoticed. It signalises to the popular mind the consequences of changed political conditions, and marks the progress of the social revolution which began with Emancipation, passed since through many phases, and has not yet approached its term. When one of the spacious mansions of pre-Union date, dishonoured by neglect and fast mouldering into ruin, suddenly assumes a grimly renovated air and becomes the bureau of a public department; or when a titled house is turned into a vast mercantile concern, or leased to a tenant whose fortune is, perhaps, hardly large enough to keep the mansion in repair, though his family goes far towards peopling its apartments, the occurrence may provoke a remark touching an absentee gentry and anti-Irish aristocracy; but when, on the other hand, one of these relics of the past falls into the possession of a religious body, and is made the centre of a Catholic organisation, the public voice not merely acquiesces in the transfer, but is jubilant over it. And naturally it is so. In Ireland, religion and nationality are fast bound together. The Catholic Church and the Gaelic race shared the same afflictions and survived through the same length of intolerable years. Each new token of inextinguishable life in [illegible] ver

Ui

of the other; on this soil, at least, they are a common cause.

If, like archæologists of a certain school, we took our data from stone monuments, we should find it easy to trace the history of Dublin during the last one hundred and fifty years. At the very outset, one is struck by the shortness of the period during which the city maintained in any degree the character of a splendid capital. Nearly all the noble buildings which adorn its streets were erected within a period of fifty or sixty years. The Parliament House, commenced in 1729, was finished, according to the original design, ten years later; but the eastern front of the House of Lords, with its fine surmounting statues, and the western front in Foster Place, were not erected until the century was drawing to a close Between 1741 and 1796, the Exchange, the Custom House, the Four Courts, the King's Inns, and Carlisle Bridge, were built. Tyrone House, Leinster House, Lord Powerscourt's mansion, and the residence so creditable to the Earl of Charlemont's taste, are of the same date. From the era of the volunteers to the enactment of the Union, private speculation as well as private enterprise were actively engaged in making Dublin a handsome city. The loss of legislative independence, one of the first consequences of which was the withdrawal of nearly all the nobility and gentry from the chief city, gave a check to the erection of public buildings, and put an end to the opening of new streets. Isolated blocks of houses, standing about on the north side of Dublin, still indicate the lines by which it had been designed to extend the city towards the then fashionable outlets of Glasnevin and Drumcondra

It should not be forgotten that Dublin owes a great deal of its beauty to one man,—a member of the Beresford family,—whose personal and political influence enabled him to carry out undertakings which his good taste and his public spirit made him feel to be desirable and expedient.

The Beresfords were the most powerful section of the oligarchy that misruled Ireland all through the eighteenth century. The family first obtained a footing in a vast field for social and political ambition when Tristram Beresford came over, in the reign of James I., as manager of the Society of the New Plantation of Ulster. This gentleman settled at

Coleraine, managed well for the Corporation of Londoners who had become possessed of the fair territories of the banished and despoiled native chiefs, and turned to the best account the opportunity which his position afforded of pushing on the fortunes of the family. They prospered immensely. Tristram's son was created a baronet; his descendants formed alliances with noble families.[1] The fourth baronet having married the Baroness De la Poer, daughter and heiress of the Earl of Tyrone, was advanced to the peerage as Baron Beresford and Viscount Tyrone, and created Earl of Tyrone. His son inherited the barony of De la Poer on the demise of his mother, and was created Marquess of Waterford in 1789.

The Beresfords had long families, and were a long-lived race, and they excelled all the birds of foreign plumage that ever swooped down on the plains of Leinster, or alighted on the wooded slopes of Ulster, in the art of feathering their own nest Vast territorial possessions, accumulated wealth, and a strong principle of clanship, secured them a prominent and powerful position in Ireland at a period when the people were held in worse than Egyptian bondage, and the parliamentary government was carried on by means of, or, as the case might be, in spite of, the fierce rivalry of faction, and a system of almost unexampled corruption. Having in their hands most of the Government patronage in three of the provinces, and to a great degree in the fourth,—where, however, Lord Shannon disputed their sway,—they were able to secure lucrative posts for themselves, and to provide for their friends, retainers, and electors.

The Church rivalled the State in promoting the interests of the Beresfords. Benefices, like pocket-boroughs, were at the service of the hosts of younger brothers; while rich episcopal Sees were looked upon as the heritage of their elders blessed with a vocation for the pastoral office. At one time there were three Beresfords together on the bench of bishops A son was seen to succeed to a mitre which his father had worn before him. Young Beresford bishops were promoted from See to See until they had advanced to archiepiscopal dignity, or happily reached primatial eminence. William Beresford,

[1] Sir Tristram Beresford, the third baronet, married a daughter of Lord Glenawley. He is mentioned in the *Book of Days*, in connection with "an uncon

Ur

brother of the first Marquess of Waterford, was successively Bishop of Dromore, Bishop of Ossory, and Archbishop of Tuam; and then, as if to give a tonic temporal flavour to the full cup of purely spiritual honours, his Grace was raised to the peerage and created Baron Decies. Thrice within a century the primatial throne of Armagh has been filled by a member of this truly episcopal family; for the Church remained faithful to the Beresfords long after the State had ceased to hold them in exorbitant esteem; and in our own time, on the death of the Most Reverend John George, who had ascended to Armagh by Cork, Raphoe, Clogher, and Dublin, and had ruled the primatial See for forty years, the vacated dignity and its enormous revenues were conferred on his cousin, Marcus Gervais, the then Archbishop of Dublin.[1]

From first to last, while power remained in their hands, the Beresfords strenuously discountenanced all recognition of popular feeling, and opposed to the utmost every concession to Catholic claims. Protestant ascendency, the rule of an oligarchy, and the interests of the family, were inextricably bound together. And yet, bigoted and domineering, and insatiable in pursuit of the good things of the world, as they proved themselves to be, they were not held in such dread detestation as some men of lesser mark among their compatriots most certainly were. One thing counted in their favour: they were a handsome race and of stately stature, and the populace have ever shown a disposition to forgive much to tyrants who really look like kings of men; and then there was occasionally a breadth and even magnificence in their ideas which carried them beyond the mere concerns of family aggrandisement. There have been just landlords and good employers among them; and they did not always carry into the details of private life that odious intolerance which, displayed on the theatre of public life, aggravated the evils that scourged the land, and led up to the tragic end of many a story.

The man to whom, as we have said, Dublin owes so much of its beauty, was the Right Hon. John Beresford, second son

[1] In the *Freeman's Journal* "Church Commission Correspondence, 1867–1868," since reprinted in book form, will be found an excellent sketch of the Beresford churchmen, and some details of the vast incomes enjoyed by [illegible] of the family.

of the Earl of Tyrone, brother of the Marquess of Waterford, a member of the Privy Councils of Great Britain and Ireland, representative in Parliament of the county of Waterford during forty-four years, and Commissioner of the Revenues in Ireland for more than thirty. Able, energetic, indomitable, and backed by the overwhelming family interest, Mr. Beresford enjoyed more actual power than any man in Ireland. It was said of him that he had the law, the army, the revenue, and a great deal of the Church in his possession, and that he might be considered the king of Ireland.

With the British viceroys—and there were as many as eleven chief governors at the Castle in the space of twenty years—he generally maintained excellent relations. A most remarkable exception, however, was in the case of Earl Fitzwilliam, whose coming to Ireland, with the avowed purpose of bringing peace to the distracted land and preparing the way for Catholic emancipation, was the cause of exceeding joy, but whose recall, after a few months, dashed to the ground the nation's newly-awakened hope. The new viceroy was of opinion that it would be impossible to effect any good in Ireland until the power of the Beresfords had been destroyed; and one of his first acts was to deprive the Chief Commissioner of His Majesty's Revenues of the important and lucrative post he had held for many years, and to exclude him from his seat in the Privy Council. The earl's recall to England anticipated by a few weeks the reinstalment of Mr. Beresford at the Board and in the Council. The family influence remained unimpaired, and the commissioner continued to be reputed fortunate in his public career and happy in his private relations.[1]

Mr. Beresford had large ideas with regard to the improvement of Dublin, and was determined to carry out works calculated to add considerably to the public convenience, and greatly beautify the then very irregular city.

[1] Left a widower with eight young children by the death of his first wife, the daughter of General Count de Ligondes, Mr. Beresford obtained, two or three years later, the hand of Barbara, the second daughter of Sir William Montgomery, Bart. This lady was one of the three beautiful sisters who were the originals of Sir Joshua Reynold's picture, The Graces. Another of the lovely trio became Marchioness of Townshend, and the third married Mr. Gardiner, afterwards Lord Mountjoy, who was killed by the rebels in '98 at the battle of New Ross. By his second marriage Mr. [illegible] children

Gradually, after the power of the Wicklow septs had been so completely crushed that the marauding descents of the Irish of the mountains were no longer to be dreaded, the city had begun to extend, though in a very straggling way, outside the fortified walls. The old town long remained compact on the high south bank of the river, under shelter of the Castle, and clustered round St. Patrick's and Christ Church. But streetways had, in course of time, been opened beyond the Parliament House and the College, St. Stephen's Green had been enclosed towards the end of the seventeenth century, and the erection of houses in Merrion Square had been commenced about ninety years later; while on the north bank a new quarter had recently sprung up—many of the nobility occupied houses in Rutland Square and Sackville Street, and a great number of aristocratic families resided in the adjacent streets.

At the time that Mr. Beresford began to form plans for the improvement of the city, direct communication between the Sackville Street quarter and the neighbourhood of the Parliament House was carried on by boats; gentle and simple wanting to cross the river at that point should alike be ferried over, the bridge nearest the sea was Essex Bridge, which had been rebuilt about the middle of the century. On the east side of the bridge stood the Custom House, and not far off, the noble Exchange was fast approaching completion. The government and municipal offices were in the same locality, as well as the theatres, and the warehouses and residences of the merchants and traders. From Essex Bridge to the sea the river followed its course, for some distance confined by walls, and then casting up brackish waters on the irregular banks in places reduced to a swamp by long neglect and tidal inroads.

Mr. Beresford's design was to widen and extend the quays, and to open an uninterrupted line from the site of the old friary of St. Saviour—near which it was already contemplated to raise a magnificent pile of buildings for the Law Courts—to the low-lying waste that stretched seawards beyond the point where Sackville Street was lost in lanes straggling down to the riverside. To throw a bridge across the water at this point, and to lay out a handsome street between it and the Parliament House, was a part of the design; as was also the erection of a new Custom House fully half an Irish mile nearer the sea than the edifice at Essex Bridge. Whatever the public may have thought of the improvement of the quays, the opening of new streets, and the building of another bridge, one part of the project provoked the most determined opposition, namely, the erection of a new Custom House in a swamp, and at so inconvenient a distance from the business centre.

All that the First Commissioner wanted, however, was an order from the Treasury at Whitehall to build a Custom House, and an architect with genius to furnish him with a noble design, and with capacity to aid him in carrying on the works. Such a man he found in James Gandon, the grandson of a French Huguenot settled in London. Gandon, whose enthusiastic devotion to his profession had already brought him into considerable notice, gave a plan which met with the First Commissioner's highest approval.

In January 1781, Mr Beresford wrote to him that he had at length obtained an order from Government for the building of a new Custom House with all expedition, and had proceeded to take possession of a large lot in a low situation. The business must, he said, be kept a profound secret; for the Corporation and a great number of the merchants, together with what was considered the most desperate of the mob, were violently opposed to the undertaking, while certain persons of influence on the other side of the channel would make every exertion to prevent the design being carried out. It appeared that interested persons affected to regard the change as injurious to the commerce of the city; a clamour was raised that there would not be sufficient room for shipping; and it was considered folly to attempt the erection of such a structure on a morass.

According to the instructions received, Gandon hastened to Dublin, where, however, he did not find affairs in such a condition that the works could be commenced with the expedition Mr. Beresford had imagined possible. At the last moment great obstacles were placed in the way, and exorbitant demands were made for the lots of ground[1] The architect's

[1] This district was in former times a part of the immediate demesne of the Cistercians of St. Mary's Abbey, and had been given to them with the grange of Clonliffe by Strongbow The abbots enjoyed rights of fishery and customs in this neighbourhood, and had hake nets on the North Strand. The people had been for generations in the habit of holding public games, tilting, and archery meetings, etc., on these grounds. See Introduction to Dalton's

position was anything but comfortable; he had to remain in a sort of imprisonment, unable to present his letters of introduction or to visit the friends he already knew, while he was tormented with the apprehension that his abrupt departure from London might injure his character, and his visit to Ireland prove after all unsuccessful. The only pleasant time he appears to have enjoyed was due to the kindness of the Right Hon. Burton Conyngham, who carried him to his princely residence at Slane, where, though still in privacy, he enjoyed for several days the splendid hospitalities of his good-natured host. On returning to town, the architect ventured at very early hours in the morning to walk over the grounds procured for the site of the Custom House, not without alarm when considering the difficulties of having the foundation laid.

Finally, after three months' delay, the purchase was completed, and Gandon received orders to commence forthwith the opening of the grounds; for nothing but uncommon activity in the commencement would prevent the violent opposition of a formidable party making every effort to stimulate the mob, and procure petitions. He was, furthermore, desired to send to London for clerks and assistants. He greatly regretted this hurry; but having held a meeting of the principal Dublin artificers, he found he could rely on them, and he began the work with a better heart.

The Sunday after the trenches were dug, many hundreds of the people assembled on the grounds, and it was apprehended that they would proceed to fill up the excavations. However, their inclinations took a less mischievous turn, and they amused themselves swimming in the trenches. The first stone was soon after laid by Mr. Beresford without any formality, lest a riot might be got up; and the Corporation ceased all opposition, thinking it impossible the structure could ever be raised.

When, however, it was seen that the foundations were going on, the High Sheriff and an influential member of the Corporation, followed by a rabble with shovels and saws, came in a body on the grounds and levelled a portion of the fence This news was brought to Mr. Beresford on a Saturday, and he immediately wrote to Gandon to replace the enclosure instantly, —to make the holes [illegible] and set his poles to put it up as fast as it was pulled down · "Prevent all opposition," he said in conclusion, "and laugh at the extreme folly of the people."

Other vexatious interruptions occurred, the works proceeding nevertheless. The architect having now fully made up his mind to settle in Ireland, went to London to make the necessary arrangements, and on his return to Dublin took a house in Mecklenburgh Street, that he might be near Mr. Beresford's residence in Marlborough Street.[1]

His choice of Ireland was the more remarkable from the fact that about the same time he had received an invitation to settle at St. Petersburg, from no less a personage than the Princess Dashkoff, who promised him, in case he should emigrate to the Czarina's dominions, advancement in his profession and military rank. This lady had been for some time sojourning in London, and was a pupil of Gandon's friend, Sandby, the water-colour artist. She had judgment enough to recognise Gandon's genius and appreciate his character. That she would have made good her words there can be no doubt, for, having shortly afterwards returned to Russia, she was appointed Director of the St. Petersburg Academy of Arts and Sciences, and President of the Russian Academy.

Gandon had no reason to regret his choice. He had a great admiration for the country of his adoption, found honourable employment in Ireland, and made many friends. The Dublin artificers, who, as a body, had pleased him so much on their first introduction to him, did not deceive his expectations, his praise of them remains on record.

While the Custom House was in course of erection, Edward Smith, a young man then occupying a very obscure position, happened to come under the notice of Gandon, who was not long in discovering in the stone-carver a talent that needed only a favourable opportunity to distinguish its possessor. The sculptured ornaments of the Custom House, and the statue of Hope surmounting the cupola, were intrusted to the young man. So fully was Gandon satisfied with his protégé's work, that he made it a condition on subsequent occasions that Edward Smith should be employed whenever there was room

[1] For tl [illegible] the building of the Custo[illegible]

for the display of the sculptor's art on the public buildings which he was himself engaged to erect.[1]

In 1791 the new Custom House was opened for public business, and in the same year the foundations of Carlisle Bridge were laid by Mr. Beresford. In the following years the Commissioners of Wide Streets directed their attention to the opening of passages from Sackville Street and Carlisle Bridge, and the laying-out of squares, streets, and places to the eastward. By Act of Parliament, a portion of St. Mary's parish was severed, and constituted the parish of St. Thomas. Before Mr. Beresford's death, in 1805, he had seen almost fully realised the city-view which, when first presented to his mind's eye, was graced with all the "glory and the freshness of a dream." If the man who imagined and accomplished so much is not, despite his political errors, remembered with sufficient gratitude by the city he thus adorned, it is owing in a great degree, perhaps, to the special odium the name incurred in the era of '98, through the cruel zeal in stamping out rebellion displayed by his son, John Claudius Beresford.

John Claudius Beresford, the third son of the First Commissioner of the Revenue, had no more cause to complain of the ill-usage of fortune than any of the host of brothers, uncles, cousins, and connections who grew up and prospered in the sunshine of the family patronage. Nothing came amiss to him that brought an increase of power, pay, or importance. In Parliament he represented, successively, the borough of Swords, the city of Dublin, and the county of Waterford. He was a Privy Councillor in Ireland, Inspector-General of Exports and Imports, secretary to the Grand Lodge of Orangemen, captain commandant of a corps of yeomanry, a Commissioner of Wide Streets, one of the Corporation for Improving the Port of Dublin, agent to the Honourable the Irish Society over their estates in Derry; a banker, an alderman, governor of the aldermen of Skinner's Alley, a trustee of the linen manufacture, and once in a way Lord Mayor of Dublin.

In 1790, being then about twenty-four years of age, he

[1] Smith's best works are, perhaps, the noble figures of Justice, Fortitude, and Liberty, surmounting the eastern front of the Bank of Ireland; and the colossal statues, so full of dignity and grace, of Moses, Justice, Mercy, Wisdom, and Eloquence, over the portico of the Four Courts The portrait statue of Lucas, in the City Hall, is also by Smith.

entered the Irish Parliament as member for Swords—a borough described as notorious in the annals of bribery and corruption, the franchise being then exercised by the Protestant inhabitants who had been six months resident in the town previous to the election. A writer, quoted in Dalton's *History of the County of Dublin*, gives, in reference to this election, a curious sketch of the way in which such matters were managed in times gone by. "General Massey," says this authority, "some time since cast a longing eye on this borough, which he considered as a common open to any occupant; and, to secure the command of it to himself, he began to take and build tenements within its precincts, in which he placed many veteran soldiers, who, having served under him in war, were firmly attached to their ancient leader. Mr. Beresford, the First Commissioner of the Revenue, who has a sharp lookout for vacant places, had formed the same scheme with the general for securing the borough to himself, and a deluge of revenue-officers was poured forth from the Custom House to overflow the place, as all the artificers of the new Custom House had before been exported in the potato-boats of Dungarvan to storm that borough. The wary general took the alarm, and threatened his competitor that for every revenue-officer appearing there he would introduce two old soldiers, which somewhat cooled the First Commissioner's ardour. Thus the matter rests at present; but whether the legions of the army or the locusts of the revenue will finally remain masters of the field, or whether the rival chiefs, from an impossibility of effecting all they wish, will be content to go off, like the two kings of Brentford, smelling at one rose, or whether Mr. Hatche's interest will preponderate in the scale, time alone can clearly ascertain." As a matter of history, we may add that the gallant general and the First Commissioner's son did pass off the stage in the aforesaid kingly fashion.

Having represented this very independent constituency for six years, Mr. John Claudius Beresford stood for the metropolitan city, and was returned in 1797. During this part of his career he distinguished himself by speaking and voting against the Union, thereby certainly representing the electors of Dublin, while going in direct opposition to the chiefs of his house, whose support—no unimportant aid, since it was calculated that th[illegible] over

Ur

about four-and-twenty seats—was relied on by the English ministry. His father was, at the same time, lending very important assistance in carrying the measure; his grandfather, the Earl of Tyrone, a staunch, though not by any means a brilliant, supporter of the Government, proposed the Union in a speech written in the crown of his hat; and his uncle, Lord Clare, was earning, by his strenuous advocacy of the cause, the sobriquet of "Union Jack." The patriotic Beresford does not appear to have got much credit for sincerity. However, we learn from the Cornwallis correspondence that his conduct at some of the Dublin meetings was so very hostile to the Union measure, that it became a question whether he should not be dismissed from his situation as Inspector-General of Exports and Imports; and, as a matter of fact, he did resign this agreeable sinecure post of £400 a year. "Mr. John Claudius Beresford this morning resigned his office," writes Lord Cornwallis to the Duke of Portland, "very liberally expressing his wish to relieve the Administration from all difficulties on his account, and desirous that the support which he intends to afford the Government on all other questions might not be attributed in any degree to his wish to retain his situation."

Unfortunately, this energetic anti-Unionist displayed more than equal zeal in a worse cause. His ultra-loyal energy in putting down insurrection found expression in very unmeasured language. A contemporary accuses him of having expressed a wish for the rebellion, in order to have an opportunity of showing the world that it might be quelled *in two days*. But, whether he did or did not use these words, he showed unbounded satisfaction when the Government proposed to adopt the most vigorous measures of repression in the month of May 1798. Oratory was not among the gifts of the well-endowed Beresfords, and on this occasion John Claudius appears to have particularly lamented his want of eloquence. Words failed him, he told the House of Commons, to express what he felt. He was glad that the Government of the country at last thought fit to adopt these vigorous measures. Leniency had failed. He was for the exertion of still greater vigour. He was for proclaiming military law at once—for trying before a military tribunal every traitor found with arms in his hands against the State, and hanging them up at once upon convic-

( )

tion. He highly lauded the good policy of crushing rebellion in the bud.

He made, however, a much more remarkable figure at the head of his yeomanry corps than in his seat in the Irish Parliament. The feelings which he could not adequately express in a speech he gave full vent to when he led his light horse into action. It will be remembered that in the reign of terror that preceded the outbreak of '98, and during the days of slaughter that followed, the military, the militia, and the yeomanry were employed in exciting the people to revolt, in seizing and torturing suspected rebels, and in slaying insurgents in the field. The British troops and the German mercenaries, let loose over the country, were active agents in carrying out the measures which Lord Castlereagh admitted were taken by Government in order to cause the premature explosion of the insurrection. Murder, according to Lord Cornwallis, was the favourite pastime of the militia; while the Orange yeomanry, fully equal in ferocity to the Ancient Britons, the Homsperg Dragoons, the Dumbarton Fencibles, and the North Cork and Armagh regiments,[1] had, owing to their intimate acquaintance with the people, still greater opportunities of destroying the innocent. Whom they would they declared suspected, and private enmities as well as party animosities could alike be gratified by the consequences—horrible torturing or disgraceful death—sure to follow such a denunciation.

The captain commandant of "Beresford's corps" took considerable pride in the efficiency of his troop. At the Sunday parades in Stephen's Green and the reviews in the Phœnix Park, their martial appearance was calculated to attract the admiration of the crowds that gathered on these occasions; for, the country being in danger, Sabbath decorum was constantly disturbed by military displays in the streets and public places For the better training of his men, he built a riding-school in the grounds of Tyrone House. Talbot Street had no existence at that date, and the large wooden building was raised on the site now occupied by Mr Quan's coach factory

[1] The Highland regiments serving at that time in Ireland were a creditable contrast in their conduct to the other troops. These regiments, says Mr. A. M. Sullivan, in the *Story of Ireland*, p. 538, "behaved with the greatest humanity and, where possible, kindliness towards the Irish peasantry."

and the National Education Model School. On one side the riding-house faced Marlborough Green, then a place of fashionable promenade, and on the other looked into the well-planted lawn of the Marquess of Waterford's residence, which, on the Marlborough Street side, was protected by a high wall that served to screen it from the pile over the way, once Lord Annesley's dwelling, but then, and until it made room for the Metropolitan Church, a barrack.

By and by, the times not improving, and the zeal of excited loyalty waxing still hotter, the commandant supplemented his force by the addition of a battalion of spies,—the yeomen were otherwise employed than in equestrian exercise, and the riding-house was turned to the same account as the Shelbourne Barracks in Stephen's Green, the old Custom House at Essex Bridge, and the yard of the Royal Exchange. Denounced by the spies, and hunted down by the Orange yeomen, suspected rebels were driven into the riding-house, suspended from a triangle, and flogged until they made "confession," true or false, or fainted away in their agony; while there stood by, like an incorrigible Saul, the captain of the rebel-hunting troop of informers and light cavalry thenceforth known as "Beresford's Bloodhounds."

The exploits of this corps of the loyal Dublin horse were somehow or another not remarkable in the field. We hear of them in a miserable affray at Rathfarnham, when the leader of a party of rebels was killed and four of his men hanged in the street; and they appear again in history, scouring the neighbourhood of Artane, and, attended by a detachment of the Coolock cavalry, triumphantly entering Dublin with their prize, —a number of pikes and fireams,—which they proceeded to lodge in the barracks. Their gallantry, no doubt, was equal to that of their comrades in arms, which was so often "difficult to restrain within prudent bounds"; possibly, like the rest, they "distinguished themselves in a high style" on different occasions, and earned, one way or another, a share of the extravagant eulogy bestowed on all His Majesty's forces on duty in Ireland by all the Government officers, civil and military. There was a good deal of work for soldiers of this kind in the city itself when the yeomanry went into permanent duty, and patrols were established through every street. Numbers of prisoners were being brought in daily, and had to be hanged, *pour encourager les autres*, on the bridges, with the gallant yeomanry in attendance. Captain John Claudius did not shirk his duty in this sphere of action. He made no difficulty about assisting at the executions with his highly-effective force. The new bridge at the end of Sackville Street (there was no sign of Westmoreland Street at that date) was desecrated by such scenes as these. The scaffolding, still erect, afforded facilities for the execution of the dreadful work. There suffered the prisoners taken at Santry by Lord Roden and his dragoons, called, from the fine horses they rode, the "Foxhunters"; and there was also put to a disgraceful death, on a bright summer afternoon, Dr. Esmond, of the old Catholic family of that name, who had been engaged in the tragic affair at Prosperous.

No achievement of the Bloodhounds and their master made so strong an impression on the public mind as their treatment of a master chimney-sweeper named Horish, concerning whom that indefatigable gleaner in the fields of history, Mr W. J. Fitzpatrick, has collected some curious particulars. Horish, it would appear, was a well-known citizen. He lived in a good house, which he himself, or his father, had built on Redmond's Hill; employed a number of climbing boys, whom he treated remarkably well, and had the best business in his line in Dublin,—having a contract for sweeping the chimneys of all the public offices, including those of the Castle. Although held in good repute, he had enemies who gave out that he was a member of the United Irish Society, and was to lend his aid in conveying some infernal machine into the Castle for the purpose of blowing up the building.[1] This was enough. The unfortunate man was seized forthwith, carried to the riding-house in Marlborough Green, and flogged unmercifully in the presence of the commandant.[2]

In strange ways did the populace give expression to the rage enkindled in their hearts by such transactions as these. One night a signboard was affixed to the door of the riding-house, with the inscription: "Mangling done here by Beresford & Co." Some, in their blind fury, destroyed the banker's notes whenever they could lay hands on them; and Mr. Fitzpatrick

[1] *Ireland before the Union*, ch. ix.

[2] Horish, according to a humorous writer, was punished for "assuming the title of Earl of Charlemont, making pikes, introducing the French, and intending

Ut

refers to instances in which a man was seen lighting his pipe, and a rebel was discovered wadding his gun, with waste paper of the same quality.

When, in 1802, an attempt was made to break the Beresford party, and Sir Jonah Barrington and Mr. Latouche contested the city of Dublin with the Orange candidates, Horish again appeared upon the scene, and in a very unexpected and effective way confronted his late tormentor at the hustings. All the chimney-sweepers in Dublin, and they were many, who had votes, polled for the Counsellor, as Sir Jonah was popularly called. "I lost the election," says the latter, "but I polled to the end of the fifteen days, and had the gratification of thinking that I broke the knot of a virulent ascendency, was the means of Mr. Latouche's success, and likewise of Mr. Grattan's subsequent return."[1] Many years afterwards, at elections in other parts of Ireland, triangles were set up in the streets, for the purpose of exciting the people against a candidate whose claims to the support of a tenantry enjoying peace and plenty under a just landlord of the house of Beresford were forgotten in the detestation attaching to the name of the master of the riding-house

But the mistakes and misdeeds of this man might have had a chance of dropping into comparative oblivion, or becoming confounded with the wrongdoings of other parties, if the attention of "an able editor," with a viciously sharp pen, had not been concentrated on the remarkable figure of John Claudius Beresford. The vengeance thus taken was prolonged and deadly. He was tracked through every path of his subsequent life, picketed on the merciless pen, triangled in every possible position, lashed with envenomed words, and gibbeted for posterity. In one of the now very scarce magazines of seventy years ago, this retributive war was carried on; and the result is that, whenever the word Beresford is mentioned in the hearing of the people, John Claudius, with his Bloodhounds and his riding-house, start up as if there never had been another of his patronymic met with in the pages of history or the walks of life. As was remarked by a worthy man who, himself an Irishman of the truest blood and feeling, had, while serving in the employment of the Waterford family, many opportunities of observing the high spirit, generosity,

[1] *Personal Sketches and Recollections of his Own Times.*

and other good qualities of the race—"John Claudius ruined the Beresfords!"[1]

Alderman John Claudius was an active member of the old Corporation. He diligently and efficiently attended to public business, without, however, letting slip any opportunity of improving his own position. He rented some of the tolls, then levied off agricultural produce conveyed into Dublin for supply of the inhabitants. How much of these were rented by him cannot at this moment be stated, but he certainly rented the tolls collected in Dorset Street. A gentleman, who then wrote remonstrances against levying the tolls, while the city was taxed, house by house, for the purposes to which the tolls were alleged to be applied, raised so strong a feeling against the exaction, that the country people at length resolved to drive the vehicles conveying their produce through the collectors by force, and the legality of the tolls having been generally disputed, the collection was abandoned. The alderman also rented the ferries, and the tolls collected on the bridges which had been built where ferry boats once had plied. For many years after Carlisle Bridge was opened, there stood a toll-house at either end, and the last remnant of the old system still survives in the metal bridge, which useful and really graceful object we owe to the much-abused toll-farmer. In conjunction with his partner, a Mr. Walsh, he threw a wooden structure across the ferry station at the Bachelor's Walk. This bridge, having been carried away by a flood, the metal bridge was cast to take its place. The alder-

[1] If we were asked to name a member of the same family as a striking set off against John Claudius, we would name his cousin, the late John George Beresford, Protestant Archbishop of Armagh and Primate of Ireland. No one who had once seen him could ever forget his handsome face and truly noble appearance. He was a man of discerning mind and generous feeling, and showed these qualities in the way in which he ruled his See, and in his relations with his clergy. The large revenue he derived from the Church he employed chiefly in its service. He contented himself with his private fortune, and died not rich. On his cathedral choir he spent £700 a year; the expenses incurred by the publication of a valuable antiquarian work were defrayed by him; and he built, at a cost of £11,000, the Campanile in the grand square of Trinity College. Our late venerated primate, the Most Rev. Dr. Dixon, had the sincerest esteem for Archbishop Beresford; and on one occasion, when speaking of him, he said: "He is a large-hearted, large-minded man, and each night in prayer I ask God to preserve his life, and to prolong the term of his benevolence and charity."

man's—or, more properly, as he was then chief magistrate, the Lord Mayor's—relentless pursuer with the envenomed pen made great fun out of the occasion, in a paragraph headed "Hanging a Bridge," and in other witty half-pages. "A neat iron bridge," we are thus informed, "being ready to be placed across the river, John Claudius Beresford, who farms the ferries as he does the tolls, is to hang his bridge: no man fitter," etc. An apple woman, who is represented to have lost her whole stock-in-trade when her standing was carried off by the fall of the bridge, said that it ought to be called Beresford's bridge; and being asked the reason, replies: Because it *whipt* away all she possessed. "The twentieth of July," we are elsewhere told, "being the birthday of his long lordship, as well as the second day of the shooting term, the same will be observed with the usual demonstrations of joy. The Beresford standard[1] will be hoisted on each boat of the ferry fleet; twenty-one rounds will be fired from each of the toll-houses, and the riding-house colours in crimson will be displayed."

For some years Mr. John Claudius Beresford's town residence was at No 2 Beresford Place, where the business of the banking firm in which he was a partner was carried on There was an inconvenient run on the bank—not for gold, however, but for window smashing—on the day Lord Camden arrived in Dublin as Viceroy of Ireland. The mob, well knowing the party that was answerable for the sudden recall of Earl Fitzwilliam, having attacked the Chancellor (Lord Clare), and nearly demolished his magnificent equipage, rushed to the Custom House, broke the windows of that part of the building in which the First Commissioner resided, and then attacked the bank, but the military, soon afterwards arriving on the spot, dispersed the crowd, without, as the report says, any more mischief occurring. It seemed hardly worth while to put on record that one man was killed, and two or three were wounded, by shots fired from the Custom House.

During the period in which Mr. John Claudius Beresford represented the county of Waterford in the Imperial Parliament, he resided, when in town, in the handsome house now so well known as the Children's Hospital, Buckingham Street.

[1] [illegible] between the horns

The mansion stood, not as now in the centre of a row, but as the end house of a block, with waste grounds in the offing, and a wide space extending between it and the palatial edifice built about the middle of the last century, at the cost of £40,000, by the Earl of Aldborough. Not long before the rebellion broke out, the eccentric earl and the future resident in the Buckingham Street mansion came into collision about certain lots of ground in the neighbourhood A suit at law was the consequence, and the case having been brought into the Court of Chancery, Lord Clare's decision was given in favour of his nephew. In an appeal carried to the House of Lords, the same chancellor being on the woolsack, the nobleman was again defeated. Thus, left without legal means of obtaining what he considered justice, the earl wrote a book attacking the Lord Chancellor. Thereupon he was cited to defend himself before his peers; but, not succeeding in doing so, he was voted guilty of a high breach of privilege and a libel on the Lord Chancellor, as chairman of the House. The end of the matter was that the earl was sent to Newgate, where he remained for some months; until, having obtained by memorial a remission of his sentence of imprisonment, he was liberated on payment of £1000.

Buckingham Street was one of the new lines laid out during the building of the Custom House. There was not even a roadway between the Strand line and Summer Hill until 1790. We find the street mentioned in *Ireland Ninety Years Ago*,[1] in the narrative of a gentleman who described to the writer of that book the way in which he had passed the night of the 23rd of May 1798. "On the morning of that day," he says, "I received a pressing invitation from my sister, who then lived in Buckingham Street, to join her family, that we might, as she said, 'all die together.' I set out in the evening for her house. The streets were silent and deserted; no sound was heard but the measured tread of the yeomanry corps taking up their appointed stations." He met an acquaintance who wanted him to go home and pass the night with him, as it was dangerous to be out. This, however, he declined to do. "While we were talking," he continues, "we heard the sound of approaching steps, and saw the attorney's corps, with solemn tread, marching towards us. My companion disappeared

Ut

down a lane, and I walked up to meet them, and when they passed me, proceeded on my way. When I reached my sister's house in Buckingham Street, I found a neighbour had called there, and given to my brother-in-law, who was a clergyman, a handful of ball-cartridges, bidding him defend his life as well as he could. So great was their alarm, they had, on parting, taken a solemn leave of each other, as people who never hoped to meet again. The only weapon of defence in the house was a fowling-piece, which I charged with powder, but found the balls in the cartridges too large for the calibre. The family were persuaded to go to bed, leaving me to keep guard; and with the fowling-piece on my shoulder and the large ball stuck in the muzzle, I marched up and down until sunrise in the morning. Meetings of the disaffected were held that night in the Barley Fields (as the neighbourhood of George's Church was then called) and on the strand of Clontarf. More than once, in the still, calm night, I thought I heard the undulating buzz and sound of a crowd, and the regular tread of a mass of men marching, but all else was awfully still"

The mansion, which a few years afterwards became the residence of Alderman Beresford, M.P., commanded, as it still commands, magnificent prospects from its upper apartments. To the north opens a view of great extent over the Clontarf estuary, the country from Glasnevin and Santry to Howth, and the Bay of Dublin east of the Poolbeg Lighthouse. Southward are seen the rounded outline of the Dublin mountains, Bray Head, with its tufted knobs, and the peaked summits of the Wicklow range; while immediately in the foreground, backed by the graceful line of those heights, the city is spread out like a map, showing conspicuously the church steeples and towers, the green dome of the Four Courts, the cupola of the King's Inns, and the Custom House amidst the shipping in the river and the docks.

The style of living which was adopted when Alderman Beresford, with his Scottish wife and troop of handsome children, removed to Buckingham Street, was "the same sort of singing, dancing, and dinnering life" so much in vogue in Dublin at that time. The master of the house, though in personal habits simple and plain enough, was generous in expenditure and magnificent in hospitality. Tall and somewhat gaunt in figure, he was not, at least at this period of his life, without a touch of the family grace about him. He had some good features, and his manners were agreeable and unpretentious. Truth to say, he was amiable and good-natured in private life, bore an excellent character as a family man, made no distinction in society or in the household between Protestants and Catholics, and was not without friends and well-wishers.[1] Indeed, if he had not possessed the goodwill of many of his fellow-citizens, he never could have held his ground after the transactions of '98.

Beauty and fashion were in the right place passing up and down the wide staircase, and sweeping through the fine drawing-rooms of the Buckingham Street mansion; while the alderman and banker's city friends, patrician relatives, and country supporters, had abundant reason to laud his cordiality and praise the *cuisine*. During his occupancy, a Dublin architect executed for him a great improvement by removing the old basement storey, laying foundations at a greater depth, which he faced with hammered limestone, vaulting the cellars and storerooms, and extending the culinary accommodations. The neighbours, unused to such architectural feats, were amazed to see the alderman's big house, supported on uprights, standing without its fandamental storey. This change being effected, there was nothing wanting to the comfort and convenience of the house, which had been built, we believe, by the First Commissioner of the Revenue.

When Mr. Beresford held hospitalities in the high and wide red house that overtops Dublin and commands splendid prospects, there were usually among his guests Sir John Stevenson and his beautiful daughters, Anna and Olivia. The composer was just then engaged in arranging the Irish airs, for which Moore was writing the immortal words. The early numbers of the Melodies were being published by Mr. Power, of Dame Street; the musical world of professors and amateurs were kept on the *qui vive*, in a state of alternate expectation and delight; and so irresistible was the charm of music and verse, that Erin and her sorrows became the favourite theme in circles com-

[1] Dr R. R Madden, in his *Lives of the United Irishmen*, says that John Claudius Beresford lived, "when he waxed old, on decent terms with Roman Catholics, nay, even went out of his way to promote the interests of some men who had suffered much [illegible] 356, 2nd ed.

Ul

posed of the betrayers of her honour, and the slayers of her sons.[1] Weep on, sang the poet to the mourning children of the nation—survivors of the day of disaster and disgrace—

> "Weep on—perhaps in after days
>   They'll learn to love your name,
> When many a deed shall wake in praise
>   That now must sleep in blame!
> And when they tread the ruin'd aisle,
>   Where rest, at length, the lord and slave,
> They'll wondering ask how hands so vile
>   Could conquer hearts so brave."

Sir John Stevenson, who enjoyed as much as any man the convivial meetings in Mr. Beresford's great dining-room, was also quite at home among the evening guests, who talked and sang beneath a blaze of wax lights in the drawing-room. He was of middle height and slight figure, handsome, and invariably well dressed. At times, when he had his company manners on, he was a little pompous, but more frequently he lapsed into those boyish and paradoxical ways, which Moore tells us used to make the matter-of-fact English people stare whenever he visited the sister island. Under the influence of lyric inspiration, as in the hour he sang "Give me the Harp of Epic Song," or touched the tender chords that sighed o'er "Faithless Emma," or set the anthems for the choirs of St. Patrick's and Christ Church, he cast the spell of poetry on all around him. His voice was full of charm; and the violin, his favourite instrument, responded under his hand to the soul of music within him. Both his daughters had the gift of beauty,

[1] "Les Irlandais aiment à faire de la patrie un être réel qu'on aime et qui nous aime, ils aiment à lui parler sans prononcer son nom, et à confondre l'amour qu' ils lui vouent, cet amour austère et périlleux, avec ce qu' il y a de plus doux et de plus fortuné parmi les affections du cœur. Il semble que, sous le voile de ces illusions agréables, ils veuillent déguiser à leur âme la réalité des dangers auxquels s'expose le patriote, et s'entretenir d'idées gracieuses, en attendant l'heure du combat; comme ces Spartiates qui se couronnaient de fleurs, sur le point de périr aux Thermopyles. . . . C'est un grand titre à la reconnaissance d'une nation que d'avoir su chanter, en vers capables d'être populaires, sa liberté présente ou passée, ses droits garantis ou violés. Celui qui ferait pour la France ce que M. Moore a fait pour l'Irlande serait récompensé au-delà de ses peines par l'estime du public et par la conscience d'avoir rendu service à la plus sainte de toutes les causes."—Augustin Thierry, *Dix Ans d'Etudes Hi*

but one, Olivia, likewise possessed pre-eminently the gift of song. No one better understood the spirit of Moore's songs. It used to flatter the poet greatly when, apropos of one of his new lyrics, Stevenson would exclaim, "How finely Olivia would sing that!" Destined to become the wife of a nobleman, she had just then to receive the addresses of humbler suitors. One of these became enamoured at the parties in Buckingham Street, and, full of youthful confidence, made a proposal for the hand of the fair Olivia. However, as he had no particular prospects in life, save a vague expectation that his father would do something for him, his suit was peremptorily rejected by her father. Possibly Sir John preferred for a son-in-law one who had more music in his soul than this not very engaging youth, as well as a more substantial income to begin life with; and possibly, too, the lady's fancy inclined the same way. At anyrate, she soon after married Mr. Edward Tuite Dalton, a gentleman of acknowledged taste, connected with the amateur musical societies of Dublin, and promoter of a glee club patronised by the Duke of Leinster and the Earl of Meath, for which Moore, an honorary member, wrote a charter glee, set to music by Stevenson. Mr. Dalton held some post in the Custom House, and was, therefore, in a rather better position than the rejected suitor, who, however, in after years found himself in more independent circumstances than his early rival. Moore, who counted Mr. Dalton among his dearest friends, dedicated to him his "Sacred Songs," many of which were set to music by Sir John Stevenson In the poet's journals and correspondence one frequently notes the affectionate terms in which he speaks of the Daltons; and in the "Rhymes on the Road" there is a burst of loving recollection, quite touching to read even now. The bard is in Italy—in places which should be "thrilling alive with melody." Yet he has heard no music—

——"not a note
Of such sweet native airs as float,
In my own land, among the throng,
And speak our nation's soul for song."

Nor even in higher walks, where art makes richer the gifts that are scattered by the wayside, does any taste win his perfect praise like his dear friend Dalton's, or any voice charm his ear lik[illegible]

"She, always beautiful, and growing
 Still more so every note she sings—
Like an inspir'd young sibyl, glowing
 With her own bright imaginings!
And thou, most worthy to be tied
 In music to her, as in love,
Breathing that language by her side,
 All other language far above."

And then his thoughts revert to the days when her father led their evening choir, and Time itself seemed changed to music, and they lived in song! How graceful is the tribute to Stevenson—

"He who, if aught of grace there be
 In the wild notes I write or sing,
First smooth'd their links to harmony,
 And lent them charms they did not bring."

Lord Byron knew the Daltons, and used to meet them at London parties. On one occasion, writing to Moore, he tells him that Mrs Dalton sang one of his (Moore's) best songs so well that, only for the appearance of affectation, he could have cried. Moore wonders what was the song; was it, "Couldst thou look?" Mr. Dalton died of a lingering and painful disease, and, after two years of widowhood, Olivia, still young and beautiful, became Countess of Bective. This event gave occasion to an impromptu "attributed" to the facetious Lord Norbury, who, having heard of the marriage, is reported to have answered—

"Yes—Stevenson always was good at a *glee*,
 But the daughter excels at a *catch!*"

Moore still continued to keep up cordial relations with the countess, as well as with her sister Anna, who was married to Mr. Lambert of Beaupark. We find in his journals such entries as this: "Sang with Lady Bective and her daughter some of the songs she and I sang together before that daughter existed, I believe." And again "Lady Bective's daughter Adelaide sang some Italian things with the true hereditary taste and feeling."[1] In due course the Earl of Bective

[1] It is, of course, the daughter of Mr. Dalton who is here referred to. The countess's second family were not, however, without a share of the gift of song [illegible] in September 1846,

succeeded to his father's title, and his charming wife became Marchioness of Headford. To her, under her new title, Moore dedicated the tenth number of the Irish Melodies, recalling once more the happy circle that met to sing the earlier numbers together under her father's roof. Stevenson had gone to another world at that date; but, with true and faithful feeling, the poet made the last of all the Irish Melodies a song of sorrow for the friend who first suggested to him the work in which their names are indissolubly associated, and which has done so much to "preserve to their country the only grace or ornament left to her out of the wreck of all her liberties and hopes."

"Silence is in our festal halls
  Sweet son of song! thy course is o'er;
In vain on thee sad Erin calls,
  Her minstrel's voice responds no more.
All silent, as th' Æolian shell
  Sleeps at the close of some bright day,
When the sweet breeze, that waked its swell
  At sunny morn, hath died away.

"Yet, at our feasts, thy spirit, long,
  Awaked by music's spell, shall rise;
For name so link'd with deathless song
  Partakes its charm and never dies:
And ev'n within the holy fane,
  When music wafts the soul to heaven,
One thought of him, whose earliest strain
  Was echoed there, shall long be given.

"But, where is now the cheerful day,
  The social night, when, by thy side,
He, who now weaves this parting lay,
  His skilless voice with thine allied;
And sung those songs whose every tone,
  When bard and minstrel long have past,
Shall still in sweetness all their own,
  Embalm'd by fame, undying last?

---

tells his correspondent that a most agreeable addition to their own special circle were two nice girls, the Ladies Taylor, daughters of Lord Headford. They were of the party that visited the convent of the Great St Bernard 'Their mother was daughter (I think) of Sir John Stevenson, and Moore dedicated one part of the 'Irish Melodies' to her. They inherit the musical taste, and sing very well."—Forster's *Life of Dickens*, vol. ii.

"Yes, Erin, thine alone the fame—
  Or, if thy bard have shared the crown,
From thee the borrow'd glory came,
  And at thy feet is now laid down.
Enough, if Freedom still inspire
  His latest song, and still there be,
As evening closes round his lyre,
  One ray upon its chords from thee.'

But the singing and dinnering life was destined to come to a sudden termination in Buckingham Street. Mr. Beresford, though so many resources were open to him,[1] some way or another did not manage his affairs well. He became an insolvent, his name disappeared from the banking firm with which he was connected, his seat in Parliament was left vacant, and his effects, including his valuable library, were brought to the hammer.[2] A grimly fantastic turn was given to this day of distress by the appearance once more upon the scene of Horish's fraternity. The sweeps purchased the alderman's carriage, and in their sooty livery drove the elegant equipage up and down the streets of Dublin. It was not, however, to be supposed that a member of so powerful a house could be irretrievably ruined by one stroke of ill-fortune. Though no longer a banker or a county member, he still held his place in the Corporation. He gave up his town residence, but only to retire to a splendid retreat. He removed with his family to Drumcondra House, a stately mansion in Portland stone, erected about the middle of the last century by the Earl of Charleville, on the estate of his wife, the only daughter and heir of James Coghill, LL.D., of the Yorkshire family of that name.

The new resident's editorial tormentor affected to take a great interest in the Drumcondra establishment, making

[1] His numerous offices and pursuits were thus burlesqued "Mr. Beresford has been a banker, a brickmaker, a limeburner, a distiller, miller, and a lamplighter, but became insolvent."

[2] The library contained all the British classics, from Chaucer to Gibbon and Johnson, and a beautiful collection of French books. There were also in it valuable artistic works, foreign galleries, etc. Well chosen as this library was, it still could not compare with that of the Right Hon. John Beresford, which was sold after the death of its owner. The collection of engravings sold with the books was choice indeed, and did honour to the fine taste of the First Commissioner of the Revenue. The catalogues of these tw[illegible]

observations on the way in which the pleasure-walks were being laid out, and suggesting that it might suitably be named Mount Horish, in compliment to a friend who had once held a triangle situation under the proprietor in the riding-house. The singing-hall, it was ascertained, had been tried by the vocal powers of Mr. Spray, who declared the echo would be unparalleled as soon as the croppy skulls were inserted in the walls. But stories to the effect that the stucco ornaments of the breakfast and supper rooms were to be designed in triangular and whip-cord patterns were pronounced to be malicious fabrications, for it was known the proprietor was determined that no visible marks of such materials of Irish history should be introduced, either to gratify the whipping visitors or frighten the whipped ones.

There could hardly be a nicer house for a family to grow up in than this. The rooms, not too vast or splendid for comfort, were panelled in brown oak, and opened five *en suite*; the ceilings were good, and the chimney-pieces of beautiful design; while the large, deeply-recessed windows looked out on well-planted, well-kept grounds. A door in the boundary wall, which on one side ran near to the house, gave admission to the enclosure of the parish church, and a pathway across the graveyard[1] afforded the family easy access to their place of worship. Mr. Beresford's children, treading their way along the path, and taking their places in the pew belonging to the owner of Drumcondra House, used to be as familiar a sight to the congregation as was the minister in the pulpit.[2]

[1] Drumcondra churchyard is, even to the present day, the burial-place of some Dublin families. It is the last resting-place of the poet, Thomas Furlong. Francis Grose, the antiquary, is buried here; and in the same vault lie the remains of his friend, James Gandon. There appears a very strange inscription on the tablet erected to the memory of the writer, whose unfinished work on the *Antiquities of Ireland* is, perhaps, like a broken column, his best monument on Irish soil. Not a line marks the resting-place of Gandon. His name, indeed, might fitly be inscribed, although he needs no "pompous epitaph upon his marble" as long as those noble buildings shall remain, in perfect beauty or in picturesque decay, upon the riverside

[2] Some years later on, another troop of children, for whom the public (at least those outside the church) had more welcome, used to trip along the same path and sit in the same pew. These were the grandchildren of Lord Edward Fitzgerald. Major-General Sir Guy Campbell, Bart., who was married to the younger Pamela, resided for some years at Drumcondra House.

The stables, a remarkable block, with groined roof supported on stone pillars, stood at right angles to the house front, and in very unusual proximity to the dwelling, from which, however, it was screened by a row of trees. More than once it has been asserted that these stables were built for "Beresford's Bloodhounds"; certain spots are indicated as the scene of tragic incidents, and one of the fine old trees is pointed out as the gibbet on which rebels were hanged by order of the master of the house. We are, however, bound to say that we can find no trace in history of any such proceedings. The stables, which are, to all appearance, of an older date than the era of the rebellion, may possibly have sheltered some yeomanry corps at the time when the royal troops were stationed in the village to protect the northern route. It is not impossible that some private hanging may have been accomplished in the neighbourhood while military law was the only law of the land. By the Drumcondra Road, no doubt, Lord Roden's Foxhunters brought into town the miserable rebels taken in the affray at Santry, and afterwards hanged on the bridges. One thing, however, is certain, namely, that Mr. Beresford did not live at Drumcondra House until fourteen or fifteen years after the rebellion. Nor do we believe that anything more remarkable occurred in the house and premises during Mr. Beresford's occupancy than the brilliant illumination of the establishment, in rejoicing for some victory won by British arms in the Peninsula—a victory in which we may be sure Marshal Lord Beresford, a greatly distinguished general and a close connection of the Waterford family, had had a creditable share.

Alderman Beresford was residing here when, in 1814, he was elected Lord Mayor of Dublin,—an office which, by the way, he appears to have filled to the complete satisfaction of the citizens. When his equipage, as newly-installed chief magistrate, appeared in the streets, the crowd looked in wonder at the crest painted on the doors, presenting between a stag's horns the image of the crucified Redeemer, with the motto, *Nil nisi cruce.* "Beresford," said a contemporary, "wore on his coach more Christianity than he would allow in his parish church."

The present condition and character of the fine town house and the handsome country residence of Mr John Claudius

Beresford afford as striking an example of the vicissitudes of fortune as any of the instances already cited. The Buckingham Street mansion, we need hardly repeat, is the locale of the Children's Hospital. In the upper storeys with the beautiful prospects, dwell the sisters of the community to which the institution belongs. The bright drawing-rooms are considered the best possible place for the sick children, who lie there in their pretty white cots, to have their temporary ailments cured and their crooked limbs made straight, or, if death have already cast its shadow across their little span of life, to have the passage smoothed for them to the heaven peopled with the saints of the Isle of Destiny and the martyrs of the Gaelic race. Above the mantelpiece, in the front room, hangs suspended a large sculptured crucifix, signifying there something very different from the crest of La Poer. The lofty lower rooms that once re-echoed with convivial laughter, the clinking of glasses, and "the glorious, pious, and immortal memory," drunk with three-times-three, are now respectively the reception-room of the convent, and the chapel wherein reigns the reverential silence that befits the sacramental presence of the Saviour of men.

Drumcondra House and Park became, in 1842, the property of the Missionary College of All-Hallows, having been purchased from the Corporation during the mayoralty of Daniel O'Connell. The mansion remains unaltered in external appearance. Over the doorway is still conspicuous the Coghill crest, a cock with wings expanded. Handsome as the house is, with its surmounting balustrade, the originally imposing elevation is considerably dwarfed by the high-pitched roof and the square tower of the new collegiate buildings.[1] The stables, deprived of their leafy screen, fitted with glazed windows and a clock dial, look like nothing so much as just what they are—a distinct, though integral, part of the educational establishment, in which are the class-rooms and the chapel of the junior students.

From out the postern door no phantom Bloodhound horses issue forth with mailed hoofs to stamp out insurrectionary pride. Through the wicket no one cares now to pass into

[1] See the Rev John O'Hanlon's *Lives of the Irish Saints*, vol. i. p 348, for an excellent view of All-Hallows, including the old mansion, the chapel, and the new college.

Ui

the pathway to the church. But, year after year, through wide open gates, marches out a chosen army of the Lord, to plant on eastern plains and western shores the standard of the holy cross, and turn upon and soil the streams of living water from founts that never yet ran dry in the land of faith and sorrow.

AROUND AND ABOUT THE ROTUNDA

SHOULD the muse of history, when embodying, some eighteen or twenty years hence, the record of our much-vexed era, find herself obliged to say or sing that the hundredth anniversary of the Convention of Dungannon passed over without any worthy commemoration, what a shame it would be for Ireland!

Certain it is that no adequate memorial of the volunteers signalised the year of grace just passed away. Neither was there very much said during that term in allusion to an event which one hundred years ago aroused the spirit of long-suffering nationality, and shook the land from sea to sea.

And yet we doubt whether so ominous a blank will mar the page that must ere long be written. History concerns herself hardly at all with motives, intentions, and omissions; she takes up the pen to narrate facts mainly; and it is quite possible that posterity, glancing through the chapter for which we in Ireland are now enacting the scenes, will simply take it for granted that the exhibition opened at the Rotunda last autumn [1] was designed to be, and was in fact, an expression of the nation's sympathy with, and undying memory of, the men of '82.

Unquestionably there were circumstances connected with the planning, the inauguration, and the conduct of that exhibition which forcibly recall transactions of the earlier period, and tend to show that the spirit of the volunteers arose once more to quicken—not a section merely of the population, but

[1] [illegible]

the mass of men who are in fact the nation. This impression is scarcely lessened by the reflection that certain analogies between recent and remote occurrences were at the moment unobserved, while certain no less significant contrasts likewise passed without a comment

That the National Exhibition created so vivid an interest and proved so complete a success, sufficiently indicates that the *motive* of the enterprise must have been something very different from that which commonly prompts the getting up of a glass palace crammed with raw materials, wrought fabrics, objects of art, and relics of antiquity. The world, indeed, is pretty well tired of manufacture exhibitions, pure and simple.

Although the circumstances are still fresh in the memory of our readers, we may be allowed, nevertheless, to refer in a passing way to one or two points in the history of the recent exhibition.

At a moment of great political excitement and serious disruption of the *status quo*, it was a happy idea, certainly, to divert men's minds into the ways of peace, to bring under general notice the stores of natural products possessed by Ireland, to collect specimens of manufacturing skill and successful handicraft produced in the country, to show by examples in what paths of high art Irishmen have acquired renown, and to excite that spirit of trade enterprise which unfortunately for many years past has lain dormant in this island. As originally planned in the autumn of 1881, the enterprise promised well. Personages of distinction in Church and State lent their countenance to the undertaking; corporations and merchants of high standing expressed a readiness to assist in a practical way, a suitable building was placed at the disposal of the committee; and a guarantee fund of £25,000 was readily subscribed.

However, before a month had elapsed, the hopes thus excited were dashed to the ground. The promoters of the arts of peace quarrelled over a question of patronage and ceremonial. One party, standing out for a strict adherence to forms hitherto observed, and insisting that royal favour should be besought, was encountered by another party which regarded such a proceeding as a piece of useless flunkeyism, and firmly declined to solicit the countenance of the head of the realm, or that of any other personage royal or viceroyal. Both parties turning out irreconcilable, disruption ensued. Those who dreaded even the faintest suspicion of disloyalty, whose interests might seem imperilled, or whose respectability ran any risk of being sullied, forthwith retreated. The aristocracy vanished, the merchant princes strode away, one important body of men refused to contribute either in money or in kind, a host of guarantors of various gradations of solvency and standing hastened to relinquish all participation in the possible glory and the certain risk of carrying the enterprise to completion

At the very moment when the movement seemed virtually abandoned, a few gentlemen, inspired by genuine patriotism, set to work to kindle from the ashes of the extinguished project a spark of life and hope. Their energy and confidence happily proved contagious, and their appeal to the nation met with a generous response. A limited liability company was speedily formed, and a Board of Directors appointed Shares to the amount of nearly £30,000 were taken, and every part of the country proffered aid and encouragement. In fact, a truly national movement was set on foot, and the promoters announced that an Exhibition of Irish Manufactures would open on the 15th of August 1882, the day fixed for the unveiling of the O'Connell monument

Still, all difficulties had not been vanquished by the resolution to dare and do. A new embarrassment presented itself when it was made known that the old exhibition building in Earlsfort Terrace would neither be let nor lent to the new company. At all hazards, then, a site must be procured and an edifice erected. One effort after another to obtain a conveniently-situated plot of ground on the south side of the city having failed, an arrangement was made with the governors of the Rotunda Hospital, by the terms of which they consented, on payment of £1500, to permit the erection of a temporary building in the garden of Rutland Square, and to allow the historic Rotunda and the adjoining public rooms to be used for the purposes of the Exhibition.

From the 11th of May, when the first sod was turned and the builders' work commenced, to the date fixed for the opening ceremony, there remained but eighty-three working days for th[illegible] the

Rotunda rooms, and the allotment to intending exhibitors of 100,000 square feet of space.

From whatever source hitches or hindrances may have arisen,—and in minor matters they failed not to crop up as the work proceeded,—the artisans engaged on the building could not be accused of creating obstruction. The conduct of the workmen all through was singularly creditable. From the outset they put their heart into the work, laboured early and late, cheered and encouraged one another, and, as each part neared completion, talked of the achievement as of something in which they were themselves personally and proudly concerned. The first authority in this matter, the Board of Directors, has in a graceful manner placed on record its testimony to the energy and skill of the tradesmen employed on the works, as well as to the untiring zeal of the professional and official staff.[1]

According, therefore, as the summer days hastened on, the green sod swarmed with busy, spirited "hands," the architect's design took form, and the shimmer of glass walls and roof began to show among the giant elms of the square.

Disadvantages there were, no doubt, in the configuration of the ground. Architectural skill was severely taxed in overcoming the obstacles presented by the inequality of the surface. It detracted from the dignity of the new structure that it should be approached by a descent from the circumjacent roadway. Moreover, it was not possible to connect the glass building with the Rotundo rooms in an effective and harmonious way. But these and other disadvantages were more than counterbalanced by the appropriateness of the situation, for the spot on which the company devoted to the cause of Irish Arts and Industries flew its flag and set up its trophies, is historic ground, and can boast of associations which no other place, spoken of as suitable for the National Exhibition, can claim.

About the middle of the eighteenth century, the area now occupied by the hospital, the Rotunda and adjoining buildings, and the garden of the square, was a piece of waste ground with a pool in the hollow, and a few cabins on the slope. Great Britain Street, a space on the north side of which this plot is appropriated, passed over the head of Sackville Street,

[1] [illegible] the *Complete Official Guide.*

and stretched its length as far as the church of St. George, that is to say, the old pile now standing derelict in Lower Temple Street. Beyond lay a suburban region remarkable for its lovely view and salubrious air, and having detached residences embowered in trees, and tenanted by people of fortune. Orchards flourished on the site of Cumberland Street and Mecklenburgh Street. Immediately north and east of the present Rutland Square, nothing was to be seen but open country. Dorset Street properly so-called extended not so much farther than the spot on which the Bethesda stands, and then the line of road assumed the name of Dorset Lane until it merged into the completely rural Drumcondra Lane. But that the city had some notion of spreading itself northward might be assumed from the fact that a row of mansions already proceeded up the hill almost in a straight line from Sackville Street, and, although having no better foreground than the waste plot already described, took the aristocratic name of Cavendish Street. Sackville Street, inhabited exclusively by families of high rank, extended no farther than Henry Street, and had in the centre a space, enclosed within a low wall, planted with trees, frequented as a promenade, and designated the Mall. In Marlborough Street, Henry Street, and Mary Street, very distinguished families resided. Henrietta Street was one of the most fashionable quarters of the town, and Dominick Street held the same rank, with its mansions and large gardens ranged on one side only of the roadway.

Altogether, this part of Dublin had an aristocratic air perfectly in keeping with the quality of its inhabitants. There was no crowding. Green openings and full-grown trees held their ground, and all the houses had gardens in the rear. The wretched masses of the population kept to their native lanes on the other side of the river. It was only now and then that daring scouts of the standing army of 2000 beggars advanced as far as the patrician quarters at the north side of the city. Capel Street was the most public part of the town thereabout, forming, as it did, the main line of communication with the thoroughfares in which stood His Majesty's Castle, the Houses of Parliament, the tholsel, and the cathedrals. Essex Bridge, the nearest bridge to the sea in those days, and a tumble-down unsightly structure, was about to be rebuilt in a style suitable to its importance as the chief pass between the two great divisions of the city.

Meanwhile, the piece of unoccupied ground skirting Great Britain Street, and facing Sackville Street, had attracted the attention of a citizen who coveted its possession with a not unholy greed, imagined a splendid structure rising on its front, and beheld, in his mind's eye, the desert background blossoming as a rose. The worthy individual who set his heart on this vineyard, and yet thereby endangered no man's peace, was Dr. Mosse, a physician practising in Dublin, and enjoying high esteem for his professional ability and singularly benevolent disposition.

Bartholomew Mosse, a native of Maryborough, in the Queen's County, was born in the year 1712. Having studied medicine and devoted himself to obstetrics, he settled early in life in the Irish capital. His active charity brought him into daily contact with the impoverished and suffering classes of the population; his compassion became strongly excited by the wretched condition of poor women when the time of their confinement approached, and they found themselves without medical aid or any kindly succour; and he resolved to do all in his power to have an hospital established, in which the relief and nursing they stood in need of should be gratuitously supplied. When, therefore, at the outset of his career, he visited England, and travelled into France, Holland, and other parts of Europe, with a view of perfecting his studies in surgery and midwifery, he laid himself out particularly to inquire into and observe the hospitals of the different countries he sojourned in.

On his return to Dublin, being determined to begin his benevolent work on a small scale, he took a house in St. George's Lane,[1] furnished it with twenty-four beds, and in 1745 opened there the first hospital of the kind ever established, it is said, in the British dominions. In the first instance, it would appear that he did not receive much assistance from fellow-members of the medical faculty, but was left

[1] The present South Great George's Street. On that line in former days were the mansions and parks of wealthy and distinguished people. The house taken by Dr. Mosse stood opposite Fade Street, and was occupied not long before by Madame Violante, the celebrated pantomimist.

( )

almost unaided in his attendance on the poor women who gratefully availed themselves of his charity The expenses of the undertaking were defrayed by his own purse chiefly, and by the proceeds of lotteries, plays, concerts, and oratorios.

Dublin was exceedingly musical in those days, and as charitable then as it is even in our own generation; and a great part of the funds spent on the hospitals and other charitable institutions of the city were provided through the exertions of the several "Charitable Musical Societies" then existing. It will be remembered that shortly before this date Handel had been invited over, and that under his superintendence a public performance of the *Messiah*—the first ever given of the great oratorio, as is now generally admitted—took place in the Fishamble Street Music Hall, for the benefit of Mercer's Hospital, the Charitable Infirmary, and Imprisoned Debtors.[1]

Foreign vocalists and instrumentalists often crossed the sea to perform in the Irish capital, and some of the number took up their abode permanently among the music-loving citizens. It therefore surprised no one that Dr. Mosse should take much trouble in getting up concerts and oratorios, or that he should bring over the Italian Castruccio as an attraction at performances got up for the benefit of his work of predilection.[2]

[1] The visit to Dublin of this renowned composer had more than a transitory effect. "It became the custom to perform his oratorios and cantatas, for the benefit not only of the charitable institutions already existing, but also of several medical charities, which, about this time, were established in the Irish metropolis. This custom was kept up for many years Besides Mercer's Hospital and Infirmary, the Lying-in Hospital and the Hospital for Incurables derived repeated benefit from frequent performances of his music Perhaps the works of no other composer have so largely contributed to the relief of human suffering as those of this illustrious musician."—*Account of Handel's Visit to Dublin*, by Horatio Townsend.

[2] Castruccio remained in Dublin, but for some reason or another sank into penury and oblivion. He was often seen gathering sticks to make his fire, dressed in the suit of black velvet which he usually wore when he appeared in public. His poverty was not known to those who could relieve him, and he died in 1752. It adds to the pathos of the story that his funeral was superb, and was graced with the presence of some of the first characters in the nation. The procession formed a fine concert, vocal and instrumental, through the streets. So great was the concourse of people in St. Mary's Churchyard (Jervis Street), where the interment of the musician took place, that the parish beadle was crushed to death.—See Walker's *History* [illegible] *Keeffe.*

Wider sympathy was enlisted by the publication of annual reports giving statistical and other details; the institution attracted attention; and Dr. Mosse had not been three years carrying on his charitable work when he received from London an application for the plan and regulations of his hospital. This inquiry was preparatory to the establishment of a kindred institution in the English metropolis in 1748. A couple of years later, two other hospitals of the same kind were opened in that city.

George's Lane house was, by this time, quite unable to accommodate the numbers seeking admission, and Dr Mosse revolved in his mind one scheme after another for raising money to purchase a site and build an hospital. Just at this juncture he cast his eyes on the piece of waste ground in Great Britain Street. A better site for the handsome and capacious building which he longed to see erected could hardly be hoped for. There was a greater area, no doubt, than was wanted for building purposes; but then the ground might be turned to account, and made to produce a quota of the much-needed funds. At anyrate, on the 25th of August 1748, he took the plot, consisting of 4 acres 19 perches, on a lease of lives renewable for ever, at the yearly rent of £70; and immediately began, at a cost of about £2000 of his own income, to lay out a garden, which he hoped would become an attractive place of promenade and recreation for the nobility and gentry residing in the neighbourhood.

Shrubberies were planted, ornamental walks laid out, pavilions and a coffee-room erected, fountains and waterworks set going. Statues and coloured lamps adorned the walks, and an orchestra, expensively decorated, graced the upper part of the enclosure. Animation being imparted to the scene by the performance of a band of music, nothing seemed wanting to the attraction of the New Gardens. The earls and the countesses, the viscounts and the barons, the right honourables and honourables, with the crowd of gentry residing in Dublin, began at once to take advantage of the enjoyment offered to them, assembled on summer evenings in the pleasure-ground prepared for their patrician presence, and, by the very fact, made the speculation a complete success. A constant resort of company during the season kept up the fashion and the charm, and the charity obtained through that source alone profits to the amount of several hundred pounds annually.

So delighted was the doctor with the beauty of the garden, that he employed M. Giezoni to paint a picture of the scene, introducing the company, the musicians, and every available accessary. He paid one hundred pounds for this picture, which was considered a masterpiece, and he intended to have an engraving of it executed, which would sell for three half-crowns each copy. The work was sent to France to be engraved, but, unfortunately, it was seized on being landed there, and never was recovered.

Meanwhile, Dr. Mosse had little leisure for contemplating the beauty of the New Gardens. The question of ways and means had become engrossing George's Lane house must be supported, the building of the new hospital had to be provided for, serious schemes carefully elaborated did not always prove successful, and, as a matter of course, the philanthropist met with contradictions from some who could not enter into the feelings which animated his own charitable heart. However, he had reason to count on the aid of a few influential friends; and a promise of popular support might seem to be indicated by the fact that a number of persons of different occupations subscribed four shillings and fourpence a year, paid quarterly, for the erection of the new hospital Timber and other materials were collected: a noble design was obtained from Mr. Cassels, the architect,[1] and with about £500 in his hands and a great hope in his heart, Dr. Mosse resolved at all hazards to set the builders at work.

As the hospital was mainly intended for the relief of the poor of the city, the doctor considered it only proper to give the Lord Mayor the honour of laying the foundation-stone. Accordingly, the chief magistrate was invited to perform the ceremony. On the 4th of June 1751 he rode to the New Gardens with his attendants, went through the prescribed forms, and subsequently partook, in the parlance of the period, of a "genteel and liberal entertainment" provided by the founder.

[1] See a curious account of the German architect who made Ireland his home, in Whitelaw's *History of Dublin*. His principal designs were the town and country mansions of the Duke of Leinster, Viscount Powerscourt's residence in the county of Wicklow, Tyrone House, and Dr. Mosse's.]

Many persons, understanding that the new edifice would cost about £20,000, and knowing that funds were not lodged for that purpose, looked on Dr. Mosse as a madman, or a builder of castles in the air. It does not, however, appear that anyone questioned his right to set up his hospital in the company of lordly mansions. No one begged leave to remark that property would suffer deterioration, and the fitness of things be infringed, by the erection of an eleemosynary institution right in the face of Sackville Street. The aristocracy of the land displayed no such illiberality in a matter concerned with the interests of the poor, as the aristocracy of the desk has manifested in days nearer to our own. Neither the fashion of the locality nor the prestige of the New Gardens was likely to be at all affected by the presence of Mr. Cassels' elegant structure.

As far as the funds permitted, the work was carried on with vigour. The doctor expended his whole personal fortune on the undertaking, mortgaged his estate, and raised all the money he could on his own credit. Up to the end of 1755 he had procured or collected £11,694, chiefly by means of plays, oratorios, and lotteries, for the support of the George's Lane house, and the building of the new hospital. Now, however, the failure of one of his schemes brought on embarrassment, his resources were quite exhausted, and he was in hourly danger of arrest and imprisonment. At this juncture, some persons of high rank, to whom he had communicated his situation, encouraged him to make an application to the House of Commons, and pray their aid to pay off the debts he had contracted on account of the hospital, and to enable him to finish the undertaking. Accordingly, a petition, with full statement of accounts and a report of the condition of the hospital, was presented to the Irish Parliament on the 23rd of March 1756. In response to this application, a grant of £6000 was voted for the specified purposes.

Later in the same year, a charter was obtained to incorporate a number of noblemen and gentlemen as governors and guardians of the hospital; and, before another twelve months had elapsed, the governors and guardians having again petitioned Parliament, the honourable House granted, on the 11th November 1757, a further sum of £6000 for the building, together with £2000 to Dr Mosse in recognition of his exertions in the cause of humanity.

By this time the hospital was nearly finished, the upper floor was furnished with fifty beds, and the founder wished no longer to delay the opening of the institution. As the head of the municipality had been invited to lay the first stone of the edifice, so now the representative of royalty was requested to perform the concluding ceremony. The Duke of Bedford, Viceroy of Ireland, his duchess, and a great number of the nobility and gentry, assembled at the hospital on the 8th of December 1757, and, the institution having been thrown open with all due form, were entertained at breakfast by the now joyous founder. Music, as was customary and proper, lent a charm to the proceedings, and during the repast the distinguished company were delighted with a concert of vocal and instrumental music.

The institution being now established on a permanent basis, countenanced by the legislature, and befriended by the aristocracy of the land, Dr. Mosse proceeded to add to the splendid edifice he had raised such details as would ensure its being in every way worthy of the spirit of philanthropy to which it owed its origin, and a credit to the capital of Ireland.

He was determined, for example, that the chapel should be as beautiful as money and art could make it, having the intention, it is said, that it should excel anything of the size in Europe. At great expense he had the stucco figures and other ornaments of the ceiling executed by M. Cramillion, an artist living at that time in Dublin. In the centre compartment and the four shields he purposed having religious subjects delineated, and with this view entered into a correspondence with M Cipriani, who was then in London, about designs For the centre, a representation of the Nativity of our Lord was deemed most appropriate; and for the shields it was considered that such scenes should be selected as the Daughter of Pharaoh taking Moses out of the Bulrushes, Christ blessing little Children, Hagar weeping over her expiring Child and calling on God for Relief, and the Midwives before the King of Egypt. Difficulties, which naturally arise when Art and Protestantism essay to work in concert, did not fail to present themselves in the course of the correspondence, and Dr. Mosse takes care to make M. Cipriani understand that his brush must keep clear of Catholic reminiscences. "As this chapel," writes, tl [illegible] estant worship, I would have the painting entirely free from any superstition or Popish representation." Unfortunately, the doctor died before the negotiations with the painter had been brought to a conclusion, and his successors appear to have thought it unnecessary to undertake the expense of painting the ceiling. An organ ordered for the chapel was not finished in the founder's lifetime, and afterwards, being considered too large and loud for its destined position, was erected in the new music-room or large Rotunda.

The doctor also ordered a chiming clock and a peal of bells for the steeple of the hospital; but it stands recorded that some ladies who lived in the neighbourhood insisted that neither bells nor clock should be fixed there, lest the sound should disturb them on mornings. He also intended to fit out an observatory in the tower, and had provided a telescope for it.

Nor did this worthy man confine his cares to the perfecting of the material structure His mind was occupied with plans for increasing the resources of the institution, and extending its influence for good. Thus the Grand Jury and gentlemen of the Queen's County having, at an assize, made a collection towards erecting and supporting a bed in the hospital out of compliment to the founder, whom they considered an honour to that part of the country, it occurred to him that it might be well to apply to the other counties in the kingdom, and endeavour to induce each of them to support a bed. Again, he conceived the idea of having nursed, clothed, and maintained, all the children who should be born in the hospital whom their parents should consent to intrust to his care. A school was to be opened, provided with Protestant masters, and the children were to be instructed in useful trades and manufactures. As a beginning of this comprehensive scheme, he, at his own expense, put out some children to be nursed.

All this time the gardens were not neglected, but were further beautified, and rendered still more productive as a source of revenue. Van Nost, a native of Dublin, though of foreign extraction, and a sculptor of repute, was commissioned to execute figures in marble and metal for the gardens, as well as for the interior of the building and the pavilion in front. On gala days, illuminations were got up with great splendour; and as f[illegible] nothing was left undone to provide the best. In one year, £1240 were expended on payments to musicians.

According to the original plan, the hospital was now solidly established, and destined, in all human probability, to go on and prosper for many a generation. It was not granted, however, to the kind-hearted founder to witness for long the happy results of his disinterested labours. Intense study and application of mind, close attention to the business of the hospital, and the fatigue of frequent journeys to London to forward his lottery schemes and other pecuniary matters, seriously impaired his health. In the beginning of the winter of 1758 he grew very ill; and in February 1759 he died, literally in the height of his work and in the midst of his days—"poor as to wealth, but rich in the blessings of the needy, and of those who were ready to perish."

We have condensed the foregoing sketch of the life-work of Bartholomew Mosse, occasionally adopting the very words of the narrative, from a remarkably interesting paper contributed, in 1846, to the *Dublin Quarterly Journal of Medical Science*. Turning now to other sources of information, we shall see the world of rank and fashion gathering round the hospital, and observe how the more it pleased folks of quality to amuse themselves, the better it turned out for the funds of the institution, which, as it so happened, became the promoter of a great deal of the gala life that distinguished Dublin before the Union.

No better proof could be given of the solid character of the institution planned, founded, and developed by Dr. Mosse than the fact that his death brought about neither a collapse nor an interruption of the work. His appointment as Master of the Hospital for life had seemed, in so far as human prevision could effect, to ensure him an opportunity of perfecting the organisation he had formed for the relief of suffering humanity, the advancement of medical science, and the support of an expensive and important establishment. But his early death deprived the institution at a critical moment of the wise control and generous self-devotion of its founder, and threw a heavy responsibility on the shoulders of his successors, whose term of office in each case must necessarily be limited to a very few years' duration. Still his spirit survived, and all that governors, [illegible] from that day to this may be summed up in the phrase, that they maintained or extended, according to circumstances, the high character and the beneficent operation of the institute which it was his noble ambition to make comprehensive and enduring [1]

In regard to the important question of funds, the governors and guardians had to see that the best means were taken to induce the public to keep the treasury supplied. Fortunately, fashion displayed, for once, a timely readiness to further a good cause; and it would have been a sin against common-sense not to take the tide at the flow and afford the arbiter of the gay world every opportunity of doing a good action. Perpetual May cannot be looked for in any clime,—least of all in Ireland,—and the governors soon saw the wisdom of seriously considering how the company frequenting the gardens might be sheltered and amused on wet evenings in summer, and lured to the vicinity even after winter had set in. Various expedients were resorted to, with more or less success; but at length, in 1763, the erection was commenced of a circular building in connection with the hospital, eminently suited for concerts, balls, and promenades, and capable of containing 2000 persons. Exteriorly, the design was plain enough, displaying no ornamentation save some emblematic entablatures, and a curious frieze in Wedgewood representing heads of oxen and festoons of drapery. The interior, however, had much that was pleasing to offer to the eye. Unlike other large halls of the same configuration, this Rotunda had no support for the roof in the centre. Fluted Corinthian pilasters, enriched windows, a tastefully decorated ceiling, a splendid orchestra, and all the effects of toned colour and brilliant lighting, combined to make this one of the most magnificent public rooms that could anywhere be seen.

Owing to its excellent acoustic properties, the Rotunda

[1] This hospital is the largest chartered Clinical School of Midwifery in the United Kingdom, and is in high repute all over the world. The charter provides that the Master of the Hospital for the time being shall be always some experienced practitioner; and that he shall have two assistants, to be proposed by him and approved of by the governors. Dr. Lombe Atthill is the present master, and the assistant physicians are Dr. Alex. Duke and Dr. Andrew J Horne. Among the students attending the classes are, we understand, a Spaniard, a Portuguese, a Swede, and six Americans. The hospital has always been largely frequented by English st[illegible]

became a favourite place for musical performances. The governors of the hospital, men of the first rank and the highest cultivation,[1] showed liberality, enterprise, and judgment in providing enjoyment for the nobility, gentry, and citizens of music-loving Dublin. The best performers of the day who came to England were brought over to Dublin to sing or play, as the case might be, at the Rotunda Invariably the audience appeared in full dress at these concerts, and, consequently, the scene was as brilliant as the entertainment was delightful.

From the beginning the gardens had been thrown open to the public on Sunday evenings; and, although music was not provided for the Sabbath promenade, the crowded attendance showed that the worthy governors, in offering a harmless recreation on the day of rest, had struck on a profitable vein. As soon as the Rotunda was built and decorated, its brilliant area (80 feet in diameter) was included in the promenade; while, tea and coffee being provided in the recesses, the company could enjoy their mild refreshment beneath the splendid chandeliers. Some criticism, no doubt, the governors had to sustain on the head of this Sunday dissipation; but they met the objection by quietly suggesting, in the style of the period, that as a considerable Maintenance had been derived by the laying open the Gardens and Public Rooms on the evenings of Sundays, the Hand that would repress the latter should hold out an Equivalent! In fact, the Sunday promenade cost little, and eventually realised a clear profit to the charity of about £1000 a year.[2]

The Rotunda, when not otherwise engaged, was likewise thrown open on the week-day evenings dedicated to garden amusements. A striking and agreeable feature of the evening

[1] The Royal Charter nominated as governors, the Lord-Lieutenant for the time being, the Primate, the Lord Chancellor the Speaker of the House of Commons of Ireland, the Lord Mayor of the City of Dublin, the Archbishop of Dublin, the Commander-in-Chief of the Forces, the Earls of Kildare for ever, and a number of others, distinguished by their rank in Church and State.

[2] Dr. Campbell (*Historical Survey*, Letter III), speaking of the Sunday promenade, does not undertake to determine whether this entertainment is strictly defensible in a religious point of view; but he wonders how it is that London, so fond of amusement, and so ready to adopt new fashions of dissipation, has not struck out something similar for passing those hours which on some people sit so heavy, and [illegible] in a much worse

recreations was the harmonious mingling of classes in the promenade. In those days the aristocracy dined early and had a long evening to dispose of. Staying at home did not suit their taste. They were social, loved movement, and shrank not at all from the admiring gaze and near contact of a crowd. Possibly, also, they may have flattered themselves that their condescension conferred a public benefit, and that by their presence they "awed into propriety" the meaner multitude. On the other hand, the citizens highly enjoyed the sight of the titled notabilities and their following of landed and official gentry; and here, in the gardens and the Rotunda, they were free to gratify their curiosity at a very trifling cost. The admission, on open evenings, was the fivepenny coin of the realm. All, therefore, who occupied a commonly decent position, could afford themselves the enjoyment of the music, the gapeseed, and the novelty of the promenade. Reminiscences of foreign civilisation must have struck those visitors who were acquainted with the habits of continental life and dwelt with an observant eye on the scene. Anyhow, an air of graciousness and freedom prevailed, and lent a charm to these gatherings of the high and mighty, the simple and the unrenowned.

And, undoubtedly, the fashionable and distinguished company were worth looking at. If we could see them as they then appeared, we should fancy that they had issued forth from the theatres rather than the lordly mansions of the town, such were their airs and graces, such the splendour and variety of their costume. Fashions, of course, changed from time to time, but considerable freedom was enjoyed throughout the eighteenth century. People chose the colours and adopted the style that satisfied their taste, or suited their figure and complexion. This was particularly the case with men of noble birth or otherwise distinguished. They might be recognised in a crowd by their garb alone. A portly figure, dressed in scarlet, with full-powdered wig and black velvet hunting-cap, could be no other than Lord Trimbleston; a suit of light blue announced Lord Gormanston; and Mr. Coote (afterwards Earl of Belmont) made himself conspicuous by his silk coat, satin shoes with red heels, and elegant feathered hat. Even in his old age, Lord Taaffe preferred to wear a whole suit of dove-coloured silk; while Lord Molesworth dressed in groom style, with coloured silk kerchief; and Lord Clanricarde invariably donned his regimentals. Macklin, the actor, adhering to the fashion of 1720, appeared with stockings rolled over his knees, long flaps to his waistcoat, enormous cuffs, and so forth; but Geminiani, the musician, attired himself in blue velvet, richly embroidered with gold.[1]

In the matter of hairdressing, too, some personages took extraordinary liberties. At a time when everybody else powdered and frizzled very much, Mr. Conolly of Castletown wore his long hair combed down and without powder; and Lord Harcourt, the Viceroy, looked particularly venerable with his grey locks all about his shoulders. Even ladies showed at times a daring spirit of innovation in this capital affair. Beautiful Anne Cately took a fancy to wear her hair plain over her forehead, in an even line almost to her eyebrows, and the Dublin ladies, following her example, had their hair Cately-fied.[2]

Masquerades became the fashion not very long after the Rotunda was built; and the governors lost no time in arranging so that these brilliant entertainments might take place within their precincts. The Fishamble Street Music Hall was sufficiently well adapted for such festivities; but the Rotunda had the advantage of an easier approach and greater space, and consequently became a favourite scene of revelry. On masquerade nights the neighbourhood, and indeed the whole city north and south, was in a state of commotion from seven o'clock in the evening. It was customary on these occasions

[1] Macklin was well known, off as well as on the stage, in Dublin. He had a residence in Drumcondra Lane. Geminiani, of whom there is an interesting account in Hawkins' *History of Music*, was offered the post of Master and Composer of State Music in Ireland, but declined from conscientious motives, as the situation could not be held by a Catholic. He died in Dublin.

[2] Miss Cately obtained an engagement at the Dublin theatre at £40 a night, and remained a considerable time in Dublin, living with her mother in the same neighbourhood as Macklin. O'Keeffe, in his *Recollections* gives some highly amusing traits of Macklin and Miss Cately during their abode in Dublin. A dramatist by profession and something of an artist by taste and training, O'Keeffe had acquired the good habit of using his eyes intelligently and noting the little incidents and traits that bring out or indicate character. He seldom omits in his description of men of eminence, an accurate sketch of the style of dress they affected. We are indebted to him for the ...

for the various characters to visit and walk through the state apartments of the mansions of the principal nobility and gentry in the city, which were thrown open for their reception and entertainment [1] Humbler folks were thus afforded an opportunity of feasting their eyes and passing their comments on the masqueraders, descending from their coaches, or carried past in their sedans on their round of preliminary calls About midnight the company came crowding into the Rotunda, and for hours the merriment knew no check.

By this time it was quite plain that the hospital, with its circular *annexe* and lovely gardens, had made the fortune of the circumjacent district Fine houses in a stately line had risen up on the north and west sides of the enclosure; and these, like the mansions in Cavendish Street, were greatly in request as residences for the nobility and gentry. Lord Charlemont, resolving to build a town house in a better situation than that occupied by the family mansion in the immediate vicinity of St. Mary's Churchyard, could fancy no position more desirable than a site adjacent to Cassels' stately fabric. Accordingly, he purchased a plot north of the grounds, and commanding a full view of the garden front (or, as we have seen it designated, the *back-front*) of the building.[2] Charlemont House, finished in 1773, was designed by the noble owner, who had a singularly correct taste in architecture, and was much admired for its simple and effective style. Speaking of the lately completed mansion, a writer of the time remarks, that nothing could be more elegant than the structure or more delightful than the situation, on a little eminence exactly fronting Mosse's Hospital, with those beautiful gardens lying between, where the genteel company

[1] See Dr. Gilbert's *History of Dublin*.

[2] Inadvertently, a description of the structure was omitted from the first part of this paper An outline-sketch may be thus supplied: The central building, constituting the body of the hospital, is a handsome fabric, 125 feet in length by 82 in depth. The principal front is composed of mountain granite. The centre, decorated with four Doric columns on a rude basement, and supporting a beautiful entablature and pediment,—the whole crowned with a domed steeple,—has a truly elegant effect. Ornamented colonnades communicate with the wings, which have also Doric columns and vases at top—that to the east serving as an entrance to the Rotunda and new rooms The front towards the gardens is also of mountain granite, but is judiciously devoid of ornament.—Cromwell's *Excursions through Ireland*, 1820; Brewer's *Beauties of Ireland*, 1825

walk in summer evenings, and have concerts of vocal and instrumental music thrice a week.[1]

In course of time the Rotunda was found worthy of being something more than a scene of revelry, a concert hall, and "a polite place of public resort on Sunday evenings." It was destined to receive the prouder title of "The Forum of Ireland." Undoubtedly, the most striking scene that ever took place within its walls was that enacted on the 10th of November 1783, when the delegates of the volunteer corps of the four provinces assembled to inaugurate the congress known in history as the Rotunda Convention.

At noon on that day the delegates met, as prearranged, in the Royal Exchange; and, having elected the Earl of Charlemont president, and John Talbot Ashenhurst and Captain Dawson, secretaries, adjourned to the Rotunda, as a building better adapted for the accommodation of a very large deliberative assembly. Truly imposing was the procession which took its way forthwith across the city amidst the booming of artillery and the clangour of regimental bands. Corps of the volunteer army lined the streets, arms presented and colours flying, while other detachments of the same force took part in the procession. Among those moving in the line of march were a troop of the Rathdown Carbineers, headed by Colonel Edwards of Oldcourt; the Liberty Brigade of Artillery, under the command of Napper Tandy; a company of the Barristers' Grenadiers, with a national standard; another brigade of artillery commanded by Counsellor Calbeck, and escorted by the Barristers' Corps in scarlet and gold; and the cavalry corps of the Cullenagh Rangers, attending the delegates as a guard of honour, and led on by young Jonah Barrington. The chaplains, in their cassocks, walked with their respective corps. Lord Charlemont, accompanied by a squadron of horse, advanced at the head of the delegates, who walked two-and-two, each in the uniform of his respective corps, carrying his side-arms, and having a broad green riband across his shoulders. The rear was brought up by the Lord Bishop of Derry (Earl of Bristol), in an open carriage drawn by six splendidly caparisoned horses, and escorted by a bodyguard of light dragoons, raised by his nephew, George Robert Fitzgerald. An enthusiastic crowd occupied the streets, filled the windows and covered the housetops, cheering the delegates and showering green ribands on them as they passed.

According as the troops of the national army arrived at the Rotunda, they took up their position within view of the building. Presently the firing of cannon announced the approach of the delegates, and the doors flew open to receive the representatives of 100,000 volunteers. Each man as he entered doffed his helmet or his hat, while the multitude without filled the air with their joyous acclaim.

Within the scene was brilliant. The great circular room had been arranged for the assembly; seats in the manner of an amphitheatre were ranged round the chair, and the orchestra was filled with ladies. One hundred and sixty delegates took their seats, their escorts massed around them. But on such a day of intoxicating excitement, formal deliberation was out of the question. A resolution was passed affirming the fundamental principle of the Dungannon Convention; all business was adjourned till the morrow; and the evening closed with illuminations, music, and high conviviality.[1]

During three weeks the Convention held its session: the Rotunda daily embracing within its ample circumference an assembly of citizen-soldiers which formed, in a scenic sense, hardly less motley and picturesque a gathering than the masquerading gentry who had lately quit the stage. Invariably the delegates appeared in their respective uniforms. No two men were dressed or armed alike. Cavalry, infantry, grenadiers, and artillery were mingled together; generals and sergeants, colonels and privates, sat side by side. The greater number were men of rank and fortune, many were members of Parliament, Lords and Commons; but some of inferior position debated with the rest. Individually, men figured in that scene at one and the same time in different characters. Lord Charlemont was at once president of a deliberative assembly and commander-in-chief of the volunteer army. Flood thundered forth his senate-house eloquence in the scarlet uniform, with green facings, of the Dublin Independent Volunteers, of which the parliamentary leader was lieutenant-colonel. Richard Lovel Edgeworth, the man of letters from Longford County,

[1] See the account of the day's proceedings in MacNevin's *History of the Volunteers*; but more particularly in Barrington's *Rise and Fall of the Irish Nati*[illegible] borrow freely

( )

had to support the character of aid-de-camp to the generalissimo. The Bishop of Derry (Earl of Bristol), and delegate of the county of Derry, figured first and before all things as a princely democrat. Of course, he donned no uniform, but the elegance and singularity of his dress distinguished him in the assembly. He robed himself entirely in purple, wearing diamond knee and shoe-buckles, and white gloves with gold fringe and tassels.[1] He was eccentric, he was magnificent, he cherished the wildest ideas. One of the wildest of all was the idea that the Catholics of Ireland might safely be intrusted with the elective franchise, and ought forthwith to have that right conceded to them! This was more than the renowned patriots Charlemont and Flood could conceive or countenance.

One day there came to the Convention—not as a delegate, but as a visitor—a tall, thin man, dressed in a complete suit of brown, with white stock and powdered wig. As he entered the building, the volunteer guard turned out and received him with a full salute of rested arms. The whole assembly rose when he appeared, and he marched up the hall amidst the deafening cheers of the delegates. This was the honorary chaplain of the Irish Brigade (Volunteer Corps), the gifted Capuchin, "the great Romanist priest," Father O'Leary.

Meanwhile the town was a scene of excitement, festivity, and military parade. Detachments of country corps had come up with the delegates. Serving without pay, self-clothed and armed, these patriot-soldiers had supplied themselves with new dresses and accoutrements for the pacific campaign in Dublin. A great proportion of the cavalry were mounted on hunters, the Bishop of Derry's escort being provided with the finest chargers that could be procured. The duty of the volunteer force seemed to consist in escorting the delegates and careering about in all directions. Grenadiers were ordered to mount an officer's guard at Charlemont House; the magnificent bishop had a guard of horse in front of his residence; and dragoons patrolled the entire city. Open-house was kept for the gallant visitors by the hospitable citizens. In a word, the volunteer uniforms were to be seen in the private

[1] The bishop rode to the Convention in regal state, "displaying the self-complacency of a favourite marshal of France, on his way to Versailles rather than [illegible] nd." Hardy's [illegible]

houses, in the streets,—everywhere. This military occupation of the capital, contemporaneous with the sittings of the Convention, was long remembered in the domestic annals of Dublin, and undoubtedly had a considerable effect in developing the taste for lavish expenditure and unrestrained conviviality for which the citizens were already becoming remarkable.

While the pride of life was thus mastering the thoughtless crowd, conflicting passions were agitating the centres of political and governmental action. The Convention, sitting at the Rotunda, pledged to digest and publish a plan of parliamentary reform, and to pursue such measures as might appear to them most likely to render it effectual, considered and debated, voted and contended, throughout the anxious three weeks' session. The Parliament sitting in College Green, watching with jealous eyes the doings of the Congress on the other side of the river, and fully determined not to reform itself, prepared for the inevitable conflict. The Lord-Lieutenant and Council, sitting in His Majesty's Castle, distracted by the perils of the hour, hardly knew what to do or what to expect.

At length, the Reform Bill, drawn up at the Rotunda, was ready. In the afternoon of Saturday, the 29th of November, it was ordered that Henry Flood, accompanied by such Members of Parliament as were also members of the Convention, should immediately go down to the House of Commons and move for leave to bring in a Bill, the facsimile of the one just approved of, the Convention at the same time declaring its sittings permanent until the fate of the Bill should be decided

Extraordinary was the sensation created in the House, where several of the minority and all the delegates who had come from the Convention appeared in their uniforms. A tempestuous debate ensued, waxing wilder as the hours rolled by; until at last, as day began to break, the calm of a settled resolution succeeded to the rush of oratory and the storm of contention. Parliament denounced the idea of a Bill introduced at the point of the bayonet, repudiated the dictation of a body of armed men "sitting in all the parade and in the mockery of parliament in that pantheon of divinities, the Rotunda"; and affirmed its fixed determination to maintain its privileges and rights against any encroachments whatsoever. Flood's motion was lost on a division of 157 to 77.

In the [illegible] wore on the silent hours. Vainly

awaiting the herald of victory, exhausted and desponding, the Convention at length relinquished the vigil. Slowly and sadly the members withdrew.

Next day, Sunday, a large number of the president's particular friends met him at Charlemont House, and a plan of action, or rather an attitude of inaction, was agreed to. Different accounts are given of what took place at the Rotunda on Monday, the 1st of December. One thing, however, is certain: the Convention there and then adjourned *sine die*.

The defeat of the Rotunda Convention, in its contest with the Parliament sitting in College Green, was a fatal blow to the volunteers. Their prestige vanished. For some years, no doubt, they maintained their organisation unbroken, and continued on every available occasion to display their martial pageants, and to hold their jovial meetings. But Government ceased to regard the patriot-soldiers with serious alarm, and the Nationalists of that day relinquished the high hopes they had founded on the military character assumed by the civic ranks.

In fact, the volunteers had failed in strategy by attempting with undue precipitation to follow up the successes they obtained in 1782. They had talked and vaunted and attempted too much, and their imprudence seems only to have furnished their wary adversary with motives for a sinister and far-reaching plan of operations, designed for the subversion of the structure so proudly raised by the men of '82

The author of a curious book, entitled *The Irish Abroad and at Home*, writing about fifty years ago, says that, on a hundred occasions, he has heard contemporaries of the men who freed the foreign trade and achieved the legislative independence of Ireland, maintain that the patriots, instead of proclaiming their success, should have dissembled their estimate of it; instead of announcing projects for further steps towards complete independence of the sister kingdom, should have assumed an attitude of content, and used every possible means for removing from England and her Government all sense of soreness from the concessions torn from her; and, instead of revelling in the interval succeeding the fortunate struggle, should have applied all their sagacity and energy to ensuring, at least, the undisturbed enjoyment of the fruits of it. "There [illegible] ested to England, by the declaration of Irish Independence, and by the conduct of the popular party subsequently, fear for the connection: an impression which determined, I have always heard, a defensive attitude in the first instance, and ultimately measures for the recovery of British domination in Ireland, and then for securing its permanency." And furthermore, he refers to a startling, though not, he thinks, an unjustifiable surmise, that the Duke of Rutland, who was appointed Lord-Lieutenant of Ireland immediately after the adjournment of the Rotunda Convention, was sent "with a view to the demoralisation of its patriotic aristocracy," and for the purpose of "diverting the public mind from grave concerns," so as to "render the resumption of British power practicable and facile."[1]

It seems monstrous to attribute motives so malign to Mr. Pitt, the youthful statesman, who, on becoming First Minister of the Crown, desired that the Duke of Rutland should undertake the government of Ireland. We are not called upon just now to enter into the question, but the fact must nevertheless be emphasised, that with the break-up of the Rotunda Convention the era of the volunteers virtually ended, and "The Rutland reign" began.

Although some five years older than the Premier, His Grace of Rutland was not yet thirty years of age. Between them a warm attachment had long subsisted, to the influence of the duke, Lord Chatham's son was indebted for his first seat in the House of Commons; and when it became known that young Pitt was to have the seals, rumour added that the rich and handsome peer was to have Ireland In the month of February 1784, the duke set out for his government, accompanied by Mr. Thomas Orde (afterwards Lord Bolton), an excellent man of business, according to repute, and well qualified to hold the post of Chief Secretary to the Lord-Lieutenant at that juncture in the affairs of the sister kingdom.

[1] The full title of the book, now not easily procurable, runs thus: *The Irish Abroad and at Home, at the Court and in the Camp. With Souvenirs of "The Brigade." Reminiscences of an Emigrant Milesian.* It was published in New York in 1856. The "Emigrant Milesian" thinly veiled the personality of the well-known Paris correspondent of the *Times*, Mr. Andrew O'Reilly, in whose rambling chapters will be found a great deal of matter highly interesting even to the present generation of Irishmen in ever

His Grace's itinerary would give a fair idea of the pleasures of a journey to Ireland one hundred years ago. We get a glimpse of the viceregal party *en route*, in a letter written by the Hon. John Beresford, also on his way to Dublin, and dated Chester, February 22, 1784. The duke, it seems, had an ugly accident in riding from Belvoir. His horse fell, crushing the rider's leg. The hurt was serious, and the surgeon, dreading mortification, endeavoured to prevail on the traveller to remain quietly for a day, at least, in Chester. Advice, however, was thrown away. The duke would not tarry on the road, neither would he take the surgeon with him. Having arrived in Chester at six o'clock on the morning of February 20, he set forward again in the afternoon of the same day, though obliged to be carried into a chaise. Mr. Orde followed in a couple of hours. Mr. Beresford tarried behind, wondering how the viceregal party could possibly get through; for it was snowing as if heaven and earth would come together, and they would want above twenty horses—enough to exhaust the whole stock on the road. Moreover, the coach, just arrived at Chester, brought word that there was neither packet-boat nor yacht at Holyhead. His Majesty's yacht, which left Dublin at the same time as the packet, had been blown out of her course, God knows where. When the last of the distinguished travellers arrived at Holyhead, on the 22nd, they found the duke very lame, the wind very high, and no sign of the yacht. However, the packet had come into harbour, and, going on board, the viceroy, with his friends and suite, sailed for the shores of Erin.[1]

Early in the afternoon of the 24th, the vessel arrived at her moorings in Poolbeg. The duke went on board the Ringsend barge, and was safely landed on Rogerson's Quay, where he, with his whole suite, stayed to breakfast, dress, and refresh themselves, for upwards of three hours, at the Royal Marine Hotel.[2]

Young and handsome, with a well-knit powerful frame; of noble bearing, yet affable withal; a lover of the arts, and a generous dispenser of a princely fortune, the Duke of Rutland would seem to have been the *beau-ideal* of an Irish viceroy. Though not without ability and the power of applying himself to business when necessary, he left the burden of affairs to his

[1] *Beres* [illegible] 784.

Secretary, made the amenities of social life his study, and devoted his energies to the task of "drinking the Irish into good humour." Mr. Orde, indeed, to do him justice, was no way deficient in practising the art of pleasing; and when we remember what were the gifts and graces of the Duchess of Rutland, we can understand that the new Lord-Lieutenant was not badly supported in his rôle (supposing it to have been assumed) of diverting Ireland from her grievances

Mary Isabella, Duchess of Rutland, was amiable and gay, fond of magnificent surroundings, and elegant in all her tastes. She was singularly beautiful. In Ireland, she was allowed to be one of the handsomest women in the Green Isle. Elsewhere, it was said, she was one of the loveliest, perhaps, in Europe. The Court over which she presided was certain, therefore, to be splendid in no ordinary degree, and quite free from any tinge of gloom in its grandeur.

No time was lost in inaugurating the new régime. The duke made it his business to be present at a grand review of the volunteer corps of the city and its vicinity; he received a deputation from the Roman Catholics, and graciously replied to their address, and St. Patrick's festival recurring soon after his arrival, he celebrated the occasion with quite unexampled splendour; in fact, "with that respect and magnificence," to quote a print of the day, "that we would expect to see in the Court of an independent kingdom rising to its proper rank among the other nations of the earth." A banquet, at which the Knights of St. Patrick were entertained, opened the programme of the evening's festivities; a ball followed, in which the company appeared in fancy characters and dresses, and a supper was served consisting of "every curiosity that art could procure, imagination suggest, or the season furnish."

Unfortunately, the citizens of Dublin were not, during the early part of the duke's viceroyalty, in a mood to be easily cajoled. They were chagrined by the rejection of the Volunteers' Reform Bill, still further excited by the ill-success of another measure of reform subsequently framed by Henry Flood, and exasperated by the injurious condition of the trading relations between England and Ireland.[1] Though the

[1] The trade grievance of that day is succinctly stated in Mr. Walpole's lately-published and admirable *Short History of the Kingdom of Ireland*, chap. ix. [illegible] account of the great debate in the

( )

Lord-Lieutenant was not personally responsible for the evils which weighed on the community, the populace did not hesitate to visit him with their displeasure. On the first occasion when he appeared at the theatre, he was hooted and insulted, the "Volunteers' March" was struck up, a general uproar ensued, and the entertainments of the evening were brought to a summary conclusion. Things came to a worse pass in the summer of 1785, when much distress existed, and the city was a scene of tumult and disorder. Military were posted in different parts of the town, and the garrison was kept in constant readiness for action. The duke, "beholding open violence, and suspecting secret conspiracy," wrote to the Prime Minister that Dublin was, in a great measure, under the dominion and tyranny of the mob, and that he was by no means sure the corps of volunteers in the neighbourhood were not countenancing the outrages committed.[1]

However, it does not appear that, after the tumultuous scene in the theatre, the chief governor was again in danger from the personal violence of the irreconcilables. His Excellency was not wanting in courage, and this, together with the jovial strain in his patrician constitution, counted in his favour with the men he had ostensibly to govern. He was in a fair way to overcome, in the long run, the rougher element in the State. As for the more respectable body of Dublin traders, they discovered before long how blessed they were in a Lord-Lieutenant who spent so freely, made the capital city so attractive, and formed so successful a school of profitable gentry, rack-renting the country to enrich the town. And as for the gay and brilliant aristocracy, they were only too well content to sail a-down the stream of time in the same boat with His Excellency—Youth at the prow and Pleasure at the helm. If only this delightful régime were lenthened out, what might not be expected in the interests of the metropolis and the nation!

Meanwhile the governors, guardians, and trustees of the

Irish Parliament on the trade question will be found in a letter from Mr. Woodfall, the first parliamentary reporter, to Mr. Eden, dated Dublin, Aug. 16, 1785, and given in the first volume of *The Journal and Correspondence* [illegible]

[1] Stanl [illegible]

hospital founded by Dr. Mosse were not asleep. On the contrary, they were fully awake to the fact that the sun was shining, and that it was their duty to work while it was yet day. They experienced no difficulty in enlisting the magnificent viceroy's interest in their charitable work. The Duke of Rutland subscribed handsomely to the hospital, and proved so good a friend that a fine ward was named after him, and adorned with his escutcheon. To supply the wants of the noble and fashionable part of the population by helping them to "fill up the vacant intervals of time," the governors now projected a scheme for increasing the accommodation afforded by the ball and concert-room, and so fully availed of by the gay world. It was resolved to erect a new building in connection with the Rotunda, which would enable the leaders of society to hold assemblies "public" in a certain sense, but protected with all the safeguards so dear to the spirit of exclusiveness. It would have been rather too much for the governors to undertake, unaided, the expense of the new erection. Therefore the distinguished parties to whose use the building should be dedicated, came forward with prompt and acceptable aid. Two hundred of the leading members of the aristocracy subscribed towards building the new rooms and establishing the assemblies. Among the original subscribers we find a duke or two, and a pair of duchesses; ten earls and nine countesses, twelve viscounts and six viscountesses, with a proportionate following of lords and ladies. Of course, the Duchess of Rutland favoured the undertaking in every way. The duke gave a large subscription, and came in person to lay the foundation-stone of the building, in commemoration of which generosity and condescension, his crest, encircled by the collar of the garter, was subsequently carved in the tympanum of the edifice, where the not inappropriate device, a peacock in pride, still remains, though so begrimed with dirt as to be hardly discernible.

Mr. Richard Johnson, an architect already rising to distinction, gave the design for the new rooms. During their progress the works were carefully superintended by one of the governors of the hospital, Mr. Frederick Trench, "a gentleman of large fortune and great taste in the Fine Arts, who devoted his time, and by his unwearied exertions [illegible] r [illegible] in his power, the improvement of every department of this noble charitable institution."[1]

When finished and decorated, the building was acknowledged to be eminently suited to its purpose, and worthy of the distinguished company who were to dance and play, drink tea and coquet within its precincts. A writer of the time describes this addition to the architectural group of the hospital and its adjuncts as superb, consisting of two principal apartments, one over the other, each 86 feet long, by 40 feet broad · the lower, with its elegant Corinthian pillars, being the ballroom, and the upper, suitably enriched, the supper-room, while there were smaller rooms for tea, cards, etc., and a convenient range of kitchens and offices.

Arrangements were made for holding six assemblies annually, from the 20th of January to the 20th of April, on weeks alternate with those of the Castle balls. From the list of original subscribers, twelve ladies were named to hold subscription-books for each year; and twenty of the gentlemen, whose names figured in the same category, were appointed to act as stewards. Among the ladies first marked as holders of subscription-books, were the Duchess of Leinster, the Countess of Shannon, the Countess of Charlemont, the Countess of Ross, the Viscountess Delvin, and the Viscountess Kingsborough. On those gala evenings the amusements began at eight o'clock, with a concert of instrumental music in the Rotunda. Tea, coffee, lemonade, etc., were served in the recesses, and the cardrooms prepared for reception. Precisely at nine o'clock a band struck up in the ballroom, and English country dances commenced; while, at the same time, another band began to play in the Rotunda, where French country dances were formed. Supper was served at twelve o'clock, on twenty tables for fifteen persons each, "covered alike to prevent crowding, and to avoid any question of preference." The caterers undertook to provide articles of excellent quality, but "convenience and cleanliness were to be attended to rather than show" Among his duties, each of the twenty stewards had the charge

[1] *Life of James Gandon*, chap. vii. The writer adds that the citizens of Dublin are likewise indebted to Mr. Trench for his exertions in carrying out other improvements in the city, and that common gratitude should long since have placed a statue to his memory in one of the niches of that capacious [illegible] hospital for whose [illegible] manent benefit be [illegible]

of providing his table with two or more servants of his own, and he was held answerable for the conduct of the men.

Dancing certainly *was* dancing in those days; and that the select company should have an opportunity of practising their steps, mastering the intricacies of the graceful maze, and advancing in the art of deportment, a rule was framed with this view. It was resolved: "That in order to assist the Instruction, and to accommodate the Pupils of the principal Masters, free Admission Tickets (not transferable) be sent to some of the principal Instructors in Dancing in this City." No spectators or servants, however, except attendants, should on any account be permitted to intrude into the Rotunda, halls, or passages.

Departures were regulated with due attention to order. Carriages drew up at the door to Great Britain Street, private sedan-chairs waited in the hospital-yard, where no numbered chair should be permitted to appear under any pretence whatsoever; and public sedans stood in Cavendish Street, the great door into which was opened immediately after supper.

That *noblesse oblige* was not forgotten by the promoters of these elegant amusements, we learn from the paragraph that graces and winds up the prospectus of the public assemblies' scheme. "It remains with Ladies and Gentlemen of the first Rank," says this document, "to determine whether this Entertainment shall be of real use to Society as well as to the Charity. Their constant Presence in the narrow Circle of a Dublin Assembly must awe into propriety and repress every Species of improper Conduct that an indiscriminate Association might occasion."

About this time a new source of emolument was opened to the infatigable trustees. By an Act of 25th George III, granted in 1785, the governors of the hospital were empowered to levy a tax on private sedan-chairs; or, in legal phrase, "to collect and levy the sum of Thirty-five shillings and sixpence sterling for every sedan-chair which any person shall keep in his or her possession, in the city of Dublin, or within one mile thereof." To families of position, in those days, one or two chairs were an indispensable luxury, almost a necessary of life. Gentlemen like Henry Grattan, for instance, did not disdain the use of the sedan; and the ladies accomplished their shopping expeditions with the aid of the same conveyance.

Sometimes the chairs were elegantly painted and ornamented, and it was considered good style to have a troop of laced lackeys in attendance, besides the indispensable chairmen or porters.

Obliged by the Act to publish annually the names, in alphabetical order, of the several persons who had taken out a licence for keeping private sedan-chairs, with their places of residence, the governors took advantage of the occasion to issue, in 1788, a small volume containing the required list, and a great deal of matter besides. In accordance with the fashion of the day, the title-page of this curious little book is in itself voluminous, running thus: "A List of the Proprietors of Private Sedan-Chairs at 25th March 1788, alphabetically ranged, with their respective Residences, published as required by Law. A List of the original Subscribers towards building the public Rooms, and establishing six annual Assemblies: to which are added the Conditions; and also a Scheme for Card Assemblies, etc., with remarks on the State of the Lying-in Hospital, its Buildings, and their present unfinished Condition. There are likewise reinserted (as it may not be necessary to intrude again on the Public), the Charter, Bye-Laws, Tables, Statements, etc. Printed by Order of the Governors of said Hospital."

Moreover, this "List of Proprietors of Sedan-Chairs" is adorned with engravings. There are views of the hospital and new buildings, a plan of the Rotunda and Assembly Rooms, a facsimile of the admission ticket, and the coats-of-arms of thirty-two of the principal annual subscribers, and of nine benefactors who left bequests to the hospital, varying from £300 to £1000.

That the trustees had their own trouble in collecting the chair-tax, may be gathered from the tone of their address to "their very respectable tenantry, the proprietors of private licensed sedan-chairs." Some of the Right Honourable and Honourable tenants are in arrear; and this is particularly inconvenient, considering that "Duties of this Nature, accruing from persons of the first rank, cannot always be collected in the ordinary Modes." However deferential they may be to these first-rank defaulters, they are no fools; and they intimate politely, but plainly, that when they "solicit their tenantry into complianc [illegible] ery trifling amount might be levied in another way, namely, by distress, sale, and suchlike methods, sanctioned by the express terms of the statute. Nay, they even venture to hint at the possibility of calling in the aid of "the executive Civil Power of this City," that is to say, the police, who are joint-proprietors with them, and who, having to collect their own moiety (ten shillings for each of these chairs), might as well get in the hospital rents at the same time.

Besides the no-renters of the first rank, there were other members of the respectable tenantry who were not above resorting to the "pitiful practice" of vacating a number when in arrear, and taking a new one. Very properly the trustees put a stop to this abuse, by considerably increasing the fine on taking out a licence. In spite of all drawbacks, the chair-tax appears to have increased the hospital income by about £440 per annum.

Part of the fund thus derived was spent on improving the approaches to the Rotunda. None but really stupid people could fancy that this was other than a useful and effective piece of work, but the way in which the trustees deprecate any attempt at faultfinding is curious. "Those who recollect," say they, "the Termination of Sackville Street, half obscured by a shed for Chairmen, the ruinous wall and Entrance to the Rotunda, and the Deformity of its roof, must possess uncommon Prejudices not to be sensible of some Change."

Improvements of a more extensive character had been undertaken some time before, when the high wall enclosing the gardens was taken down, and its place supplied by a dwarf wall surmounted by a railing, thickly set with lamps. In 1787 all these improvements were completed, and the governors might well be excused if they surveyed their domain with pride. Handsome houses, fit dwellings for the noblest in the land, had been erected in regular line on the north and west sides of the enclosure, forming thus, with the hospital and Cavendish Street, a complete square. These new rows of mansions were known respectively as Palace Row and Granby Row; but it was thought that so elegant a square should have rank and title as such, and receive an appropriate name. The responsible parties did what was right and proper under the circumsta[illegible] was the title formally conferred on the gardens and the rows of mansions overlooking the enclosure.

There were forty-eight tenements in all, regularly built, and numbered in the same order as at the present day. Each house made an annual payment to the hospital: the sums varying according to the contents of each frontage and the number of private lamps at the door. One shilling and ninepence per foot was paid by these tenements for the lights on the garden rails, and as a percentage to the hospital; and threepence per foot was levied for painting said rails. No house had less than two private lamps in front. Some had three. One only, Lord Charlemont's, lighted four. Each lamp was rated at £1, 14s. od. The smallest house in the square was number 48, and its payments under the above heads amounted to £5. os. 4d. The largest, Charlemont House, paid £16, 16s. od. The governors of the hospital, being now a corporate body, undertook, besides the lighting of the square, its supervision by a proper watch and patrol.

Admirable as was the action of the governors, in thus caring for and beautifying the property under their charge, they by no means occupied a singular position in this respect. It was a season of life, hope, and movement; extensive projects were on foot for the improvement of the city, and a vast deal in this direction had been already accomplished within a very few years. Far down the river, on a waste expanse, the new Custom House was rising up in stately beauty. Higher up on its banks the new Law Courts were in course of construction. Preparations were being made for extending Sackville Street to the water's edge, and connecting it, by a bridge,[1] with a new street to be opened from the College to the river. The new front to the House of Lords was nearing completion; and, in the sculpture-yard adjoining, the colossal statues of Justice,

[1] Gandon's original design for Carlisle Bridge was magnificent. He intended it for a triumphal bridge to commemorate the achievements of the army and navy during the reign of George III. Ten thousand pounds were saved by the adoption of a simpler design. The bridge, as erected, was considered to supply all reasonable requirements. It was wider than either Westminster Bridge or Blackfriars' Bridge in London.—*Life of Gandon.* [Carlisle Bridge has been recently replaced by "O'Connell Bridge," the full [illegible] bridge in Europe.]

Fortitude, and Liberty, intended to surmount the pediment, were being executed in Portland stone.

Revisiting Dublin, after a few years' absence, strangers were astonished at the changes that had taken place in the interval, both with regard to its order and general appearance. John Kemble, for instance, staying here in July 1788, writes to his friend, Edmund Malone, who was then in England, that the city is, in every particular which his observation can reach, "incredibly improved." The lights, he adds "are as regularly sustained by night as they are in London", and though the citizens "affect to be oppressed in various shapes by the institution of the police," he knows "they keep the streets ten thousand times more orderly than the old watchmen ever did."[1] Mr. Woodfall, in the letter we have already referred to, writes thus to Mr Eden: "You, who were here so lately, would scarcely know this city, so much is it improved, and so rapidly is it continuing to improve After the talk of the misery of the people, in our Parliament, and in the Parliament here, I cannot but feel daily astonishment at the nobleness of the new buildings, and the spacious improvements hourly making in the streets I am sometimes tempted to suspect appearances, and to think I am at table with a man who gives me Burgundy, but whose attendant is a bailiff disguised in livery In a word, there never was so splendid a metropolis in so poor a country."[2]

To the general waking-up of the nation, effected by the volunteer movement, and to the liberality of the House of Commons in undertaking the cost of public works, this commendable activity and its admirable results were mainly due. Much, also, must be set down to the professional ability and to the disinterested exertions of individuals. The Hon. John Beresford, First Commissioner of the Revenue, and James Gandon, the architect, did more for the improvement of Dublin than any other men of that day or of more recent days.[3] In justice,

[1] *Life of Edmund Malone.*

[2] The writer concludes his paragraph with a query worth producing here. "Why," he asks, "do not those who see this and say it, fairly apply a remedy—encourage their tenantry, dispel the national sloth and indolence of the lower orders of the people, promote industry, and teach their inferiors the blessings of independence, and the happiness of living comfortably [illegible]?"

[3] See "[illegible] this volume.

it must also be said that the Duke of Rutland did all that a viceroy, of such taste, judgment, and princely spirit, might be expected to do for the encouragement of the elegant art of architecture, and the improvement of the seat of his government. Gandon, in jotting down his recollections of this period in the history of Dublin, thus speaks of the Lord-Lieutenant's influence on art and on society.

"During the progress of the new Custom House, Docks, Stores, House of Lords, etc., Ireland was fortunate in having a Chief Governor, one of the most illustrious noblemen who have resided in this country, in the person of His Grace the late Duke of Rutland. The entire country seemed animated by his influence and splendid hospitality. The city of Dublin assumed an unwonted gaiety, and the tradesmen and manufacturers of every description hailed with exultation the arrival of such an illustrious Chief Governor. All public amusements were patronised in such a manner as not only to gratify the public, but the parties volunteering for public approbation; the most eminent theatrical performers and composers of that time sought the Irish metropolis; nor were painting, sculpture, nor, more particularly, architecture, neglected, as ample encouragement was given to the professors of eminence in the different branches of the Fine Arts. In consequence, several eminent artists were induced to settle in Dublin. During the many years I have resided in Ireland, the Duke of Rutland was the only Chief Governor who could find leisure to pay the least attention to the Fine Arts. In England, His Grace had employed and encouraged several of the most eminent painters of his time. Shortly after his arrival in Dublin, he ordered all the old pictures which were in the Lodge in the Phœnix Park to be taken down, and supplied their places with part of his collection of modern painters."

Meanwhile, the lovely duchess, and the gay crowd following in her train, lent animation and picturesqueness to the scene. She, to whom men thought that Burke's description of Marie Antoinette might well be applied,—"glittering like the morning star, full of life, splendour, and joy,"—was the centre of attraction wherever she appeared. Her favourite drive was the North Circular Road, and a brilliant scene that country avenue presented [illegible] ...ton, drawn by [illegible] preceded by outriders in splendid liveries, might be expected to issue from the Park. Sunday was the great day for the drive Lord Cloncurry tells us, in his *Personal Recollections*, that it was the custom on that day for all the great folk to rendezvous in the afternoon upon the North Circular Road, and that he frequently saw three or four coaches-and-six, and eight or ten coaches-and-four, passing slowly to and fro, in a long procession of other carriages, and between a double column of well-mounted horsemen. "Of course, the populace," he adds, "were there, too, and saluted with friendly greetings, always kindly and cordially acknowledged, the lords and gentlemen of the country party, who were neither few in number nor insignificant in station." His lordship further notes that the evenings of those Sundays were commonly passed by the same parties in promenading at the Rotunda. "I have frequently seen there," he says, "of a Sunday evening, a third of the members of the two Houses of Parliament"

But the elegant equipage and the charming duchess were to be seen occasionally in quarters not so fashionable as the North Circular Road. In some way or another it had reached Her Grace's ears that there was actually in Dublin a handsomer woman than herself; and one day she drove to Francis Street, an important trading centre in those days, and, alighting from her carriage, entered the shop of a woollen draper named Dillon, whose wife it was that had the reputation of surpassing even the Duchess of Rutland in beauty. On asking for Mrs Dillon, Her Grace was ushered into the parlour, and received with perfect ease by the object of her curiosity: a tall, magnificently-formed woman, all sweetness and dignity. It was the duchess who was embarrassed in the *rencontre*. Soon recovering herself, however, she took Mrs. Dillon's hand, and frankly told her the object of her visit. She had been under the impression, she said, that she was herself the handsomest woman in Ireland, until someone told her that in face and figure Mrs. Dillon far surpassed her. Now she knew how true this was. "You are, indeed," she exclaimed, "the most beautiful woman in the three kingdoms!"[1]

[1] The "Emigrant Milesian" gives this little scene in full detail. Much more, too, he has to say of the brilliant duchess—and many a piquant trait he gives of the duke. Between forty and fifty years afterwards he saw Her Grace in [illegible] ity."

Contemporary newspapers and memoirs treating of the period give us glimpses of "His Grace, the Lord-Lieutenant and our vice-queen," on the occasion of visits made in the provinces. They were in Limerick in October 1785, and at an assembly in that city the duchess danced with Mr. Beresford, son of the Bishop of Ossory. During the same season they visited Cork, and graced a similar entertainment. On that occasion the duchess was attired in light pink silk, with diamond stomacher and sleeve knots, and had on a large brown hat trimmed with red ribbon, and decorated with a great quantity of jewels. In this costume she opened the ball with the Honourable Richard Hely Hutchinson. His Excellency appeared in fawn-coloured waistcoat and breeches, and a green coat, trimmed with gold, and wore the insignia of the Order of St. Patrick.

Next year the duke and duchess joined a Christmas party at Dangan Castle, and were the guests of Colonel and Mrs. St. George, to whom, on their marriage two months before, Lord Mornington lent his noble residence in Meath. In the viceroy's suite came Lord Westmeath, Lord Fitzgibbon, General Pitt, General Conyngham, "some of the prettiest women and a group of the gayest young men." The bride, then but a short way in her nineteenth year, thought herself in Elysium for half the first week, but soon grew weary of the ceaseless round of dissipation. Night was turned into day, "for no obvious reason, as all hours in the twenty-four were equally free from interruption"; the conversation of some of the ladies was not very edifying; and it was tiresome work "playing commerce with a party of women, impatient for the hour of eleven, —which usually brought the men," said the fair hostess, "in a state very unfit for the conversation or even the presence of our sex."[1]

There was no exaggeration, he says, in the compliment paid to Mrs Dillon by her noble visitor. He saw her in her country house, at a place called Roper's Rest, and never forgot the admiration her appearance created in him It appears that Mrs. Dillon was as much distinguished by modesty, grace, and charity as she was by her singular beauty. Mr. Dillon was connected by birth with the family of Viscount Dillon. But, like nearly all the well-to-do Catholics of his time, he was glad to be allowed to live unmolested, and work in obscurity. The woollen trade, however, in all its branches, took precedence of every other trade in Ireland, and r[illegible]

[1] *The Re*[illegible] which

Towards the close of 1787 the duke visited the north of Ireland. He was magnificently received by the Marquis of Downshire, the Earl of Moira, and other noblemen and gentlemen, and superbly entertained by the town of Belfast. This, however, was the last of the viceregal progresses. An illness, "the consequence of too much conviviality," attacked the duke on the road, turned to putrid fever on his return to the capital, and speedily closed his days. One more pageant, grand but melancholy, and the Rutland reign was over. On the 27th of November, the minute guns in the Phœnix Park commenced firing at six o'clock in the morning, and the bells of the churches rang their dead peals during the day. The duke's remains, which had lain in state in an anteroom of the House of Lords, were borne in a long procession through the streets to the platform on the North Wall, where the barge waited with the king's boat to receive the body, and convey it to His Majesty's yacht Nothing so imposing in its way had ever been seen in Ireland. Eight horses drew the mourning chariot, which was preceded by the town major, attended by a troop of horse. A train of Irish artillery, and, in fact, the whole army establishment, formed part of the procession. Standards of the Order of the Garter and of the Order of St. Patrick were borne on lances. The rectors and vicars of the city, the Lord Mayor, the Lords Justices, the Governors of the Bank, the nobility—all took their place in the sad cortege.[1]

Thus was brought to a sudden termination the short but brilliant viceroyalty of Charles Manners, Duke of Rutland. The Marquis of Buckingham succeeded as Chief Governor. Society, sobered for a moment by the untimely death of its leader, speedily resumed its air of careless gaiety, pursued unchecked its round of dissipation, and contrived to ignore,

began with a honeymoon at Dangan, was happy, but of very short duration. Mrs. St. George was a widow at twenty-two years of age. After some years she married Mr. Richard Trench. Their distinguished son, Archbishop Trench, published, when Dean of Westminster, selections from his mother's Journals, Letters, and other papers. The book portrays, incidentally, a very charming character, is full of interesting sketches of Irish, English, and continental society, and gives many a portrait in words of personages remarkable in their day, and in some cases famous still.

[1] Such is the account given in the *Annual Register*, 1787. A detailed description of the funeral procession may be found in Walker's *Hibernian Magazine* o

( )

conveniently, the signs of the times forecasting the Insurrection of 1798 and the Union of 1801. Thanks to the charity that covereth a multitude of sins, the hospital treasury was liberally replenished. Fortunately, also, its affairs were prudently administered, and its troop of friends constantly recruited from the ranks of the powerful and energetic. Year after year fashion maintained its headquarters in the neighbourhood of which the hospital, with its annexes, formed the veritable centre.[1]

Among those who had residences in Rutland Square during the twenty years preceding the Union, may be mentioned the Earls of Charlemont, Bective, Grandison, Farnham, Carhampton, Erne, Enniskillen, Darnley, Wandesford, Ormonde, and the Countess of Longford; Viscount Wicklow, Viscount Caledon, and Lord Templeton; the Bishop of Limerick, the Bishop of Kilmore, and the Bishop of Leighlin and Ferns, to say nothing of a host of Right Honourables, Honourables, and Members of the House of Commons

In Sackville Street might be found at home the Earls of Westmeath, Drogheda, Glandore, and Altemont; Viscounts Bangor, Netterville, Gosford, Pery, Belmore, and Southwell, Lord Leitrim and Lord Sunderlin; and fifteen Members, at least, of the House of Commons.

Gardiner's Row included the town residences of the Earls of Carrick, Ross, Aldborough, and Arran; and the domicile of Lord Norbury.

In Great Denmark Street dwelt the Earl of Belvidere, the Earl of Fingal, Viscount Charleville, and Lord Tullamore.

Viscount Kenmare and Viscount Dunlo, Lords Kilconnel, Ougley, and Lismore lived in North Great George's Street.

The Marquis of Waterford and the Earl of Annesley occupied mansions in Marlborough Street.

Morning, noon, and night this aristocratic population kept circulating, as the French would say, within and without the Rotunda, the new buildings, and the favourite gardens. Subscribers had access to the gardens at all times, and thither

[1] Referring to this subject, a contemporary publication says: "The Lying-in Hospit[illegible] of the city, and i[illegible]

resorted the dames of high estate to take their exercise in the morning and early afternoon, while the lords and gentlemen played at bowls in the lower part of the grounds. Assemblies, masquerades, concerts, and promenades attracted the gay throng on week-day evenings. On Sundays they came in the forenoon to attend divine service, and occupy the seats they rented in the beautifully decorated chapel; and at a later hour they made their appearance, as we have said, in the brilliant promenade.

The average receipts from the Gardens, the Rotunda, and the Public Assembly Rooms, from 1789 to 1796, amounted to £4000 per annum.

Certainly it was a strange vocation for an hospital, this office of catering for the amusement of its circumjacent population of aristocrats. As already observed, the nobility and gentry objected not at all to the presence of a charitable institution in the heart of the locality sacred to rank and fashion. But how strange it must have seemed to the patients, that an hospital should be kept up in the midst of such surroundings. What with the rolling of coach-wheels far into the night, the shouting of the chairmen, and the cries of the link-boys; what with the flashing of carriage-lamps, and the flaring of flambeaux, the accustomed silence and the natural darkness of the midnight hour must have been completely chased away.

Gaily thus the years sped on, until, one day, the joyous movement ceased, and the brilliant spectacle vanished like a scene of a panorama. During 1798, and the following troubled years, the Rotunda and Assembly Rooms were turned into a barrack; and the door-posts of the houses bore the unmistakable signs of a state of siege, namely, a list of the persons (good and faithful subjects, be it understood) dwelling in each mansion. The district which shortly before had been the vortex of fashionable life, looked like nothing so much as a section of Paris during the Reign of Terror.

Then followed the Union, making the desolation permanent. When Ireland lost her legislative independence, Dublin lost the titled and territorial magnates who had made the city a brilliant capital. The hospital was well-nigh ruined by the change, which deprived the institution of the liberal aid of the Irish House of Commons, the patronage of a resident and charitable [illegible] ing of the Rotunda and its adjuncts as long as there remained a wealthy and a pleasure-loving population to seek amusement within the area set apart for music and dancing, play and promenade.

Later, the Rotunda assumed a new and far from unimportant office, and was the scene of many a memorable meeting and many a stormy debate. But into its subsequent history we shall not enter in these pages

IRISH WOOL AND WOOLLENS

I.

FOUR or five years ago, having occasion to open a history of Florence in search of some information relating to the trade guilds of that famous seat of liberty and commerce, I came upon an interesting account of the style of living prevalent among the citizens of Firenze la Bella in the fourteenth century of our era. Their dress, their dwellings, their entertainments were minutely described; and the prices of sundry articles of daily consumption and various materials for clothing and house furnishing were likewise quoted. Among entries of manufactured goods imported by the merchants of the republic, my eye caught the words, "white Irish serge, five and fivepence farthing per ell."

Can it be possible, thought I, that any product of Irish industry found for itself a demand in the luxurious Italy of five hundred years ago?

Forthwith, I looked through all the books I could lay my hand on which seemed likely to furnish information concerning the manufacture and export of Irish serge in days gone by. Not finding what I sought in my calf-bound authorities that talk in type, I addressed myself to a walking encyclopædia of my acquaintance, a gentleman of prodigious memory, whose knowledge of Irish affairs—historical, antiquarian, political, and domestic—seems altogether inexhaustible, and whose reservoir of archaic lore overflows in a torrent of living speech in answer to any demand made by an intelligent querist, be he adversary [illegible] ...ly short time I obtained all

( )

the information I could have hoped for anent the woollen exports of mediæval Ireland, and furthermore became enriched with a miscellany of *viva voce* notes on Irish trade in general, and the Italian poets of the age of Dante in particular, the illustrious Earl of Charlemont, and the flocks and herds of ancient Erin; the patriots of '82, and the historians who *love and make a lie*, the mistakes and misdeeds of which this country has been the victim from A.D. 1169 even to the hour when the query about Irish serge was propounded by the present writer.

However, the ascertained points most germane to the matter are the following, namely, that Fazio degli Uberti, a celebrated Italian poet, who towards the middle of the fourteenth century wrote a description, in *terza rima*, of the countries he explored in the course of his travels through the world, relates, in his poem entitled *Ditta Mundi*, how, having seen England, he passed into Ireland—a country *worthy of renown*, as he says, *for the beautiful serges she sends us*; that, in the *Dizionario della Crusca*, under the heading of "Saia" (serge), an example is given of the use of the term "saia d'Irlanda" from an old ledger, in which is charged "a piece of Irish serge to make a dress for Andrea's wife"; and that the patriotic Lord Charlemont having, during his lengthened sojourn in Italy, come across a copy of Fazio's extremely rare work, transcribed the interesting passage above alluded to, and subsequently brought it under the notice of the recently founded Royal Irish Academy, as a remarkable evidence of the extent of Irish commerce and the success of Irish manufactures at a remote period of our history.

From that day forward, whenever, in the course of desultory rambles over the highways and byways of Irish history, I came on any reference to Irish wool or Irish cloth, forthwith I made a note thereon, without any more definite purpose, however, than to store up, against some possible eventuality in the future, facts which, if not seized on the moment, might elude research in the hour of need.

Only the other day, when inquiring for a certain statistical treatise in a library stocked with works on arts and manufactures, I learnt by chance that a reader—presumably a gentleman of the press—had just been asking whether some book on the Irish woollen [illegible] be laid

Ur

before him, but had received for answer that no such work was procurable, although the collection numbered several volumes on the cognate subject of the linen trade. I could not but think that, although no special work on Irish woollens might be named by the aid of which an article could be got up in hot haste for a morning paper, there nevertheless exists, both in public and private libraries, ample material for an essay on that highly important subject, if one had only time and patience to run through histories, pamphlets, statute books, travels, and memoirs, set in order the gathered notes, and reduce the mass of information to a readable form.

The Irish wool trade has a history far from deficient in variety and incident. It was dealt with, in a fair spirit generally, by English legislation from an early period of the Anglo-Norman occupancy to the reign of William and Mary. But from 1699 to 1779, it was proscribed by statutes as inimical to social happiness and public morals, as was the penal code directed against the religion of the majority of the population. Possibly the laws that annihilated the wool trade wrought more destruction than the legislation that aimed at stamping out the Catholic faith; for the Trade Acts snatched bread from the mouth, filched hope from the heart, and wrenched power from the hands of the industrial sections of the community.

But though the trade was sentenced to destruction, the spirit evoked by the deed was not set at rest for generations. Irish wool assumed an importance seldom enjoyed by a staple of manufacture. First, it was a party cry, fierce and minatory, and then it swelled to a national outcry, which artillery could not silence. English Parliaments were convulsed by it, and Irish Parliaments were disgraced or immortalised according as they sacrificed or set free the wool. The question wove itself into the checkered web, one hundred years long, of Irish history. This it was that rallied the volunteers. The air they marched to had words set to it with a refrain ringing of the wool, and Napper Tandy acted under the same inspiration when he suspended from the necks of the volunteer guns labels inscribed with the words, *Free Trade or Speedy Revolution!* If not dyed red as scarlet on ensangumed fields, the wool had at anyrate a tinge of romance imparted to it by the adventure connected with its contraband transport to foreign countries, and its association with the flight of the Wild Geese and the escape of hunted priests under favour of the smuggler's sail. Popular songs kept alive the pathos and the pain of the story. In winter evenings beside the hearth, and on summer nights beneath the moon, the peasants sang, to strains of native music, wild and plaintive, the lament of the hapless maiden ruthlessly robbed of the *Suisin Buidhe*,—the "Yellow Blanket,"—which cloaked in allegory the legend of the ruined trade.[1] Literature, too, had a thread of wool run through its pages. An essay of inconsiderable length, but a masterpiece of the English tongue, thrown off in obedience to a generous impulse to retrieve the fortunes of the injured wool, received the distinction of being branded by a grand jury as a scandalous, seditious, and factious pamphlet. A small volume, dictated in a singularly calm and reasonable spirit, as would be thought in our days, but discoursing plainly of the wool, earned a yet severer penalty, and was publicly burned by the hands of the common hangman. And these pieces of "dangerous" and ill-treated literature were not the production of men undistinguished by their character, capacity, and position, but were the work respectively of Jonathan Swift, Dean of St. Patrick's, and William Molyneux, member for the University of Dublin.

It is not my intention, I need hardly observe, to endeavour to write an exhaustive paper on Irish wool and woollens, though I fancy I can discern the lines on which such an essay might run, and very much wish that someone would do the industrial cause so good a service. But as, at this moment, the subject of home products and manufactures occupies a good deal of attention, the wool as usual coming to the front, I think it just possible that Irishmen at such a juncture may not be unwilling to refresh their memory of past readings, and to lend me their attention while I run through some rough notes, and open at marked passages a score or so of volumes lying conveniently at hand.

[1] The air of *Suisin Buidhe* will be found in the valuable and enlarged edition of Bunting's *Ancient Music of Ireland*, published in 1840. "Very old; author and date unknown," is the note given in the margin by the compiler of the work. There are persons still living who remember in their childhood hearing the country people singing, with extraordinary feeling, the [illegible]

II.

In the day when Lord Charlemont wrote his paper on the antiquity of the woollen manufacture in Ireland,[1] it was thought a great deal to cite, in support of the thesis, records of the date of Edward III., bearing evidence to the high repute, at home and abroad, of Irish friezes, serges, and stuffs in that monarch's reign. Further inquiry led to the conclusion that woollen garments were in use among the natives many centuries before the English landed on these shores. Not, however, until our own day were proofs positive forthcoming of old Erin's possession of a home manufacture of cloths of great value and beauty, as well as of fabrics of coarser style. Within the last forty years the labours of our antiquaries, the publications of our archælogical societies, and, above all, the deciphering of the ancient laws of Ireland, have revealed, as existing in the past, a state of things hitherto unimagined, and thrown a strong light on the social and domestic life of the primitive, but by no means barbarous, inhabitants of the land of the Gael.

References to the teasing, carding, combing, and other processes by which the wool was prepared, and to the spinning, weaving, napping, and dyeing of the cloth, occur in the Brehon Laws. The woollen manufacture in all its branches was carried on by the women of the tribes; and these laws lay down very precisely the divisions of the raw material, and of the cloth in different stages of its manufacture, which a woman should be entitled to take with her in case of separation from her husband, the proportions being adjusted evidently by an estimate of the amount of labour expended by the wife on the wool or on the fabric. Equally with the fleeces, the dye stuffs were of home growth, and great attention was devoted to the procuring of pure and beautiful colours, in a variety of shades. A fine blue was much admired, green was a favourite colour, and a plant, now unknown, was grown in ridges for dyeing cloth a "splendid crimson red." Party-coloured, striped, and spotted cloths were also esteemed. Industry and art enabled the spinning and weaving women not only to keep up the stock of material required for the ordinary clothing of the tribe, but also to provide the splendid mantles in which the kings and chiefs figure so conspicuously in song and story. These mantles were considered princely presents, when offered by one great man to another; and the provincial kings, valuing them as so much treasure, took them in form of tribute from their subordinate chiefs. In fact, as an article of revenue, manufactured cloth appears to have ranked next to live stock. In the *Book of Rights*, wherein "the revenues of the principalities and the laws of the rights of the provincial kingdoms, and of the tributes and rents given to them and by them," are precisely stated, we find cloth and cattle set down together. Thus, the King of Cashel is entitled to receive from one of his tributaries 1000 cloaks and 1000 milch cows; while from others, together with hogs or cattle, he exacts cloaks with white borders, or napped cloaks trimmed with purple, or mantles all variegated. Connaught is not behindhand in the quantity and quality of the cloth produced by her petty states. One tributary is taxed to the amount of thrice fifty superb cloaks, and others must find royal cloaks, or cloaks of strength, or speckled cloaks, or purple cloaks of fine brilliance. Dye stuffs were likewise taken in tribute Ancient legends, poems, and lives of saints, also abound in references to the manufacture and use of woollen garments in Ireland, and to the importance assigned to the princely mantle. For example, in the *Táin Bó Chuaighne*, an epic poem of considerable antiquity, a description occurs of the personal appearance and dress of the Ulster chiefs as they arrive, with their hosts, at the camp of Connor. A comely champion, with deep red-yellow bushy hair, and sparkling blue laughing eyes, appears on the scene with a red and white cloak fluttering around him, fastened at the breast with a golden brooch; while another warrior, dark-visaged and black-haired, proudly advances, leading on his company, and wearing a red shagg cloak with a silver fastening. A white-hooded cloak, with a flashing red border, and many other varieties of the ample and splendid garment, are also described. Other ancient MSS are also rich in word-pictures of this kind. The ladies' flowing mantles are, of course, not left out of the tableau. For instance, the poet does not forget to record that the heroine of a story appeared in all the splendour of "a lustrous crimson cloak of dazzling sheen." [1]

[1] O'Curry, ... *ish*,

For centuries succeeding the heroic period, Irish kings and warriors continued to display in Court and camp these much-prized mantles. Sometimes, too, the splendid garments strewed the field when their owners lost a battle. Thus it is recorded, that among the spoils left by the sons of Brian Roe, when they fled from Mortogh, in 1313, were "shining scarlet cloaks." Military mantles, of a style better suited to a rough campaign, were adopted on occasions by soldiers equipped for hard service. Mr. Halliday, in a posthumous work,[1] notes, from the *Annals of Ireland*, that in A.D. 938 a chosen army of 1000 men marched from Aileach, prepared for a winter campaign by sheep-skin mantles provided for them by Muirchedach, who thus gained the name of Muirchedach of the Leather Mantles.

While the upper ranks in Ireland prided themselves, throughout the Middle Ages, on the fine texture, rare fringes, costly trimmings, and elegant clasps of their mantles, and, moreover, indulged in a profusion of linen, the humbler classes of the population were habited in a garb almost entirely composed of woollen material, heavy or light in substance according to necessity. A thin stuff answered for shirting or vest; a thicker composed the tunic and the *trouse* or trowsers; and of a heavy rug or frieze was fashioned the cloak, which was as indispensable an article of attire to the peasant as to the chief. The women had longer mantles than the men, and wore them over a kirtle or gown which reached to the ankle.[2] A short cloak or cape, having a conical hood terminating in a tassel, was much worn by the men, and went by the name of *Cochal*, hence the English *cowl*, almost universally used for a hooded cloak or cape. "In the eighth century," observes Dr. W. K. Sullivan in his introductory volume to O'Curry's *Manners and Customs of the Ancient Irish*, "the *Cochal*, in the latinised form of *Cocula*, was considered, in Wales and other countries, as a characteristic of Irish dress; and the coarse long-napped woollen cloth of which it was made continued to be an important export of Ireland up to at least the middle of the fourteenth

(1873); *Manuscript Materials of Ancient Irish History*, by the same author (1861); The *Book of Rights*, edited by Dr O'Donovan, and published by the Celtic Society (1847).

[1] *The Scandinavian Kingdom of Dublin.* Edited, with some notice of the author's life, by J. P. Prendergast (1882)

[2] J. C. W[illegible] *[illegible] on the Dress, Armour and Weapons of the Irish* ([illegible])

century." The learned author adds, that the hooded cloak, until lately so common in this country, and still much worn by women in the South and West of Ireland, may be regarded as a modified descendant of the ancient *Cochal*, and that the frieze still corresponds to the description of the ancient material.

Not very long after the Anglo-Norman adventurers had made good their footing in the island, the governors of the pale became alarmed at discovering in the new settlers a dangerous tendency to adopt the Irish style of dress So objectionable did this fancy to appear in habit like the Irish seem to the maintainers of English rule, that active measures were taken to retain liege subjects in their proper apparel, and induce the native chiefs to favour foreign fashions. John, King of England and Lord of Ireland, who had had fair opportunities of becoming acquainted with the state of affairs in the latter kingdom, adopted means, which it must be acknowledged were not unprincely, of giving a desirable turn to the fashion of the day in clothes. Soon after he ascended the throne of his father, he addressed an order, as we read, to the Archbishop of Dublin, directing him to buy such a quantity of scarlets as he should judge sufficient to make robes (after the English mode it is conjectured) to be presented to the Kings of Ireland, and others of the kings' liegemen, natives of the kingdom.

Whether these personages wore with a good grace the "scarlets," cut after the pattern that seemed good to King John, history does not record; but there is abundant evidence to show that they transmitted no taste for novelty to their descendants, who stoutly adhered to ancestral and suspicious modes. "The barbaric splendour and quaintness of the Irish chiefs seems to have caught the fancy of the English settlers in the reign of Edward III., as we find the use of the Irish dress prohibited to them in the celebrated Statute of Kilkenny, passed during the administration of Edward's son, the Duke of Clarence One clause in this Act ordains that the English in Ireland shall conform in garb and in the cut of their hair to the fashion of their countrymen in England: whosoever affected that of the Irish should be treated as an Irishman, which obviously meant ill treated.""

This war of the Plantagenets was made not on Irish manufactures, be it noted, but on Irish tailoring. The red and white cloths of the country were on sale in England in the thirteenth century, and pieces of this description are enumerated as comprised in the effects of King John himself.[1] Amongst the different articles of dress stolen at Winchester by Walter Blowe-berme and Hamon le Stare, and which afterwards occasioned the celebrated duel between those gentlemen about the close of this reign, was a tunic of Irish cloth.[2] Edward III., who did more to encourage trade in England than any of his predecessors on the throne, and who made Ireland an equal participator in the advantages offered by his protection, showed particular favour to Irish frieze; for a statute passed in the twenty-eighth year of his reign exempts it from duty under the description of *Draps appellez frisewure queux sont faitz en Ireland.*

However, even the Statute of Kilkenny, though renewed in every Parliament till the year 1452, had little permanent effect in reforming the manners of the liegemen of the pale, who continued to find an irresistible attraction in the society of their neighbours across the border; and while delighting in the music, the sports, the story-telling by the hearth, and the pleasant freedom of the Irishry, shaped their beards, and arranged their hair, and cut their cloth after the fashion of the native Gael. Wrapped in their Irish mantles, these degenerate English refused to change their garments of predilection, or conform in such matters to the wishes of any king of England or any lord deputy of Ireland. An Act, passed in the reign of Henry VI., asserts that now there is no diversity in array betwixt the English marchours and the Irish enemies (*Irreys enemis to nostre seigneur le roy*), and proceeds to correct this evil.

In the reign of Edward IV. another advance was made, and not only the English of the pale, but the Irish dwelling in certain counties, were commanded to go appareled like Englishmen.[3]

[1] Gilbert, *Historical and Municipal Documents of Ireland* (English Rolls, A.D. 1172 1320). Preface.

[2] Quoted from *Kymer's Fadera* by Lord Charlemont and others

[3] "In order to counteract the efforts made by the English Government to destroy their ancient manners, the Irish exerted all their obstinacy to preserve [illegible] and refined manners [illegible] orian,

And still it seems to have been all in vain, for in the reign of Henry VII. the very lords of Ireland were wont to attend Parliament in the vesture of Irishmen. An Act was then passed ordering these personages to appear in the same parliament robes as those of England, under the penalty of a hundred shillings—a round sum in those days to levy off a lord.

Galway, a great commercial port, and a staunch English town in the main, did, nevertheless, give cause for displeasure, inasmuch as that the clothes of its inhabitants were not found of a piece with their principles. In an ordinance "gyvyn at our manor of Greenwych, the 28th day of April, in the 28th year of our reign," Henry VIII. (the first English prince, by the way, who assumed the style and title of King of Ireland), among other directions for the government of the town of Galway, enjoined, "that no man nor man-child do wear no mantles in the streets, but cloaks or gowns, coats, doublets, and hose shapen after the English fashion, but made of the country cloth or any other it may please them to buy."[1]

Other sumptuary regulations of the same reign had a more general application than the ordinance issued by the king to his well-beloved lieges of Galway. In one of these Acts, it is enjoined that no loyal woman should wear any kirtle or coat tucked up or embroidered with silk, or laid with uske after the Irish fashion, and that none should wear mantle, coat, or hood, of the said pattern.[2]

Waterford, also a prosperous and loyal town in those days, does not appear, from anything that I know, to have given the Government serious trouble on the subject of costume, although the manufacture of woollen cloths flourished on the banks of the Suir. Stanihurst, whose account of Ireland is published in Hollinshed's *Chronicles*, speaking of the Waterford men, says, "as they distill the best *aqua vitæ*, so they spin the

Froissart, 'of any amusements and polite behaviour, nor wishing to acquire any knowledge of good breeding, but to remain in their pristine rudeness.' This rudeness was but seeming: for the Irish knew how to live with foreigners, and to make themselves agreeable to them, especially if they were enemies of the English."—Augustin Thierry, *History of the Conquest of England by the Normans*. Conclusion, sect IV.

[1] The king's ordinance is given in Hardiman's *History of Galway*

[2] See reference [illegible] *[illegible]nnces and Land* [illegible]

choicest rug in Ireland", and he gives a curious instance of the value of this peculiar cloth in cold weather, and its close resemblance to a bear-skin. "A friend of mine," says the historian, "being of late demurant in London, and the weather by reason of a hoare-frost being somewhat nipping, repaired to Paris Garden clad in one of these Waterford rugs. The mastiffs had no sooner espied him, but, deeming he had been a beare, would fain have baited him; and were it not that the dogs were partly muzzled and partly chained, he doubted not that he should have been well tug'd in this Irish rug, whereupon he solemnly vowed never to see bear-baiting in any such weed."[1]

This is not the last we hear of the Irish rug or the Irish mantle. Spenser devotes some space—to use a phrase not known to the author of the *Faerie Queen*—to a description of the obnoxious garment; and Shakespeare alludes in a very marked way to the rug and the kernes who wore it. In fact, the advance of learning brought into action another engine for attacking a style of dress disapproved of by the party that had the press on its side. The mantle was stigmatised, arguments in favour of its suppression were advanced; "the Iryshe men, our naturall enemyes," had an objectionable way of concealing things, weapons and the like, under their mantle, "fit cloak for a thief"; they had a custom of wrapping the folds hastily about the left arm when attacked, "which serves them instead of a target";[2] in a foray, they would draw the hood or the cloak itself over their head, making it do service as a helmet: hence the epithet "rug-headed" as applied to the Irish;[3] nay more, this barbarous head-gear was only a too effectual mask when the worst villainy was in hand: "hooded men" meant assassins.

The mantle was written down, in a word, and became more

[1] Paris Garden, it will be remembered, was a place of public amusement in London, where the citizens enjoyed the barbarous pastime of bear-baiting. The passage from Stanihurst will be found in the work of Planché already quoted.

[2] In the *Encyclopædia of Costume* it is observed that this is a common practice in Spain at the present day. When looking through Doré's *Spain* lately, I was myself struck with the resemblance of the peasant's cloak, so frequently pictured in the book, to the Irish mantle—heavy, ample, and fringed—as described in historians' and poets' views of Ireland.

[3] "We must supplant those rough rug-headed kearns."—Richard II., act ii., ( )

than ever an object of peculiar abhorrence to the English. To strip the chiefs of their handsome mantles, and the people of their comfortable, water-tight, much-prized frieze cloaks, would have been looked on as a good stroke of statesmanship, and equal to a general disarmament of the common enemy.

But, though new means were adopted to bring the native costume into discredit, the old were not relinquished. It is amusing to read how Sir John Perrot, Queen Elizabeth's trusty Lord Deputy, took a leaf out of King John's book, and, having intimated that members habited in the Irish mantle and trouse should not be allowed to attend the Parliament he convoked in 1586, he proceeded to use the gentler arts of persuasion, and "bestowed both gownes and cloakes of velvet and satten" on some of the country gentlemen. "And yet," adds the historian, "the Irish chiefs thought not themselves so richly, or at least so contentedly, attired in their new costume as in their mantles and other country habits."[1]

Strange, indeed, would it have been, under these circumstances, if the government of Her Majesty's successor, "the Solomon of the age," did not devote some attention to the study of this philosophy of clothes. Anyhow, the importance of the question was not ignored. Reform was once more proclaimed throughout the length and breadth of the island. "The circuits of the judges were not now confined within the narrow limits of the pale, but extended through the whole kingdom, and the Lord Deputy Chichester, in 1615, directed that all sheriffs, justices of the peace, jurors, and other officers of justice, and freeholders, should attend all Sessions and Sitting Terms, wearing English attire and apparel, and that all who appeared at them in mantles, or robes, or wearing glibbs, should be punished by fine and imprisonment."[2]

[1] See an interesting note, in which this bit of history is given and a description of the trouse appended, in Archdeacon O'Rorke's *History of Ballysadare*, ch. iii.

[2] See, in Fitzgerald's *History of the County and City of Limerick*, vol. i., a preliminary view of the progress of civilisation, in which a great deal of Walker's information on Irish dress is confessedly embodied. The glibbes, so often mentioned with opprobrium, meant the Irish mode of wearing the hair in long locks hanging behind on the neck, and falling over the forehead in a manner resembling the "fringes" which ladies wear at the present day. In Ware's *Antiquities*, those who are curious in the matter will find a woodcut representing an Irishman with the long glibbes and dependent moustache so fondly cherished by the natives.

Stranger still would it have been, considering all the force and sapience expended in the attempt to reduce the Irish to a "conformitie, concordance, and familiaritie in language, tongue, in manners, order, and apparel with them *that be civil people*," if some persons in high office had not been able to persuade themselves that good government had triumphed at last, and the dawn of civilisation appeared. Accordingly, we find Sir John Davis, of happy memory, rejoicing in the successful carrying out of the late enactments. "These civil assemblies at Assizes and Sessions," writes His Majesty's Attorney-General of Ireland, "have reclaymed the Irish from their wildness, caused them to cut off their glibs and long haire; to convert their mantles into cloaks, to conform themselves to the manner of *England* in all their behaviour and outward forms." Furthermore, Sir John was led on to "conceive an hope that the next generation will, in tongue, and heart, and every way else, become *English*; so as there will be no difference or distinction, but the Irish Sea betwixt us."[1]

This interesting example of official complacency, and the art of *prophesying to us pleasant things*, would furnish a choice heading to a chapter of the history of Ireland in the seventeenth century Meanwhile, the women of Ireland continued spinning and weaving and dyeing the wool, and cutting the clothes of the nation according to the pattern handed down by their ancestors;[2] the men, and men-children, went on displaying, on every convenient occasion, a very decided and most "uncivil" preference for Irish versus English behaviour and costume; and the Fates, deaf to the thunders of royal ordinances, and the sweet persuasion of Elizabethan English, never ceased weaving the thread of Ireland's destiny into a fabric of quite another hue and texture from that contemplated in the prevision of the inspired law officer of "the wisest fool in Christendom."

1 "A Discoverie of the State of Ireland" (1613).

2 Sir William Petty, Surveyor-General of the kingdom of Ireland, speaking of the dress of the Irish peasantry in his day, says · "Their clothing is far better than that of the French peasants, or the poor of most other countries; which advantage they have from their wool, whereof twelve sheep furnish a competency to one of these families. Which wool, and the cloth made of it, doth cost these poor people no less than £50,000 *per ann.* for the dyeing it, a trade exercised by the women of the country."—*The Political Anatomy of Ireland* (1672)

III.

RETURNING to the point whence we took our departure, and diverging into another path, let us note what indications of a foreign trade in Irish wool, raw or manufactured, may chance to turn up. That Ireland, long before the Christian era, was the resort of the great trading communities of the then known world, that at the epoch of her conversion she had the advantage of well-established commercial relations with the neighbouring islands and the adjacent Continent; and that for succeeding centuries she maintained a profitable communication with Britain, Gaul, and Spain, are matters of history, and form the subject of interesting pages in Moore's *History of Ireland*, and in the work of Dr. W. K. Sullivan, which I referred to in the first part of this article.

No trace, however, of an export of cloth in those remote days have I come on; nor is there any evidence, as far as I know, that at a later period the Danes, whether in their plundering expeditions through the island or their trading settlements on the seaboard, made any store of the woolfels or the manufactured cloths of Ireland.

Authorities state, as an established fact, that Irish woollens were well known and highly valued long before England developed her cloth manufacture and acquired a foreign trade in that commodity. This, of course, supposes an export of the Irish product, at a time, too, when Italy and Flanders were at the head of the manufacturing industries of which wool is the staple. Certain it is that in the thirteenth and fourteenth centuries Ireland was much resorted to by trading companies from countries largely engaged in the wool trade. On the Dublin Guild merchant-rolls of that period we find registered representatives of almost every craft or trade from France, Brabant, and Flanders.[1] Flemish merchants, trading to Waterford, Youghal, and Cork, have left their mark in the records of the time.[2] Florentine and other Italian merchants and money-dealers carried on their operations in Dublin and the provincial towns. The Richardi of Lucca had agents at Ross, Kilkenny,

[1] *Historical and Municipal Documents of Ireland* (English Rolls, A.D. 1172–1320). Edited by J. T. Gilbert. Preface.

[2] Macpherson, *Annals of Commerce* (1805).

Limerick, Waterford, Youghal, and Cork. A petition in French from these merchants, praying the viceroy to inquire into certain losses they had sustained in Ireland, and a writ by which Edward I. directs his representatives to inquire into the allegations put forward in the complaint of his beloved merchants of the company of the Richardi, may be seen in the second volume of *Facsimiles of National Manuscripts of Ireland.* Mr. Gilbert, the editor of this splendid work, gives the facts relating to the trading transactions of the English mercantile houses in the letterpress accompanying the documents reproduced.

In those days, as from time immemorial, the great traffic of the country was carried on at fairs. Among the commodities bartered at these trading centres, cloths of various kinds are mentioned. There is even evidence to show that the Irish mantle caught the fancy of continental visitors, and was considered worthy of being transported across the Alps in days when luxury in dress was carried to excess in Italy; for it is on record that the pope's agent in England obtained a licence in 1382 for exporting certain articles custom-free, and that among these articles were five mantles of Irish cloth, one of them lined with green, and a russet garment lined with Irish cloth.

Such being the state of things, it is not so very surprising that Irish serges made their way to Florence. But that the high dames of the republic held the foreign fabric in estimation, and that the author of *Ditta Mundi* considered it worth his while to visit the remote island which produced so admired a material, are striking proofs of the excellence of the manufacture. "If in the middle of the fourteenth century," to quote Lord Charlemont, "the serges of Ireland were eagerly sought after and worn with a preference by the polished Italians, and particularly by the Florentines, it must have been for the excellence of their quality, for Machiavelli, in his *History of Florence*, says (1830) that the woollen manufacture had long been established at Florence That year the corporation of woollen weavers was the greatest and most powerful in Florence, containing in it, and presiding over, many ancillary trades, such as carders, dyers, etc." The workshops of the wool trade in Florence, we learn from other authorities, amounted to 200, and there were besides 20 warehouses of the *Calimala* or trade in the transalpine fabrics which imported more than

10,000 pieces The merchants of the *Calimala* ranked second among the *Arti*, or guilds, into which professions and trades were divided—that of the Doctors of Laws and notaries taking precedence, the bankers holding the third place, and the wool merchants, with the dyers and dressers, following. More than 30,000 souls were employed in the woollen manufacture; and it is said that, at a single fair, woollen goods to the amount of 12,000,000 crowns were sometimes sold The merchants of Florence were not only rich and powerful, but held their heads very high. They were everywhere considered fit company for princes. None of the superior trades and few of the others were beneath a citizen's attention, even in the highest families. Their sons were early placed in shops or warehouses—first in Florence and then abroad. They travelled from country to country, becoming acquainted with the world and acquiring cultivation and experience of the most valuable kind. In point of fact, every citizen, no matter what his rank, should enrol himself a member of one or another of the *Arti*.[1] Dante's parents, it will be remembered, were of the guild of wool

Who knows but that Fazio degli Uberti, noble though he was, may have known something otherwise than by hearsay of the Saia d'Irlanda? Who knows but that he may have seen something of the world beyond the Alps even before he made the circuit commemorated in the *Ditta Mundi*?[2]

[1] Napier, *Florentine History*, vol. ii (1846): Arthur Young, *Travels during the Years* 1787–88–89, second edition (1794). The last-named writer traces the excellence of the Florentine fabrics to the Friars Umiliate, who came to the city, in 1239, to improve the manufacture of woollen cloth. They made the finest cloths of the age. He says that he was assured, when at Florence, that an assessment of one shilling a week on the wages of the woollen manufacturers alone built the cathedral.

[2] Fazio was the grandson of Farinata degli Uberti, the renowned leader of the Ghibelines of Florence, and the conqueror of the Guelphs at the battle of Monte Aperto. Readers of the *Divina Commedia* will remember the terrible and pathetic scene in Canto X., when Farinata "uprose erect with breast and front, e'en as if hell he had in great despite." Fazio, driven into banishment by the triumphant faction of the day, took the opportunity to travel abroad. On his return he wrote the *Ditta Mundi*, a historical and geographical description of the world, probably in the year 1350 Having spent many years of his old age in Verona, he died in peace there, and there was buried Tiraboschi, in his *Storia della Literatura Italiana*, tome v., having given a sketch of the poet's career, says, in conclusion [illegible] especially in force [illegible] Fazio's

By a natural progression the woollen manufacture, as a great trade, extended to the northern countries of Europe. "Venice and the other Italian States," says a well-informed writer,[1] "carried on the woollen manufacture when the rest of Europe remained ignorant and uncivilised; but when other countries that produced wool began to manufacture their own materials, the Italian manufactures declined. The Flemings first perceived their advantage for a commercial intercourse with the north of Europe; and though they were without wool of their own, yet, being nearer to the countries that produced it, particularly England, they were enabled to procure a raw material on cheaper terms, and in a short time to undersell their rivals, and to supersede them in the foreign market." England, in course of time, likewise awoke to a sense of her own advantages and interests. Her exports of raw material may have been considerable, but she was far behindhand in weaving wool, until Edward III. directed his energetic mind and strong will to the fostering and extending of a profitable trade. Taking advantage of discontents among the manufacturers of Flanders, he invited Flemish weavers to come and settle in England. Seventy families of Walloons crossed the sea, and established themselves in different towns, but principally in Norwich, where they were frequently visited by the king, and his consort.

canzone, "portrait of his Lady Angiola of Verona," is a love-song not perhaps surpassed by any poem of its class in existence, and he gives a translation of it in *Early Italian Poets*. I have never seen the *Ditta Mundi* Quaritch's catalogues some time ago contained a fine MS. on vellum of the work, price £25; a copy of the first edition, likewise on vellum, price £5; and one or two copies, with some leaves stained, at a lower figure. However, the *Ditta Mundi* has disappeared from the latter issues of the catalogue. In the Quin collection, Trinity College Library, there is a splendidly-bound copy of the first edition; but as far as the reading public are concerned, No.70 in that collection of rare and beautiful volumes might as well be entombed with Fazio degli Uberti at Verona, for the donor made it a condition of the bequest that no one should be allowed to consult any work in the collection except in the presence of the librarian. One would perhaps think twice before undertaking a journey to Italy in search of a copy of an early edition of the *Ditta Mundi*, but certainly one would think three times before asking the learned and urbane librarian of T C. D. to stand by while a reader endeavoured to seize the meaning of what are described as almost unintelligible pages. An edition, "ridotto a buona lezione," was published at Milan in 1826

[1] Preston, *Prize Essay on the Natural Advantages of Ireland, etc.* (1803).

their countrywoman, Philippa of Hainault. These expert manufacturers soon taught the English to work up their own wool into fine cloths. Edward conferred many privileges on the industrious and skilful strangers, and caused various ordinances to be made for the encouragement of the trade. It was enacted that "no man nor woman, great nor small (except the king himself and a few privileged persons), shall wear no cloth other than is made in England, Ireland, Wales, or Scotland." The prices of cloth were fixed by edict, and the fabrics specified which should be worn by the various classes of the community Moreover, the quality of the woollen shrouds people were to be buried in was prescribed. The king derived a large income from the duty paid on every sack of wool exported. This duty was collected at places or ports called staples, where "the king's staples" were said to be established, and to which all goods should be brought, for payment of the customs, before they could be sold or exported. A Statute of Staple was passed, appointing certain towns to be in future the staple for wools; the first chapter directing that, for Ireland, staples "shall be perpetually holden at Develin, Waterford, Cork, and Drogheda, and not elsewhere." By other ordinances of the same reign, a staple or market for English wool (Irish, of course, being included) was established at Calais, Bruges, Brussels, Louvain, and Mechlin.[1]

About this time there turns up another remarkable testimony to the excellence of our Irish serges. The promoters of the woollen manufacture in the British Isles found reason to complain that in Spain the industrious and enterprising Catalonians were manufacturing serges, and supplying the fabric to the French as Irish. "The stuffs called *sayes*, made in that country (Ireland), were in such request that they were imitated by the manufacturers of Catalonia, who were in the practice of making the finest woollen goods of every kind."[2]

In course of time the woollen manufactures of England acquired a high character, and were much in demand on the Continent. In the Dutch market, "English serges" were held in superior estimation. But the goods so classed were in reality, to a great extent, Irish; and the author of the prize

[1] Longman, *History of the Life and Times of Edward* III., vol. i. (1869). *Annals of Commerce*, vol. i. Smiles, *Th. Hu* [illegible] 1867).

[2] *Annal* [illegible]

essay on "The Natural Advantages of Ireland" shows how it was that our native manufacture, in this instance, lost its identity. The criterion of the buyer, he remarks, was a particular manner of folding and packing. Quantities of Irish serges used to be sent to England. They were then new-folded and packed by the English factors, who received a percentage for their trouble, and finally were exported to the Dutch market, under the denomination of English serges.

However, the Irish did not by any means pass all their products through the neighbouring island. Their merchants had establishments at the Brabant marts, or fairs, and dealt in a great variety of commodities, among which wool and fells of hides are enumerated. Towards the end of the fifteenth century, trade with foreign countries was greatly facilitated, for Ireland as well as England, by the conclusion of a treaty of peace, commerce, and alliance between Henry VII of England and the Archduke Philip, sovereign of the Netherlands. By the provisions of this treaty, liberty was allowed on both sides to trade to each others dominions without asking for licence or passport, and to carry all manner of merchandise, whether wool, leather, victuals, arms, horses, jewels, and other wares, either by land or water, from Calais, England, and Ireland to the countries of Brabant, Flanders, etc. That the flourishing city of Waterford carried on a direct trade in wool with Brabant, and enjoyed valuable privileges in connection with its wool exports even before that treaty was concluded, is evident from an inquiry that took place in the same reign (referred to in Molyneux's *Case of Ireland*) regarding a Waterford vessel, carrying wool to Sluice (l'Ecluse, the port of Bruges), which was driven by stress of weather into Calais, and seized there by the governor. It was pleaded by the owners that the merchants of Waterford and their successors had a licence from the King of England to carry wool where they pleased.[1] Traces of an

[1] Campion, writing in the reign of Elizabeth, describes Waterford and Dungarvan as full of traffic with England, France, and Spain, by means of their excellent good haven. A writer in the *Ulster Archæological Journal* (vol. vi.) gives an interesting sketch of the city, its extensive trade in days gone by, and the attractions it possessed for foreigners at all times The writer, the Rev. T. Gimlette, among other remarks, makes in substance the following.—From the earliest times Waterford afforded a home and shelter to the foreigner The Danes made it one of their first settlements. Norman knights established themselves there [illegible] ghts of

Irish trade with this part of Europe turn up at the date of Elizabeth's reign. Guicciardini, in his description of the Netherlands (quoted in the *Annals of Commerce*), says that Antwerp takes from Ireland skins and leather of diverse sorts, and some low-priced cloths.

IV.

THE foregoing sketch, slight though it is, shows plainly enough that Irish weavers were not unskilled in remote days, and that the serges, friezes, and other stuffs they produced were of no mean value. And yet, some writers would lead careless readers to imagine that the inhabitants of Ireland knew little of arts or industry until the fortunate day when the province of Ulster was planted with English and Scottish farmers, traders, weavers, and labourers, in the reign of James I. Mr. Froude, for example, says that the new colonists "went over to earn a living by labour in a land which had produced little but banditti": and that then, "for the first time, the natural wealth of Ireland began to reveal itself; commerce sprung up, . . . busy fingers were set at work on loom and spinning-wheel; fields, fenced and drained, grew yellow with rolling corn, and the vast herds and flocks which had wandered at will on hill and valley were turned to pro-

St. John, on their return from the Crusades, settled in the city on the Suir, and Dominicans and Franciscans from France and Spain had convents and churches in the midst of the population. In the days of Henry VII. the Irish traffic with the south of France for Gascoigne wines was almost monopolised by Waterford, which became in succeeding reigns the great port of transit, not alone to England and Wales, but also to Flanders, Spain, and many parts of France Continental traders in the middle of the sixteenth century discovered the peculiar advantages of a residence in the town, and settled there. Later on the Huguenots founded families which long maintained an honourable position in the land of their adoption.

It may be interesting to note that a city which in times nearer to our own sank to a low position as a trading port ("Busy as a Waterford merchant—doing nothing," was a common saying in the south not so long ago), is every day rising in commercial importance. The quay has a busy character added to its native picturesqueness; and at Kilmacthomas, not many miles from the city, is the seat of a flourishing woollen manufactory, one of the few of which Ireland now can boast.

fitable account." Assuredly, the author of *The English in Ireland* was wool-gathering himself when he discovered that the arts of spinning and weaving were a novelty to the aborigines of the island, and that the vast flocks of Erin had from time immemorial wandered up hill and down dale, idly consuming their own fleeces.

If such had been the case, what could be the meaning of a proposal seriously made in the very reign of the monarch who decreed the Plantation, to the effect that a restraint should be laid upon the wools and woolfels of Ireland, the exportation of which was calculated to interfere prejudicially with England's foreign trade?[1] Commerce could not have been created and extended with such amazing celerity, in a country inhabited by lawless men and useless animals, as to become already a danger to the State which had undertaken to civilise the dependent province. A trade which included exports to Spain and Portugal of hides, wool, yarn, rugs, blankets, and "sheep-skins with the wool," in the early years of King James's successor, was surely not a growth of yesterday's date. Again, fighting with windmills was hardly one of Strafford's foibles; and he, at anyrate, when his turn came to do something for Ireland, would not have given himself so much trouble in planning the destruction of a trade which was only new-born.

Strafford's scheme for holding Ireland in subjection, and draining her resources for the benefit of a ruined exchequer and a faithless king, was at once bold in outline and comprehensive in detail. If, instead of legislating for a nation, the Lord-Deputy had been maliciously bent on taking all the savour and sweetness and warmth out of the life of a colony of galley-slaves, he could not have devised anything more likely to effect his purpose. He strove to secure for the government in Ireland a monopoly of salt and a monopoly of tobacco; he contemplated imposing a tax on bees; and he was determined to prevent the Irish from exporting their wool, or manufacturing it at home for their own use. "Wentworth resolved," says his biographer, "that all the wool manufactures

[1] This was in 1622. Referring to the circumstance, Smith, in his *Memoirs of Wool* (1747), makes the following remark:—"Here, then, by the way, it may be noted that the exportation of wool from Ireland is a complaint of [illegible] commonly observed."

of Ireland should be stopped, in order to compel her to purchase them from England. The Irish were not to be allowed to weave or spin their own wool, but this same wool was first to be taken to England, where it was to pay a heavy duty, and, when turned into cloth, carried back to Ireland, where again a duty was to be imposed, thus absolutely doubling the customs."[1]

The writer of a recently published pamphlet,[2] which includes a good deal of information of a useful and seasonable kind, having referred in general terms to Strafford's system of legal spoliation, seems greatly to wonder how so grave a historian as Leland should impute to a statesman like Wentworth the design of restraining the Irish from indraping their own wool, for the direct purpose of reducing the people to such a strait that they could not revolt from their allegiance to the Crown without nakedness to themselves and their families Mr. Blackburne scouts the notion that Wentworth, who, "whatever his failings and prejudices may have been, was unquestionably a man of intellect and talent," should have originated the notion of "strengthening the connection between the two countries by the inability of the nation to revolt in consequence of their having no clothes." One can hardly read this part of the pamphlet without a smile The pity is, that two or three such pages did not fall in the way of the modern Clothes Philosopher when that master of trenchant satire was engaged on his *Sartor Resartus*.

Making excuses for Strafford in this matter of the wool is simply labour lost His own words leave no doubt as to his intentions or the heartiness of his endeavour "I am of opinion," he says, "that all wisdom advises to keep this kingdom as much subordinate and dependent upon England as possible; and holding them from the manufacture of wool (which, unless otherwise directed, I shall by all means discourage), and then enforcing them to fetch their clothing from thence, and to take their salt from the king (being that which gives value to all their native staple commodities), how can they depart from us without nakedness and beggary?" Lord

[1] Elizabeth Cooper, *The Life of Thomas Wentworth, Earl of Strafford* (1874), vol i

[2] Edward Blackburne, *Causes of the Decadence of the Industries of Ireland* (1881)

Ui

Strafford's biographer justly remarks that such a sentence as this would alone be sufficient to wipe out the memory of a thousand benefits, and wonders at "the cold cruelty of binding, in the fetters of contingent rags and famine, the 'little sister' whose wealth was to enrich the 'more excellent' by means of her silver mines," etc.

The scheme for compelling the Irish to take from the king alone the salt without which they must starve, since they depended so much on salted provisions for their subsistence, fell to the ground when it was discovered that the profit would be too small to compensate for the trouble of carrying it into execution. Nor did the earl wear his head long enough to mature the plan for making the Irish dependent on England for their clothing, and hindering them from continuing their exports of woollens, which, he conceived, were likely to beat, by their cheapness, the English out of the trade

As a set-off against this base attack on Irish wool, I must note that, during Strafford's administration in Ireland, the native fashions in beards and clothes were freed from the penalties imposed on them by former Governments. In the session of 1634–35, an Act was passed in Dublin "for Repeal of divers statutes heretofore enacted in this kingdom of Ireland," and, as the preamble sets forth, to put an end to the distinction between subjects, since now the happy change of times allowed of such abolition One of those Acts, which "shall be from henceforth utterly repealed and made voyde of none effect to all intents, constructions, and purposes," was that made in the twenty-fifth year of the reign of King Henry VI., whereby it was ordained "that he that will be taken for an Englishman shall not use a beard upon his upper lip alone," under penalty of being dealt with as an Irish enemy. Another of the repealed Acts was one passed in the fifth year of Edward IV., the plain meaning of which was that anyone arrested under suspicious circumstances "in the county Meath" might be killed offhand, unless he had in his company a "faithful man of good name or fame in English apparel."

Thus, after a conflict of more than four hundred years between Irish obstinacy and English statutes, the natives and their mantles remained in possession of the field

A French gentleman, who came here soon after the Irish war broke out, and wrote an account of his travels through the country, describes the dress of "the Irish whom the English call savages." "Their breeches," he says, "are a pantaloon of white frieze, which they call trowsers, and for mantles they have five or six yards of frieze drawn round the neck, the body, and over the head." "The women," he observes, "wear a very large mantle, the cape being made of coarse woollen frieze, in the manner of the women of Lower Normandy." The traveller notes also that the Irish, who import wine and salt from France, sell their strong frieze cloths at good prices.[1] Massari, Dean of Fermo, who, as secretary, accompanied the Papal Nuncio Rinuccini on his embassy to Ireland, describes in his journal the dress of the Irish women. He remarks that the costume somewhat resembles the French mode. "All wear cloaks," he says, "with long fringes; they have also a hood sewn to the cloak, and they go abroad without any other covering for the head; some wearing a kerchief as the Greek women do." The Italian traveller does not fail to observe the sheep of the country, "from which fine wool is made."[2]

Another testimony to the estimation in which the Irish fleece was held in the seventeenth century is given in Drayton's allusion to the Leinster wool—

> "Whose staple doth excel,
> And seems to overmatch the golden Phrygian fell."

Already I have given Sir William Petty's observations on the domestic manufacture of woollen cloths later in the same century; but, apropos of the people whom the English call savages, I cannot help calling to mind another sentence or two from the *Political Anatomy of Ireland.* The writer says: the diet, housing, and clothing of the 16,000 families who are computed to have more than one chimney in their houses, "is much the same as in England, nor is the French elegance unknown in many of them, nor the French and Latin tongues, the latter whereof is very frequent among the poorest Irish, and chiefly in Kerry, most remote from Dublin."

Before leaving too far behind the Earl of Strafford's era, a word about Irish linen and his services to that trade may be

[1] *The Tour of the French Traveller, M. de la Boullaye le Gouz, in Ireland,* A.D. 1644. Edited by T. Crofton Croker (1837).

[2] Rev. C. P. Meehan, *The Irish Hierarchy in the Seventeenth Century* Fifth ed. (18[illegible]

permitted. Unquestionably, he did much to improve the cultivation of flax. He invited Flemish and French artisans to settle in Ireland and devote their better skill to the production of superior linens. Furthermore, he embarked £30,000 of his private fortune in the trade. But it is a mistake to speak of his having "introduced" the manufacture among the Irish, and "set our women to spin," as we hear so often repeated. Linen was, in point of fact, an article of clothing in very early times in Ireland. Lenas, or vests of linen, were worn by the higher classes of the ancient population, and "kingly linen" is a term met with in old poems. Among the commodities on sale in the thirteenth century at town markets and fairs, linen is mentioned. "Linen cloth falding" is one of the articles enumerated as being imported into Chester from Ireland in the fifteenth century; and linen cloth was sold in the same period in the Irish establishment in the Brabant marts. Extravagance in the use of linen in their apparel was more than once the subject of complaint against the Irish, and furnished matter, too, for legislation. In 1539, an Act of Parliament limited the quantity for each shirt to seven yards. Somewhat later, Spenser described the thick-fold linen shirts of the native Irish.

Strafford and his interest in the linen manufacture may be dismissed in the words of Dr. Smiles, who says it was greatly to the credit of the earl that he should have endeavoured to improve the industry of Ireland by introducing the superior processes employed by the foreign artisans; and had he not attempted to turn the improved flax manufacture to his own advantage by erecting it into a personal monopoly, he might have been entitled to regard as a genuine benefactor of Ireland."[1]

Despite of heavy duties, and Strafford's ominous hostility, the woollen manufactures of Ireland continued to flourish. Considerable injury, however, was inflicted on the trade by the wasting of the stock throughout the country during the Civil War and the Cromwellian devastations.[2]

[1] *The Huguenots.*

[2] In *Whitelock's Memorials* (quoted in *Memoirs of Wool*), under the date of 6th April 1652, appears the following summary of news from Ireland:—"Letters of the Forces of the Parliament about Eniscorfy (Ireland) burning the corn, and every morning the houses they quartered in the

Cattle and wool rose to a high price in England, owing to the failure of the supplies from the neighbouring island. And yet, as if Ireland still possessed the glorious prerogative of youth, prosperity returned with the Restoration, and the trading industries not only revived, but gave promise of advancing to a position of the highest importance. Energy and hope had a fair field for a few short years; and then the cattle trade received a fatal blow, and the wool entered on a new chapter of its history.

V.

For a long time previous to this date, an extensive trade in the export of live cattle from Ireland to England had been carried on. Since the war had come to an end, these exports had greatly increased, and formed, in fact, a chief source of Irish wealth. On inquiry it was found that at this period there had been about 61,000 head of great cattle brought over annually from Ireland. Rents having fallen in England soon after the Restoration, the calamity was erroneously attributed to the importation of Irish stock; and the landowners demanded that British should be closed against the Irish cattle dealers. The House of Commons determined to carry a prohibitory Act, in spite of the remonstrance of the Duke of Ormonde, Viceroy of Ireland; in opposition to the Upper House, in which the Lord Chancellor of England and the Duke of York (afterwards James II.) both spoke against the measure; and in open contempt of the king, who considered the proceedings impolitic for England as well as prejudicial and grievous to Ireland, and publicly declared that he could not give his assent to so unjust a thing. To such an extreme was the animosity of the country party in England carried, that when the Corporation of London petitioned Parliament to be allowed to accept a present of 20,000 (or, as some say, 30,000)

night before; killed and took many Irish; that he was an idle soldier who had not a veal, lamb, poultry, or all, for his supper."

The Civil War "almost annihilated every manufacture in Ireland; and that country, which had so abounded in cattle and provisions, was, after Cromwell's *settlement* of it, obliged to import provisions from Wales."—Lord Sheffield, *Observations on the Manufactures, Trade, and Present State of Ireland* (1785).

live cattle subscribed by the Irish people for distribution among the sufferers by the Fire of London, matters were so contrived in the House of Commons as to oblige the Corporation to consider it a more prudent course to decline the gift[1]

The contest was not protracted In 1663 an Act was passed absolutely prohibiting the importation from Ireland, at all times, of cattle (dead or alive), sheep or swine, beef, pork, or bacon, under pain of forfeiture of one-half to the use of the seizer or informer, the other half to the poor of the parish where the said should be found or seized. Three years later, this Act was made perpetual, with a clause introduced against horses. To make the ruin complete, butter and cheese were added to the commodities that in future should not be exported from Ireland to the parent country.[2]

Ireland was thrown into consternation by this enactment. Deep distress ensued. The price of horses fell from thirty shillings to one shilling, and that of beeves from fifty shillings to ten shillings. Despair overwhelmed the people; but the Duke of Ormonde threw off the incubus, making "no doubt but Ireland would by time, peace, and industry recover itself from the blow it now received from England." In the development of home industries he saw the best resource for such a crisis. He turned his attention to trade in general, and to the

[1] See the *Eighth Report of the Royal Commission on Historical Manuscripts* (1881).

[2] Carte, in his great work, comments on this example of paternal government. "The English seem never to have understood," he says, "the art of governing their provinces, and have always treated them in such a manner as either to put them under necessity, or subject them to the temptation, of casting off their government whenever an opportunity offered. It was a series of this impolitic conduct which lost them Normandy, Poictou, Anjou, Guyenne, and all the dominions which they formerly had in France. . . . When Rochelle, Saintes, Engousleme, and other towns in those provinces, submitted to the kings of France, they took particular care to insert in their capitulations an express article, that, in any circumstances or distress of the affairs of France, they should never be delivered back into the power of the English. It is not a little surprising that a thinking people, as the English are, should not grow wiser by any experience, and after losing such considerable territories abroad by their oppressive treatment of them, should go on to hazard the loss of Ireland, and endeavour the ruin of a colony of their own countrymen planted in that kingdom"—*Life of James, Duke of Ormonde*, vol. vi.

Carte, an Englishman and a Protestant minister, died in 1754. He could not have dreamed that the revolt of the American colonies would add ano[illegible] parent State

manufacture of woollens in especial. Not that the wool trade, any more than the cattle trade, had been left unmolested by jealous interference. It was clogged by vexatious disabilities. Wools could not be exported to England except by the particular licence of the Lord-Lieutenant; and by a manœuvre, which can only be described as despicable trickery, Ireland was deprived by the amended Navigation Act of 1663 of the colonial trade which she had previously enjoyed,[1] and which, in such a juncture as the present, might open up for woollens as well as for other commodities a profitable outlet.

Still, there were opportunities which might now be taken advantage of, and possibilities which might serve to animate and encourage all who had the interest of the country at heart. The king, anxious to compensate Ireland in some degree for the injustice and injury inflicted on her so much against his will by the ruin of her cattle trade, directed, by a letter dated the 23rd of March 1667, that all restraints upon the exportation of commodities of the growth and manufacture of Ireland to foreign parts should be taken off, and this favour was notified by a proclamation from the Lord-Lieutenant and Council.[2] Thus, though New England was barred, France, Spain, and Portugal were rendered more accessible. Again, if the Irish manufacturers could be taught to produce fine broadcloth as well as the friezes, stuffs, and serges for which they were already celebrated, English woollens might be entirely excluded. Sir William Petty, as we read in Carte, presented to the Duke of Ormonde a memorial for the encouragement of woollen fabrics, "chiefly recommending the setting up of manufactures of fine worsted stockings and Norwich stuffs in all parts of the nation for making the best advantage of their wool and employing their poor." The Council of Trade approved of this proposal, and the viceroy lent his aid, not merely by the bestowal of fair words, but by taking on himself both trouble and expense in carrying out the plan suggested. He established a woollen

[1] For an account of the way in which this act of legislative treachery was performed, see the speech of Lord North in the British House of Commons, November 13, 1799. On that occasion the Minister of the Crown exposed in clear terms "the commercial restrictions of which Ireland so justly complained." The speech will be found in Plowden's *Historical Review of the State of Ireland*, vol. i. (1803).

[2] Hely Hutchinson, *The Commercial Restraints of Ireland*, etc. (1799). Cheap reissue recently published by M. H. Gill & Son, Dublin.

manufactory at Clonmel, the capital of his county palatine of Tipperary, bringing over 500 Walloon families from the neighbourhood of Canterbury to carry it on, and giving houses and land on long leases, with only an acknowledgment instead of rent from the undertakers. Also, in Kilkenny and Carrick-on-Suir, the duke established large colonies of those industrious foreigners, so well skilled in the preparation and weaving of wool.[1] About the same time a number of clothiers (master manufacturers) from the West of England, "finding their trade decaying, removed themselves and their families over into Ireland, invited by the cheapness of wool and of livelihood." Some of the English immigrants established a manufactory in Dublin, while others fixed themselves at Cork and Kinsale. In Limerick, new vigour was infused into the trade by the arrival of a colony of sixty families from Holland; and the manufacturing population of Waterford was increased by the accession of some Frenchmen, who established a drugget factory in the city.

Capital being now freely invested and new markets found, rapid progress was made. The towns assumed a busy, thriving air. Even the face of the country was changed, for, in order to keep up the supply of wool, vast tracts of land were turned into sheep-walks. Naturally, the peasantry looked with anything but favour on this advance of trade at the expense of agriculture. They did not like being driven

[1] The first migration of Walloon weavers to England took place, as already stated, in the reign of Edward III.; another settlement was made under favour of Elizabeth, who welcomed to her dominions the artisans of the Netherlands, driven out by the Duke of Alva's persecution, and granted her protection, at the same time, to the French Protestant refugees. The Walloons on this occasion settled in large numbers at Canterbury and other places, and employed themselves in manufacturing various kinds of cloth. A place of worship within Canterbury Cathedral was granted to them, and to the foreign refugees of all nations settled in the place. Numerous bodies of foreign artisans passed over into Ireland during the same reign, and settled in Dublin, Waterford, Limerick, Belfast, etc. Restrictions were imposed by Act of Parliament on the exportation of raw wool and woollen yarn from Ireland, to this end among others, "that artificers may, by the abundance of the commodities within the realm, be allured to come into the same to work them within this realm, and thereby to give example to others to use that trade to the great commodity and profit of the realm." Early in the reign of James I. other detachments of Flemings and French crossed over into Ireland and added new strength to the [illegible]

into the mountains, bogs, and woody parts, to make way for the fleecy flocks. "I have myself," writes a contemporary, "very frequently heard them curse the English sheep with all the bitterness and rancour imaginable." Presently, when the War of the Revolution burst over Ireland, the evicted agriculturists took an insane revenge, killing hundreds of the sheep in the fields, driving off the flocks of the Protestant proprietors, slaughtering until they had consumed all, and, to quote the same authority, producing by their reckless proceedings so great a scarcity in the country that, if the Irish army had not been plentifully relieved from France, a great number must have perished of famine.

With the return of peace on the triumph of the Williamite cause, the wool-growers and the manufacturers retrieved their losses with amazing rapidity. The security which a settled Government seemed to promise animated the trading communities to renewed activity, and the losses which the country had sustained by the Cattle Bill were now fully made up. Although the woollen manufactures were almost exclusively in the hands of Protestant settlers, the general population benefited largely by the extension of trade. Catholic artisans, albeit excluded from trade privileges, had nevertheless their share of work in the inferior branches of the industry. Catholic wool-growers followed their profitable avocations in the pastoral districts, finding in their old connection with France a ready outlet for any surplus store which might remain after the home demand had been supplied. Catholic traders in the towns flourished with the rest. "So thriving and prosperous were the affairs of the Irish," says the authority above quoted, "that apprehensions were entertained that the estates of the Protestants would ultimately fall into their hands by purchase." In fact, some of the lands forfeited in the Revolution War had been actually purchased back by the Catholic traders whose rightful heritage they were. Even the peasantry felt that a good time had come, and gave up "spoiling the Egyptians" in the barbarous fashion they had devised. The late war and the later peace had brought about a change in the state of affairs which opened up for the poorer classes an opportunity of bettering their condition. The Protestant properties, as Matthew O'Conor observes, had become much embarrassed by di[illegible] during the continuation of the contest, and the proprietors, being unable to stock their lands after the peace, were under the necessity of leasing them to the peasantry at low rents, and for long terms of years. The peasantry thus acquired valuable interests, and became a rich, a sturdy, and independent yeomanry; even that miserable race known by the name of cottiers, the working slaves of the Irish gentry, were in a more thriving and prosperous condition in those days than at any subsequent period. Most of them were in the possession of a cow, one or two goats, and six or seven sheep.[1]

Thus a new era seemed to have dawned—an era of healthy activity and remunerative industry. Well-nigh two hundred years have passed since then, and we who live in the distracted Ireland of to-day are left to conjecture how different the state of things might be if the Treaty of Limerick had never been violated; if "the ferocious Acts of Queen Anne" had never been promulgated; and if the wool trade had been suffered to develop into a great national industry.

VI.

It could hardly be supposed that the passion for monopoly which had its triumph in the Cattle Bill was laid to rest, once and for ever, by the consummation of that deed of iniquity. The jealousy of the country party in England may, indeed, have been pacified by the ruin of the Irish cattle-feeders, but the national vice broke out before long in another direction. Apprehensions were now aroused in commercial circles by the success of the Irish woollen manufactures. Reason might have suggested that the prosperity of Ireland could not in the longrun be an injury to England, and that even in the wool trade the two countries might work in fair emulation, command new markets for their improved fabrics, and together carry on a splendid rivalry with the manufacturing nations of the Continent. Such wide views, however, were not entertained by more than one man in the million. Unreasoning selfishness carried the day. As early as 1673, Sir William Temple, at the request of the Earl of Essex, then Viceroy of

Ireland, publicly proposed that the manufacture of woollens (except in the inferior branches) should be relinquished in Ireland, as tending to interfere prejudicially with the English trade. In all probability, the Irish manufacturers of broad cloths would gain on their English rivals, and the improvement of woollen fabrics in this kingdom, argued the statesman, "would give so great a damp to the trade of England, that it seems not fit to be encouraged here."

Sir William's suggestion was not immediately acted on, but it showed the way the wind blew in high quarters. By and by there were ominous mutterings of the storm in lower levels, and in response to popular clamour, several Acts were passed, early in the reign of William and Mary, restricting the exportation of wool and woollens from Ireland. However, elated by the success they had already achieved, the Irish clothiers disregarded all penalties, found means to elude the vigilance of the authorities, and got off their wool and woollens in spite of Acts and prohibitions. This state of things could not continue long. Agitation in England became more violent. Petitions from the excited centres of British commerce showed Parliament what kind of legislation was expected from the representatives of the trading nation. Both houses addressed the king.

The Lords represented that: "The growing manufacture of cloth in Ireland, both by the cheapness of all sorts of necessaries of life and the goodness of material for making all manner of cloth," having made the king's loyal subjects in England very apprehensive that the further growth of it would greatly prejudice the said manufacture here, and lessen the value of lands; they, the Lords, besought his most sacred Majesty to be pleased, "in the most public and effectual way that may be," to declare to all his subjects of Ireland, that "the growth and increase of the woollen manufacture there hath long been, and will ever be, looked upon with great jealousy by all his subjects of the kingdom of England," etc.

The Commons of England, in Parliament assembled: "Being very sensible that the wealth and power of this kingdom do, in a great measure, depend on the preservation of the woollen manufacture as much as possible entire to this realm," [illegible] stors.

Ui

to be jealous of the increase and establishment of it elsewhere, and to use their utmost endeavours to prevent it. "They cannot without trouble observe that Ireland should of late apply itself to the woollen manufacture, to the great prejudice of the trade of England. . . . Parliament will be necessitated to interfere to prevent the mischief that threatens. . . . His Majesty's protection and favour in this matter is most humbly implored," etc.

William III., of glorious, pious, and immortal memory, discovered no sign of having been visited with any disturbing sentiment of indignation or pity, such as moved even the "merrie monarch" in similar circumstances, though it is likely he may have winced under the ungenerous pressure put on him by the Lords and Commons, whose nominee he was. "The king replied briefly," says Mr. Froude, "that the wish of Parliament should be carried out, and Ireland was invited to apply the knife to her own throat. Two letters of William to the Lords Justices survive in Dublin Castle, embodying the words of the two Addresses, and recommending to the legislature the worst and most fatal of all the mistaken legislative experiments to which a dependent country was ever subjected by the folly of its superiors." [1]

Animated by the imminence of the danger, the Irish manufacturers made what remonstrance and resistance they could. Their cause was defended by an array of pamphlets, showing forth how destructive to the interests of the United Kingdom, how disastrous to the Protestant cause, how criminal in every sense would be the destruction of the woollen trade, which was the mainstay of the English colony, the English garrison, the English religion, the English dominion in Ireland! Appeals to the higher interests, the political integrity, the fanaticism of the parent country, were urged in every mood and tense. According to these desperate champions of a cause which was every moment growing more hopeless, there would be no chance of saving Ireland from the grip of the Pope of Rome, or preserving the British Isles from the clutches of the King of France if once Hibernia's wool were sacrificed. High over the heads of the forlorn hope towered one of the representatives in Parliament of the University of Dublin. He, William Molyneux, took up his position on loftier ground.

Boldly attacking Poynings' Act, he impugned England's right to make laws for Ireland [1] In his famous treatise, *The Case of Ireland's being bound by Acts of Parliament in England Stated*, he took care to say that he had not any concern in wool or the wool trade, and, in fact, he left the question altogether on one side However, no one doubted that it was the wool in danger that prompted this supreme effort, nor did he himself deny that it was the interference of the English Parliament in the woollen manufacture of Ireland which led to the publication of the book. "This," said the author, writing to his friend, the philosopher Locke, "you will say is a nice subject, but I think I have treated it with that caution and submission that it cannot justly give offence; in so much that I scruple not to put my name to it, and, by advice of some of my good friends here, have presumed to dedicate it to His Majesty." Notwithstanding all his care, he could not be certain what effect it might possibly have; for "God only knows what resentments captious men may take on such occasions." *The Case of Ireland* created a sensation on both sides of the Channel, excited the English Parliament to a higher pitch of animosity, and hastened the catastrophe. "On the 21st of May, a member of the House of Commons produced the obnoxious pamphlet, read portions of it to his indignant fellow-members, and obtained the appointment of a committee to report on its insolent defiance of the sovereign power of the English Parliament over Ireland." [2] Forthwith the Parliament of England addressed the king, beseeching His Majesty that the laws restraining the Parliament of Ireland should not be evaded, denouncing the *Case* as seditious and libellous, and praying the sovereign to discover and punish the offender. William did not concern himself to "dis-

[1] The particular statute known as Poynings' Act was one which provided that henceforth no Parliament should be held in Ireland until the Chief Governor and Council had first certified to the king, under the Great Seal, "as well the causes and considerations as the Acts they designed to pass, and till the same should be approved by the king and Council." This Act virtually made the Irish Parliament a nullity; and when, in after times, it came to affect not merely the English pale, for which it was originally framed, but the whole of Ireland when brought under English law, it was felt to be one of the most intolerable grievances under which this country suffered."—Haverty, *History of Ireland*.

[2] Bourne

Ut

cover" the member for Trinity College, but the book, by order of the English Parliament, was burnt by the common hangman.

Without delay the work of demolition then proceeded. After a bootless struggle on the part of a brave minority, the Irish Parliament gave effect to the king's recommendation to the Lords Justices, "to avoid giving jealousy to England by the further maintenance of the woollen manufacture in the kingdom," and imposed duties amounting to a prohibition on the exportation of Irish woollens. Immediately after, an English Act of Parliament (10th, 11th of William III., ch. 10) suppressed the manufacture *in toto* Irish wool and woollens were not in future to be exported to any countries except England and Wales, from which places, as everyone knew, they were already virtually excluded by heavy duties. Evidence of the activity of the doomed trade is afforded in the long list of prohibited articles embodied in the statute. Wool, woolfels, worsted, and woolflocks, woollen yarn, cloth, serge, bays, kerseys, and sayes; friezes, druggets, cloth-serges, shalloons, and other drapery stuffs are enumerated To prevent any possible infringement of the new ordinances, penalties of the severest kind are imposed on all who take any part in conveying the raw material or the manufactured articles out of the kingdom Any such commodities found on board ship shall, according to the statute, be at once forfeited. The ship itself shall be forfeited. The master of the vessel, every sailor on board, every other person knowing of the transaction, shall be fined £40 each Ships suspected of being engaged in the prohibited commerce, and wool and woollen fabrics intended for foreign exportation, wherever met, wherever discovered, may be seized by any person whatsoever. And, for the more effectual carrying out of the law, it is enacted that two ships of the fifth rate, two ships of the sixth rate, and eight armed sloops, shall constantly cruise on the shore of Ireland, particularly between the north of Ireland and Scotland, with power to enter and search any vessel; and if any Irish wool or woollens bound for foreign parts should be discovered on board, to seize ship, cargo, and crew.[1]

[1] That other reaches of the island shore required as close watching as the Ulster seaboard became apparent after some time; and in the reign of George [illegible] Encouragement of the Woollen [illegible]

This sudden and merciless blow was followed by immediate consequences which all had foreseen; but it also led to results which none could have predicted. The healthy industrial life of the population was at once paralysed. All feeling of security in the body politic vanished at this spectacle of the parent State devouring its own offspring. In Dublin and its suburbs, 12,000 English families were reduced to beggary, and 50,000 families of the same nation, as well as the settlers of continental origin scattered through the provinces, saw a like fate staring them in the face. Flight was the best resource, whether for settlers or natives, who were in a position to escape from the blighted land; and an exodus of operatives, variously stated from 20,000 to 60,000, forthwith began, depopulating districts of the South and West, and inaugurating a migration from the North which continued to flow to America all through the eighteenth century. A number of the Protestant weavers went to Germany, and, being received with open arms, settled in States where their religion prevailed, and founded manufactories for the celebrated Saxon cloths. Many of the Catholic artisans removed to the north of Spain, and began there a manufactory highly prejudicial to England. Multitudes, both of Protestants and Catholics, were welcomed by the King of France, who had lately established woollen manufactories in Picardy and elsewhere. Louis settled the Irish refugees in Rouen and other industrial centres, securing the Protestants among them in the free exercise of their religion, and founding, with the aid of this army of trained artisans, and the wool which speedily followed them from Ireland, a trade which England, from that day up to the present hour, has never ceased to suffer from. America was the refuge of the ruined Presbyterians of Ulster. They deported themselves in thousands, and

Manufactures of this Kingdom, by the more effectual preventing the unlawful exportations of the Woollen Manufactures of the Kingdom of Ireland to foreign parts," empowered the Admiralty to increase the effectiveness of the fleet of armed cruisers hanging about the coasts of Great Britain and Ireland. Comprehensive as the above list of prohibited articles may seem to be, it did not embrace all the fabrics of the Irish woollen manufacture. Wadding, for instance, and one or two other articles excepted out of the 10th and 11th of William III., were afterwards specially prohibited in the reign of George II. For some time it was the custom to allow each sailor to take with him from Ireland, woollen stuffs to the value of forty shillings, while each officer might take five pounds worth of cloth; but this privilege was subsequently withdrawn.

founded settlements in the New World which they called after their old homes. There, in a new Derry, in another Donegal, in a transatlantic Coleraine and Tyrone, grew up a generation nurtured on memories of a cruel wrong—a generation of ready-made rebels, who flocked on the first signal to the standard of revolution, and became the backbone of the insurgent army.[1]

However, all could not depart. A dispirited, disorganised, pauperised mass remained, to rear an idle, turbulent progeny: the curse of the towns and cities of the old land. Aghast at the spectacle of desolation which met their gaze on every side, the Irish Parliament now addressed the throne with a view "to give a true state of our most deplorable condition," and solicit some redress. Their deliberations were but a wail over the decay of trade, the forced emigration, the extreme want and beggary to which poor tradesmen were reduced. But they had themselves prepared the way for the overthrow of the trade, and their Judas repentance was all too late. What was all this to Queen Anne?

If all documentary record of this sad time were lost, we still should have in Swift's inimitable pages the situation pictured for us of a country where "one part of the people are forced away, and the other part have nothing to do." Says the dean in one of his sermons: "It is a very melancholy reflection that such a country as ours, which is capable of producing all things necessary, and most things convenient, for life, sufficient for the support of four times the number of its inhabitants, should yet lie under the heaviest load of misery and want, our streets crowded with beggars, so many of our lower sorts of tradesmen, labourers, and artificers not able to find clothes and food for their families." On another occasion he says, it is manifest that "whatever circumstances can possibly contribute to make a country poor and despicable are all united with respect to Ireland." First among the causes of the general misery, he places "the intolerable hardships we lie under in every branch of our trade, by which we are become hewers of wood and drawers of water to our rigorous neighbours." He dwells on the growing poverty of the nation, on the injustice of refusing

[1] Dobbs, *Essay on the Trade and Improvements of Ireland* (1729); D'Arcy M'Gee, *History of the Irish Settlers in America* (1851); and other authorities.

a people the liberty, not only of trading with their own manufactures, but even their native commodities: "Ireland is the only kingdom I ever heard or read of, either in ancient or modern story, which was denied the liberty of exporting their native commodities and manufactures wherever they pleased, except to countries at war with their own prince or state; yet this privilege, by the superiority of mere power, is refused to us in the most momentous parts of commerce." Similarly, when considering the causes of a kingdom thriving, this practical patriot places in the foremost rank, trade and industry, and a disposition to value and encourage home productions. The first cause, he says, of a kingdom thriving is, "the fruitfulness of the soil to produce the necessaries and conveniences of life not only sufficient for the inhabitants, but for exportation into other countries." The second is, "The industry of the people in working up all their native commodities to the last degree of manufacture." And another is set down as, "A disposition of the people of a country to wear their own manufactures, and import as few incitements to luxury, either in cloths, furniture, food, or drink, as they possibly can live conveniently without."[1]

Sage advices, not a few, has the dean to give to the people in reference to their conduct in this season of calamity and distress. They should renounce all foreign dress and luxury: those detestable extravagances of Flanders' lace, English cloths made of our own wool, etc., which are not fit for people in such circumstances any more than for the beggar who could not eat his veal without oranges. The women should be clad in the growth of their own country, should be satisfied with Irish stuffs for the furniture of their houses, for gowns and petticoats to themselves and daughters; and if they are not content to go in their own country shifts, may they go in rags: the clergy should wear habiliments of Irish drapery, and the weavers should contrive decent stuffs and silks for this demand at reasonable rates. The lawyers, the gentlemen of the University, the citizens of those corporations who appear in gowns on solemn occasions, should use the fabrics suitable to their wants which the native manufacturers produced. It were to be wished that the sense of both Houses of Parliament, at least of the House of Commons, were declared by some unanimous

[1] Sermon iv.; "Letter to the Earl of Peterborough": "A Short View of the State of I[illegible]

UI

and hearty votes against wearing any silk or woollen manufacture imported from abroad: every senator, noble or plebeian, giving his honour that neither himself nor any of his family would, in their dress or furniture of their houses, make use of anything except what was of the growth and manufacture of this kingdom; and that they would use the utmost of their power, influence, and credit to prevail on their tenants, dependants, and friends to follow their example. Anyhow, "let a firm resolution be taken, by male and female, never to appear with one single shred that comes from England; and let all the people say, *Amen.*" As for the weavers and traders, they should improve the cloths and stuffs of the nation into all possible degrees of fineness and colours, and engage not to play the knave, according to their custom, by exacting and imposing upon the nobility and gentry, either as to the prices or the goodness.[1]

Anonymously, in 1720, Swift entered into the strife of Irish politics, armed with his famous tract, "A Proposal for the Universal Use of Irish Manufacture, in Cloaths and Furniture of Houses, etc., utterly rejecting and renouncing anything wearable that comes from England." To this day the production is read with delight as an example of the master's trenchant style. But the fierce satire of the literary composition is, in the apprehension of nineteenth-century readers, cast into the shade by the grim irony of the incidents which its publication gave rise to. When, as Swift himself afterwards related, a discourse was published endeavouring to persuade our people to wear their own woollen manufactures, full of the most dutiful expressions to the sovereign, and without the least party hint, it was termed *flying in the king's face.* The Government considered the proposal as a sort of *leze*-majesty, and the printer, Waters, was seized and forced to give great bail. Nine times the jury who tried the case were put back, until they were under the necessity of leaving the prisoner to the mercy of the court, by a special verdict; the judge on the bench invoking God for his witness when he

[1] "Proposal for the Universal Use of Irish Manufactures"; "The Drapier's Letters"; "Answer to Letters of Unknown Persons"; "A Letter to the Archbishop of Dublin concerning the Weavers"; "A Proposal that all the Ladies and Women of Ireland should appear constantly in I[illegible]"

asserted that the author's design was to bring in the Pretender! The cause, continues Swift, was so odious and unpopular, the trial of the verdict was deferred from one term to another, until, upon the Duke of Grafton's—the Lord-Lieutenant—arrival, His Grace, after mature advice and permission from England, was pleased to grant a *nolli prosequi*.[1] "In the midst of this prosecution, about 1500 weavers were forced to beg their bread, and had a general contribution made for their relief, which just served to make them drunk for a week; and they were forced to turn rogues, or strolling beggars, or to leave the kingdom"[2] About four years later the Lord-Lieutenant and Council issued a proclamation offering three hundred pounds for the discovery of the author of the "Drapier's Letters." Harding, the printer of these obnoxious productions, was tried before the Chief Justice; but the jury would not find the bill, nor would any person discover the author. Again, when a London journalist reprinted *A Short View of the State of Ireland*, a lengthened prosecution of the printers was the consequence. Swift, referring to the vexations the printers had to undergo, takes occasion, in his characteristic way, to show how dangerous it is for the best-meaning person to write one syllable in defence of his country, or discover the miserable condition it is in. So much is this the case, continues he, that, "although I am often without money in my pocket, I dare not own it in some company, for fear of being thought disaffected."

By no means was it all talk with the Dean of St. Patrick's. He expended both time and money in visiting and assisting distressed artisans, without any distinction of creed. Five hundred pounds a year it was his wont to lend out in small portions, without interest, to necessitous but honest and diligent tradesmen, and at one time he had the gratification of believing that he had recovered two hundred families in the city from ruin. Frugality for the sake of others he knew how to practise. He would often walk rather than ride, and then would say he had earned a shilling or eighteenpence, which he had a right to do what he pleased with, and could expend on his favourite charities. The weavers considered him their special patron and legislator, and frequently came in a body to receive his advice in settling

[1] Letter from Swift to Pope. "Drapier's Letters."

[2] "Proposal that the Ladies and Women of Ireland should appear constantly in Irish Manufactures."

Ul

the rates of their stuffs and the wages of their journeymen. In every sense they were his neighbours; for the industrial population of Dublin were massed round St. Patrick's Cathedral, and still inhabited the Coombe, Spitalfields, Weavers' Square, New Street, and other localities which had been flourishing centres before the suppression of the woollen trade. A notable part of the population were of Huguenot origin, and places of worship, with a French service, had been provided for them. One of these was in Peter Street, and another was under the roof of St. Patrick's, the ancient Lady Chapel of the Cathedral being, in fact, at that time and for long after, the French church of the locality. It was Swift's habit to attend the afternoon service here every Sunday.[1] Stella, who "loved Ireland much better than the generality of those who owe both their birth and riches to it, and detested the tyranny and injustice of England in the treatment of this kingdom," also showed a good example of liberality and judgment in disbursing charity, and of simplicity in her habits and attire. The same pen that so well knew how to lash and scathe has traced with tender care such little traits of one who, "with all the softness of temper that became a lady, had yet the personal courage of a hero," as that she "bought cloaths as seldom as possible, and those as plain and cheap as consisted with the situation she was in, and wore no lace for many years."

Swift's description of the condition of the people brings us on to about thirty years from the date of the suppression of the woollen trade. Another term of thirty years passes by, and it appears that things have not much improved in the interval. Primate Stone, in 1758, describes the people as not either regularly lodged, clothed, or fed. adding that "these things, which in England are called necessaries of life are to us only accidents, and we can, and in many places do, subsist without them."

Again, proceeding down the stream of time some twenty years further, we come on Hely Hutchinson's declaration that "the present state of Ireland teems with every circumstance of national poverty"; and find the discouragement of the woollen manufactories, by the English Act of 1699, referred to as the principal cause of the distress and poverty of the land "A country will sooner recover," says this writer, "from the

[1] Life of Swift, in the edition of his works published by Faulkner

( )

miseries and devastations occasioned by war, invasion, rebellion, and massacre, than from laws restraining the commerce, discouraging the manufactures, fettering the industry, and, above all, breaking the spirit of the people."[1] The situation is summarised by the author of a prize essay already quoted, who observes that "the history of no fruitful country, enjoying peace, and not visited by pestilence and famine, during eighty years, can produce so many instances of wretchedness as appear in Ireland during a period of that length which succeeded the proscription of her woollen trade."

Meanwhile, it was not enough to inflict a fatal injury on a nation's industry, but the ill-used people must likewise be defamed. With writers of a certain class it became a habit to attack the Irish for being slothful, lazy, idle, and indolent; for their thievish, lying, slavish disposition; for their dirt, their disorder, and their mendicancy. The causes of their misfortunes were conveniently ignored, and poverty was attributed to them as a chosen and cherished vice. Other traducers, by a bold stroke, traced idleness, beggary, and the rest to the religion of the bulk of the people. Lord Sheffield's rejoinder to the accusation of idleness hits the mark in a few short words: "The Irish people are not naturally lazy; they are, on the contrary, of an active nature, capable of the greatest exertions, and of as good a disposition as any nation in the same state of improvement; but that men who have very little to do should appear to do little is not strange."[2] Bishop Berkeley seems to have been ignorant of the fundamental cause of the Irishman's sloth and backward condition. But he was too right-minded a man to be misled into supposing that the Catholic religion was accountable for the evils complained of. "Many suspect your religion," says his lordship, addressing the Roman Catholic clergy of Ireland, to be the cause of that notorious idleness which prevails so generally among the natives of this island, as if the Roman Catholic faith was inconsistent with an honest diligence in a man's calling. But whoever considers the great spirit of industry that reigns in Flanders and France, and even beyond the Alps, must

[1] *The Commercial Restraints of Ireland* (1779).

[2] *Observations on the Manufactures, Trade, and Present State of Ireland* (1785).

acknowledge this to be a groundless suspicion. In Piedmont and Genoa, in the Milanese and the Venetian State, and indeed throughout all Lombardy, how well is the soil cultivated, and what manufactures of silk, velvet, paper, and other commodities flourish! The King of Sardinia will suffer no idle hands in his territories, no beggar to live by the sweat of another's brow; it has even been made penal at Turin to relieve a strolling beggar. To which I might add, that the person whose authority will be of the greatest weight with you, even the pope himself, is at this day endeavouring to put new life into the trade and manufactures of his country. Though I am in no secret of the Court of Rome, yet I will venture to affirm that neither pope nor cardinals will be pleased to hear that those of their communion are distinguished above all others by sloth, dirt, and beggary: or be displeased at your endeavouring to rescue them from the reproach of such an infamous distinction."[1]

VII.

RETRIBUTION, in the meantime, was fast overtaking the traders who had been envious of their neighbour's good. They perceived, before long, that the result of their greed was to "starve a friend and glut a foe." Out of the ruins of the Irish trade rose, as already intimated, the great woollen manufactures of France, which, establishing a formidable rivalry with England's staple of commerce, soon beat the island factors out of the principal foreign markets, ultimately commanded a sale even on British ground, and now are actually threatening the very existence of the West of England trade in some of its important branches. The origin of the French woollen trade may be told in a few words.

Colbert, Louis XIV.'s Minister of Finance, devoted very serious attention, from 1661 to 1683, to the task of developing the industrial activity of the French nation. In his youth he had served his apprenticeship to a woollen-draper, and the encouragement of cloth manufactures became a special pursuit when he found himself in a position to carry out his plans.

[1] *A Word to the Wise* (1752).

The king aided his minister right royally, and, under the patronage of the State, the trade progressed. At this juncture Ireland, by increased wool production, was trying to make up the loss she had sustained through the stoppage of her cattle exports to England. Wool was wanted by France, and the Irish wool-growers, especially the Catholics, who knew the Continent much better than they knew the neighbouring island, took advantage of the opening thus presented, and landed their wool-packs in the French ports. Probably, however, the continental clothiers had but an imperfect appreciation of Ireland's resources in this particular until the soldiers of their nation, coming over to fight for James II., in the Revolutionary War, beheld the vast pastoral plains of the island, saw the peasantry destroying the sheep that had usurped the place of the agriculturist on the soil, and learned how inexhaustible must be the wool-supply of such a land. Wiser than their Irish allies, the French gathered up the fleeces of the slaughtered sheep, collected an immense quantity of woollen yarn, and, on their departure from Ireland, carried off so much material as sufficed, in the parlance of that age, to put their manufacturers upon a clothing trade for Turkey. Quickly on this followed the flight of the Irish weavers, and their settlement in the manufacturing towns of northern France. About the same time, on the disbanding of the army after the conclusion of the Treaty of Ryswick, a number of soldiers, who had been originally weavers, returned to their trade. These men were instructed according to improved methods, and, together with the Irish contingent, notably increased the strength of the industrial forces. Irish wool now became an absolute necessity for the French manufactures, one pack of that staple being required to work up every two packs of the material elsewhere procured. France was determined to obtain wool from Ireland, and Ireland was equally resolved that France should be supplied. Despite of armed cruisers, despite of revenue-officers, in the teeth of penalties and prohibitions, four-fifths of the Irish fleeces were carried annually to France.

This clandestine export was effected in various ways, according to circumstances. During the first years a great quantity of raw wool was transported to the coasts of Clare and Galway, and shipped in the French vessels which came to take off the recruits for the Irish Brigades. It is said that this intimate association of "Wild Geese" and wool had its origin in the fact that Captain Teigue M'Namara, an officer in the Irish Brigade, a native of Clare, and possessor of a large property in that county, took advantage of the opportunity he enjoyed as conductor of the recruiting expeditions to smuggle wool into the French ports, thus serving "the foes of Ireland's foe" in a twofold way, and benefiting the home interests not a little.[1] Later on, the shores of Kerry and West Cork became the scene of wool smuggling, conducted with the aid of privateers and fishing fleets. There were times when the smugglers' audacity knew no restraint, and the wool was carried openly to Cork city, and shipped in sight of the soldiers who were sent to prevent the transaction.[2] Early, however, in the traffic, a less clumsy method of transporting the material was devised and adapted in some of the principal ports. The wool was combed, screwed into butter firkins or beef barrels, covered with a layer of meat or grease, and, judiciously weighted with shot, passed through the custom-house as provisions. Quite early in the century, merchants of Waterford, Wexford, and Youghal brought their ships into Rochelle, Nantes, St. Malo, and Bordeaux, and made their sales in the open market, to the amazement of any English traders, travellers, or prisoners of war who might happen to be on the spot. So great was the demand for wool in France, that at certain times the Irish merchants found it worth their while to take their cargo of raw wool into the English ports and sell it there, notwithstanding the heavy duties, to factors who conveyed it to Kent and Sussex, whence the owlers of those parts smuggled it, together with fine English wool, to the opposite shores.[3]

[1] See a paper by the Very Rev. Dean Kenny, entitled "History of Drunkenness in Ireland," which appeared in the *Illustrated Monitor*, when that now extinct publication was conducted by the late Father Robert Kelly, S.J.

[2] See *Tour through Ireland of two English Gentlemen* (1746).

[3] In the appendix to Smiles' *Huguenots*, there is an interesting account of the owlers of Romney Marsh, and of the way in which the woolmen managed their business. Dr. Johnson thinks that the word owler, applied to one who carries out wool illicitly, may perhaps come from the necessity of carrying on a clandestine trade by night; but he rather believes that it is a corruption of *wooler*, by a colloquial neglect of the *w*, such as is often observed in [illegible] and other words,—*wooller*, *oolers*, *owlers*

Thus, fed by English owlers and Irish smugglers, the French factories worked at high pressure. Abbeville, Amiens, Beauvais, became centres of the cloth trade, and Rouen gloried in possessing the first woollen manufactory in the world. In less than thirty years from the day when the French soldiers carried home their load of Irish fleeces, and the ruined weavers of the island sought refuge in the dominions of Louis the Great, the woollen manufactures of France were brought to such perfection that the English clothiers could not discover any difference between the foreign fabrics and their own fine cloths. The French had not only ceased to take English woollen goods, but had supplanted the once dominant traders in the most important foreign markets. They had engrossed the Turkey trade which England once enjoyed, and were supplying Italy, Spain, Portugal, and even Barbary, with sayes, serges, druggets, and other stuffs, which formerly had been classed as English.[1]

It may not be improper to mention here that three important discoveries (but all, alas! too late) were made in the course of the last century by English traders and politicians.

First, it was discovered that a serious mistake had been made in interfering with the Irish cattle trade: "Concerning these laws for prohibiting the importation of Irish cattle, many people think them in general to be hurtful; and that it would be wiser to suffer the Irish to be employed in breeding and fattening their black cattle for us than to turn their lands into sheep-walks, as at present, in consequence of which they are enabled, in spite of all our laws to the contrary, to supply foreign nations with their wools, to our great detriment."[2]

Secondly, it was discovered that it would have been better for the British Empire if the Irish had been allowed an open trade in their wool. "Experience has taught us," says a writer in the *Daily Post* (1740), "that the more the Irish are crampt in that article (the wool trade), the more it redounds to the advantage of the French, our most formidable and inveterate enemies. By the folly, not to say the injustice, of England, France has rivalled us this many years, with a witness, in the Spanish, Portugal, Italian, and Levant trades, besides the

[1] Prior, *Observations on the Trade of Ireland.* Second edition (1729). *Memoirs of Wool*, vol. ii.

[2] *Annals of Co*[illegible]

Ul

great vent she finds for woollen goods in the Austrian Netherlands and some parts of Germany: this prodigious increase of trade has raised her to such a pitch of grandeur that she is become more terrible than ever to her neighbours." The same writer goes on to ask, whether it would not be more eligible "to let the Irish share with us in the woollen trade, nay, to throw even all our trade into their hands, than to raise up France upon the ruins of the whole British Empire"?

Thirdly, it was discovered, and in the British Parliament acknowledged, that truer statesmanship it would have been to leave all the "Papists" in possession of their estates in Ireland than to force them by penal statutes to emigrate to America, where they or their sons were at that very time fighting with the desperation of injured men in the rebel ranks.

Naturally, a question arises as to how it was that the strength of England was not adequately exerted in putting a stop to the transmission of the supplies from Ireland which kept the French factories working at a rate so injurious to rival establishments. The answer is, that British strength was indeed put forth, but could effect little against a nation obstinately bent on resistance and evasion. A code of laws and a fleet of cruisers gained little in a contest with "a nation of smugglers." "When Ireland was restrained from exporting her woollen manufactures," writes Sir James Caldwell, "the exportation of raw wool became the business not of the few, but of the many. it was no man's interest merely as a native of Ireland to prevent it, it was, therefore, not only connived at but encouraged; and those who did not unlawfully export raw wool for a pecuniary advantage to themselves were well pleased to see it done by others, from a principle of resentment and indignation against those who had subjected them to what they could not but consider as a cruel and oppressive law, which had not only impoverished many individuals whose wealth was a common benefit, but cut off bread from the mouths of innumerable industrious poor, and consequently produced national impotence and poverty." "And," adds Sir James, it is both cruel and vain "to expect that the people of Ireland will not smuggle wool, because it is forbidden by those who have already forbidden them to eat."[1]

[1] *An Inquiry Concerning the Restrictions laid on the Trade of Ireland* (1766).

Substantially similar is the view taken of the smuggling question by the author of *The English in Ireland.* As this lively writer brings the picturesque side of the situation into higher relief than does Sir James Caldwell, I take leave to brighten these pages by introducing a sketch from the work just named. "The entire nation, high and low," says Mr. Froude, "was enlisted in an organised confederacy against the law. Distinctions of creed were obliterated, and resistance to law became a bond of union between Catholic and Protestant, —Irish Celt and English colonist,—from the great landlord whose sheep roamed in thousands over the Cork mountains to the gauger who, with conveniently blinded eyes, passed the wool-packs through the custom-house as butter-barrels; from the magistrate whose cellars were filled with claret on the return voyage of the smuggling craft, to the judge on the bench who dismissed as frivolous and vexatious the various cases which came before the court to be tried. All persons of all ranks in Ireland were principals or accomplices in a pursuit which made it a school of anarchy; and good servants of the State, who believed that laws were made to be obeyed, lay under the ban of opinion as public enemies. . . . Government tried stricter methods, substituted English for Irish officers at the chief ports like Waterford and Cork, and stationed cruisers along the coast to seal the mouths of the smaller harbours. But the trade only took refuge in bays and creeks where cruisers dared not run in. If encountered at sea, the contraband vessels were sometimes armed so heavily that the Government cutters and schooners hesitated to meddle with them. If unarmed and overhauled, they were found apparently laden with some innocent cargo of salt provisions. . . Driven from Cork warehouses, the packs were stored in caves about the islands, and cliffs, and crags, where small vessels took them off at leisure, or French traders, on signal from shore, sent in their boats for them. Chests of bullion were kept by the merchants at Rochelle and Brest to pay for them as they were landed. When the French Government forbade the export of so much specie, claret, brandy, and silks were shipped for Ireland in exchange on board the vessels which had brought the wool."

For some of the above particulars Mr. Froude is indebted, as he ac[illegible] blin

Castle, bearing the date of 1730. The price of fleece wool in Ireland at that time, according to the same document, was fivepence a pound; of combed wool, one shilling. In France, Irish fleece-wool sold for two-and-sixpence a pound; combed wool, from four-and-sixpence to six shillings

It is not easy to understand why the French, who were ready to give such a high price for Irish wool, did not turn their attention to the flocks of their own country. Arthur Young described their sheep as wretchedly cared; fed, or rather starved, on straw during the winter, and lying on dung-hills, so filthy was their stabling. The fleeces were poor and of a bad quality, and three sheep were kept where there might have been a hundred. France spends, says this observant traveller, 27,000,000 livres a year on importing wool, every pound of which might be produced in the country. Of course, it was all the better for poor Ireland that France was so negligent in this particular, for, says Swift, "Our beneficial traffic of wool with France hath been our only support for several years past, furnishing us all the little money we have to pay our rents and go to market."

VIII.

If, in the interval between the Restoration and the Revolution, the conversion of Ireland into a vast sheep-walk was condemned as discouraging agriculture and forcing human beings to give place to wool-producing flocks, with much more reason was the aggravation of that system during the greater part of the eighteenth century regarded as a grievous injury to the country at large. Unquestionably, the peasantry suffered in the earlier period; but, then, there was some compensation to the general community in the lucrative employment of a large body of artisans engaged in working up the wool into cloths and stuffs for foreign markets In the later and longer period, though camlets and other woollen fabrics were clandestinely carried to Spain and Portugal, and serges were smuggled into Scotland, and the people for the most part "sheared their own wool and wore it," nevertheless no manufacture [illegible] all commensurate with the enormous

( )

production of raw material. In point of fact, there was no adequate industrial compensation for the neglect of husbandry and the low status of the agricultural classes.

Up to the middle of the eighteenth century the "pernicious sheep-walks" formed the main feature, after the bogs, of the Irish landscape. The counties of Tipperary, Limerick, and Carlow were mainly given up to wool-growing. The baronies of Corra and Terrera in Sligo, and a great part of Roscommon, particularly that part between Athlone and Boyle (30 miles long and 10 miles broad), were continued sheep-walks. There were flock-masters in Connaught who had 20,000 sheep on their farms Patches of corn and potatoes appeared like a trimming on the skirts of the pastoral plains, and amidst these patches grovelled the wretchedly-housed peasants. Arthur Young, who notes these particulars, observes that at the period of his tour (1776–78) the population had greatly increased, and was sensibly encroaching on the grazing lands. Still, the sheep farms were seldom under 400 or 500 acres, and rose to 3000 about 6000 or 7000 being then the greatest flock kept by one owner.

Among the four provinces, Connaught kept the pre-eminence in wool-growing. The greatest quantity was produced in that western region, the quality of the fleece being also superlatively good. A wool fair was annually held at Ballinasloe, in the month of July, and lasted for several weeks. On these occasions, sales to the amount of £200,000 were frequently effected.[1] It does not appear that time was reckoned as a very valuable commodity by the Connaught flock-masters and their customers, for at this fair they were wont to spend a great amount of it in bargaining. A later writer than Young says that an improved method of transacting business had recently been adopted by the Cork and Limerick buyers, who went to the growers' houses, made such bargains as they could, and paid in bills at various dates. Still the July fair held its ground, and was conducted in accordance with traditional modes. "It is," continues the author referred to, "perfectly ridiculous to see sensible men walking about the streets of Ballinasloe, the buyers on one side and the sellers on the other, for often six weeks and more. This had been carried so far sometimes that the buyers have made parties to take a tour to

[1] [illegible]

Killarney or elsewhere for a fortnight or more, thinking to tire the sellers into a bargain."[1]

Most of the Connaught wool was conveyed to Munster. Five hundred cars laden with wool might be seen at a time on the road to Cork city, and in the county of Cork half the wool of Ireland was combed. Clothiers established at Charleville, Donnerail, Mitchelstown, Kanturk, Newmarket, and other places, bought up wool, got it combed in their own houses, gave it out to be spun by the peasantry, and then sold it to the weavers, or disposed of it to the French agents. All over the South, weavers were at work, some living in cabins about the country, and others inhabiting cottages, with small gardens, in the towns.

Everywhere throughout Ireland, except perhaps in some parts of Ulster, the people prepared the raw material and made their own clothing In every cottage there was a spinning-wheel, and at the door, in fine weather, sat mother or daughter spinning and singing the while—for music, which in those days was generally an enlivener of most domestic and out-of-door avocations, was invariably an accompaniment to wool-spinning Dr. Petrie, and other collectors of our national melodies, have preserved many of these spinning tunes It was an understood thing that while the men supported the family by their labour in the fields, the women, who in those days never engaged in agricultural work, paid the rent by the profits of the distaff. Wakefield remarks that the people display great ingenuity in the manufacture of their cloth and stuffs. "Instead of using oil in the weaving, as is the case in all woollen manufactures, they extract in the summer-time the juice of the fern root, which they find to answer the purpose; and for dyeing they employ the indigenous vegetable productions of the country, such as twigs of the alder, walnut and oak leaves, elder berries, etc."[2] By all accounts, an excessive quantity of wool, far more than skilful artisans would approve, was used in the domestic manufacture of friezes, linseys, stockings, and petticoat stuffs. "The amount of the consumption of woollens in Ireland," says Lord Sheffield, "we cannot know, but it is very great, and perhaps no country whatever, in proportion to the number of its inhabitants, consumes so much. The lower orders are covered with the clumsiest woollen drapery, and

[1] Dutton, *Survey of Clare* (1808).
[2] *Ireland, Statistical and Political*, vol i. (1812).

although the material may not be fine, there is abundance of it. Besides coat and waistcoat, the lower classes wear a great-coat both summer and winter, if it can possibly be got. Not only their clothing, but their stockings, seem to contain a double quantity of wool." The women, also, he observes, wear the clumsiest woollens, their petticoats, and their cloak, when they have one, containing much wool. Whatever cloth and stuff remained after the farmer's household was supplied, found a sale at the different fairs. At Rathdrum, in the county of Wicklow, a flannel fair was held on the first Monday of every month, and the frieze fair of Kilkenny was celebrated.

Manufactories of superior cloths existed in the cities and towns; for although the production of first-class broadcloth for exportation was checked by the prohibitory statutes, it received encouragement in another direction. "When the Irish found themselves prohibited by English laws from the exportation of all woollen manufactures, they thought the grievance insupportable, and to alleviate it applied all their wit and industry to two purposes: first, to export as much manufactured wool to France as possible; and, secondly, to make fine cloths for their own consumption. These were deep wounds to the English woollen trade: the one giving our inveterate enemies a rivalship in that business, and the other taking from the English a great part of the Irish trade for fine cloths which they enjoyed before."[1]

Thus stimulated to exertion, the Irish clothiers succeeded in making a serviceable and sufficiently fine quality of cloth for the use of the easier classes. The Spanish wool required for mixing with the Irish was procured, strangely enough, through London; as indeed was also, at least at one time, the supply of that staple which the French manufacturers had need of. Swift evidently thought that in his day Irish gentlemen had no reason to consider themselves unsuitably garbed in native manufacture, and he did his best, as we know, to bring the fashion of English broadcloth into discredit. Fashion, however, reasserted its mischievous influence as time went on; and Dr. Campbell had reason to complain of the coxcombs of his day for their ignorant contempt of homespun garments, and their affectation in pretending that woollens of the country were not good enough for their own wear. The Irish, he says, are "very culpable in this affair, but the fault falls not upon

[1] Harris, *Life of William III.*

the manufacturer, but upon the consumer. The woollen manufacture, in despite of all efforts to annihilate it, has flourished in the city of Dublin, while it has languished everywhere else. But, as if the natives wished to conspire with other agents in banishing it hence also, they scorn to wear a homespun coat. Even an attorney's clerk must be dressed in English cloth; and such is the contempt of Irish woollens in Ireland, that it is common with the drapers to sell for English those which are really Irish." [1]

Thus, the growing, preparing, and smuggling of wool filled up a considerable space in the life of the Irish people during the best part of the eighteenth century; and the manufacture of cloths and stuffs, principally for home consumption, gave employment to a multitude of hands. And yet the woollen manufacture, though respectable, was immeasurably below the standard it would have reached if a free export had been allowed. "Home consumption," says the writer just quoted, "is not sufficient stimulus. The genius of trade sickens at the very thoughts of restriction, and it dies upon actual restraint." As for the clandestine trade, though a great number derived advantage from it, its drawbacks were neither few nor trifling, and its benefits were in some respects illusory. Precarious, hazardous, demoralising, it was, as a system, the very opposite of steady, open, legitimate trading. There was all the difference in the world between the constitution of a great commercial community and the enlistment of a host of trading adventurers. Sir James Caldwell, an excellent authority, points out at some length the evils that wool smuggling brought on the country, and says in conclusion. "It deprives the poor of employment, discourages industry, promotes idleness and debauchery, disposes the common people to insult Government, sows the seeds of rebellion, and quenches humanity, by making violence, and in some cases murder, necessary to self-defence." [2]

Although France was ready to pay a high price, and at times any price, for Irish wool, the mode in which the payments were made increased the general disruption of sobriety and order. As already observed, the French Government objected to so great an amount of specie leaving the kingdom as had been

[1] *A Philosophical Survey of the South of Ireland* (1777).

[2] *An Inquiry concerning the Restrictions laid on the Trade of Ireland* (1766).

transmitted to Ireland during the first years of the contraband traffic. Cash remittances were therefore discontinued, and an exchange of commodities substituted. Ireland was consequently deluged with wine and brandy, glutted with silks, laces, and suchlike commodities, and entangled more than ever in an illicit traffic, by the necessity of smuggling in French luxuries as well as running out native wool. A superabundance of good wine did not foster habits of temperance, and strangers remarked that the produce of excellent foreign vintages could be got in places where common Irish bread was not to be had. Luxurious and copious drinking on the part of the men was emulated by extravagant dressing on the part of the women. French finery suited ill with poverty-stricken surroundings, and only helped to render more remarkable the general disarray. Curious notions of Irish customs in the matter of drinking and dressing are to be found in the *Querist*. Dr. Berkeley asks, "Whether any kingdom in Europe be so good a customer at Bordeaux as Ireland?" "How many gentlemen are there in England of £1000 per annum who never drink wine in their own houses? Whether the same may be said of any in Ireland, who have even £100 per annum?" The lady's lace is a match for the squire's bottle, and the *Querist* wants to know, "Whether it be not a notorious truth that our Irish ladies are on a foot, as to dress, with those of five times their fortune in England? Whether it be not even certain that the matrons of this forlorn country send out a greater portion of its wealth for fine apparel than any other females on the whole surface of this terraqueous globe?" [1]

A considerable quantity of French silk was used, in the early part of the last century, at funerals in Ireland. The scarfs worn by the mourners were made of lustring (commonly pronounced *lutestring*), and it was computed that between £11,000 and £12,000 were annually expended in the purchase of this smuggled article. However, after some time the Cambric Company of Belfast proposed, in the interest of Irish manufacturers, that linen should be used instead of silk at funerals. This mode having been adopted at the funeral of "a late great man of the first distinction," a statistician of the day remarked that "it was well judged to bury him in character as a friend to his country and a benefactor to multi-

[1] The *Querist* was first published in 1735.

Ui

tudes."[1] Another authority of the same date remarks that, whereas silk scarfs were of little utility except for the one occasion, linen scarfs might be applied to many other uses. They could be made of all prices, from one shilling to eight shillings a yard, answerable to the quality or fortune of the deceased. Eventually the Ulster manufacture gained the day, and it became the fashion to honour the dead and serve honest trade at the same time by the display of a profusion of white linen at Irish funerals.

I daresay it would be interesting, while following the ramifications of illicit trading in Ireland, to notice instances of complicity in the traffic on the part of the gentry whose property touched on the seaboard. Those who are curious in the matter will find one notable instance of the association of a contrabandist's pursuits with the avocations of a landed proprietor in the early pages of Miss Cusack's *Life of the Liberator*.

Clearly, it was Bishop Berkeley's opinion that the Irish people would have shown more wisdom if they had accommodated themselves to circumstances, relinquished the desire of a free trade in wool and woollens, and quietly directed their commercial enthusiasm into other channels. He thought that hankering after a foreign trade, and grieving over its loss, enfeebled the national mind; and he inquires "Whether it would not be more prudent to strike out and exert ourselves in permitted branches of trade than to fold our hands and repine that we are not allowed the woollen?" and "Whether, if there was a wall of brass a thousand cubits high round this kingdom, our natives might not, nevertheless, live cleanly and comforably, till the land, and reap the fruits of it?" But it is also plainly indicated in the *Querist* that the treatment which the wool had received destroyed all feeling of security in other trades, that the people could not get rid of the idea that industries of other kinds, even though they should be "with great pains and expense thoroughly introduced and settled in the land," might be at any moment similarly uprooted, and that, therefore, "they stuck to their wool."

Moreover, nearly every other Irish industry had its grievance as well as the woollen trade. The Ulster linen manufacture received many a stealthy thrust and many an open blow from English jealousy, and was subject to disastrous fluctuations

[1] Dobbs, *An Essay on the Trade and Improvement of Ireland* (1729).

( )

which kept the passenger traffic between the North of Ireland and America busy for scores of years deporting weavers out of work. In 1772, such was the state of affairs in Ulster that, as reported to the Irish House of Commons, the best manufacturers and weavers, with their families, had gone to seek bread in America, and thousands were preparing to follow. The Irish glass manufacture was most injuriously treated. Disabling duties were imposed on the Irish hempen manufacture, which at one time had supplied the whole British navy with sailcloth. Irish fishermen were not allowed to appear off Newfoundland, and petitions were presented to Parliament by English fishermen praying that the Irish might be prevented catching herrings on the coast of Waterford and Wexford.

In fact, the only extensive and, occasionally at least, unfettered trade that Ireland enjoyed in those days was the export of salted provisions, which began immediately after the prohibition of the cattle trade with England The French took immense quantities, and it was believed that without the Irish supplies they could hardly have victualled their ships. For a number of years the French settlements in the West Indies were provided from the same quarter. According to a contemporary foreign authority, a breast of Irish beef was the greatest regale in those islands.[1] Besides beef, the French took butter, tallow, and raw hides in great quantities. Prior, in his *Observations on the Trade of Ireland*, gives an idea of the extent of the foreign exports. "It appears," he says, "from the quantity of our commodities exported to France, at a medium yearly for seven years ending 1786, taken from the custom-house books, that the French take from us, one year with another, two parts in five of all our tallow, above one-third of all our butter, a fourth part of all our raw hides, and above one-third part of all our beef, which last commodity may otherwise lie a drug upon our hands, since no other foreign nation has occasion for the same, either for their own consumption or for the use of their colonies." Later on, the British navy received supplies of Irish beef, and in times nearer to our own, as, for instance, during the Peninsular War, the British army was to a great extent victualled from Ireland.

Vicissitudes, of course, tried this trade as well as others. Although it did not excite national jealousy in any marked

[1] See the treatises of Dobbs and Sir John Caldwell already quoted.

degree, it was victimised on occasions in the interest of the English contractors. "Of all the restrictions," says Arthur Young, "which England has at different times most impolitically laid upon the trade of Ireland, there is none more obnoxious than the embargoes on their provision trade. The prohibitions of the export of woollens, and various other articles, have this pretence at least in their favour, that they are advantageous to similar manufactures in England; and Ireland has long been trained to the sacrifice of her national advantage as a dependent country; but in respect to embargoes, even this shallow pretence is wanting,—a whole kingdom is sacrificed and plundered, not to enrich England, but three or four London contractors!"

The operation of this system of embargoes may be inferred from the account given by Mac Pherson of one of these transactions, shortly told as follows: An embargo was laid, in 1776, on the exportation of salted provisions from Ireland, in the apprehension of the French furnishing themselves with a stock of Irish provisions for victualling their fleets in the impending war, and was still in force in 1779. The French suffered no inconvenience, nor did the West India Islands, for the American market was open to them. But to the Irish it was a grievous and ruinous disappointment. "Their discontent was almost converted into indignation by a belief, which prevailed very generally among them, that the measure did not originate from the professed motive, but from a design of giving enormous lucrative contracts to ministerial favourites." So great was the distress following this prohibition, that it was feared the country would become depopulated unless the commercial grievances of Ireland were speedily redressed. Multitudes went to America, where their countrymen were fighting in the rebel ranks, and the charity of the higher classes in Dublin was strained to the extremest limit by the necessity of feeding daily 20,000 poor citizens ruined by the new prohibition."[1]

Passing strange it is that the spirit of enterprise was not wholly crushed by the discouragements and injuries inflicted on the trade of Ireland during so long a period. Necessity stimulated energy; and it must be remembered that in trade lay the one chance for the Catholic body to rise from the degraded position it was held in by the penal code. Lord Chesterfield, albeit disdaining to use the vulgar arts of persecu-

[1] [illegible] of *Commerce*, vol. iii.

tion, was far from desiring to see the Irish papists acquire power of any kind. He had sagacity enough to perceive that a serious pursuit of mercantile avocations would sooner or later enable them to obtain position, wealth, influence. His policy, therefore, would have been to repeal the laws that forbade Catholics to purchase estates, lure them thus from commercial enterprises, and then rely on the Gavel Act for breaking up, by subdivision, the newly-acquired properties. Fortunately, Chesterfield's viceregal reign was too short to allow him an opportunity of carrying out his subtle schemes The temptation to exchange the office of merchant for that of estated gentleman was not just then set as a snare for ambitious Catholics Traders of that religion worked on in the industrial groove, and amassed in many cases respectable fortunes. Then foreign relations afforded them opportunities of educating their children. It was the custom to send out Catholic youths as *soi disant* apprentices on board of trading vessels; and then, when they had got some education in the colleges of France and Spain, to smuggle them back into Ireland with the brandy and Bordeaux.

IX.

But, to return to our sheep once more. All through those years the Irish never reconciled themselves to the loss of the legitimate wool trade. In vain they were told that it was unbecoming and ungrateful on their part to refuse this little compensation — the wool monopoly — to England, that great nation which had been at such trouble and expense in quelling the frequent rebellions of the Irish.[1] In vain they were invited to acquiesce in the inevitable, and give up the wool. They could not be made to recognise their obligations, and they would not accept the inevitable. For eighty years they kept on persistently *not acquiescing*, until in the end they paid off

[1] "The monopoly of wool and woollen yarn has been the greatest occasion of complaint in Ireland, of hardship laid upon it by England's ergrossing so valuable a branch of trade to itself This the English claim to be due to them upon account of the charges from time to time they have been at in reducing the natives of Ireland, as also in restoring the British interest when routed or disturbed by the frequent rebellions of the Irish."—*Dobbs.*

Ul

old scores in quite another fashion, and made the inevitable fly from before their face.

Several of the authorities we have quoted set the trade question in a fair light from time to time, between 1728 and 1766. They showed that, in order to relieve the English woollen trade, the Irish manufacturers should be allowed to join in competing for the foreign market; they pointed out how such branches as the Turkey business, for instance, might well be carried on in Ireland, while the English weavers were employed in producing finer fabrics, and they ventured to inquire how it was that England still continued to compliment the French with a trade she denied to Ireland. Reiterated observations of this kind produced some effect in the longrun Thinkers and legislators in this island began to understand that something must be done to relieve the country from the intolerable oppression that weighed it down; and a vigorous public opinion grew strong by degrees, and finally demanded a hearing. Ireland, dreaming that the wool might yet be free, was gradually preparing for a struggle: while England still maintained an impassive front, determined not to read aright the American lesson. A contest at close quarters was now inevitable. It was not destined to be a long one Let us note the points of advance and retreat, observing the order of events, and keeping close to our best authorities.

In 1770, as Mr Lecky writes, the viceroy, Lord Townshend, suggested the necessity of relaxing the commercial restrictions under which Ireland laboured, and suggested that a coarse kind of woollen cloth, which was made in Ireland but not in Great Britain, might be sent without danger to the Spanish and Portuguese markets. His efforts, however, were completely futile. In 1776 a few slight commercial concessions were granted by England. Newfoundland and other fisheries from which Irish fishermen had been excluded were thrown open to them; and the Irish were permitted to furnish the clothing of their own troops when they were stationed out of Ireland[1] In 1778 the Prime Minister, Lord North, proposed to relieve the commercial restraints of Ireland by allowing a free and general exportation of all kinds of goods, except the woollen manufacture,—"that article being reckoned too sacred to be yet meddled with." But so great was the commotion

[1] [illegible] England in the Eighteenth Century, vol. iv.

excited in the manufacturing towns of England that Lord North had to reconsider his proposal.

"A general alarm," says Mac Pherson, "spread through most of the trading and manufacturing parts of the kingdom." They considered the "admittance of Ireland to any participation in trade as not only destructive, in the most ruinous degree, of their property, but as being equally subversive of their rights. They were as little disposed to consent that the people of Ireland should cultivate their own manufactures, and dispose of their native commodities at the proper foreign markets, as they were to admit them to any limited degree of commercial participation. In short, the alarm was universal, and took such absolute possession of the public attention that, for a short time, the American War and all its brooding events appear to have been forgotten." The table of the House of Commons, as we read in Plowden's *Historical Review*, was covered with "petitions against any extension of commercial advantages to Ireland by which the trade of England should be in any way affected. Liverpool, Manchester, and Glasgow threatened to be no longer loyal if these Bills should pass.' The popular passion triumphed for the moment. The British Parliament yielded to the pressure from without, and only some slight modifications of the commercial code were effected.

Ireland was now fast assuming a formidable attitude. Her Parliament was determined to assert its rights; and the volunteers were demanding free trade with arms in their hands.

In February 1779, "the Sheriffs of Dublin represented to the Lord-Lieutenant that 19,000 persons connected with the weaving trade in that city, besides many other poor, were on the brink of starvation, and that nothing but an extension of trade and a free export of manufactures could save them." Two months later a meeting was held in Dublin, at which all present pledged themselves "not directly or indirectly to purchase any of the goods or manufactures of Great Britain that could be manufactured at home. . . . Agreements to use only domestic manufactures, and to abstain from purchasing English goods till the commercial restrictions were removed, were now entered into by the grand juries of many counties and by numerous county meetings, and were signed in most of the great towns." The viceroy, Lord Buckinghamshire, having requested the leading [illegible] l with

Ut

their opinions concerning the state of the country, Lord Lifford, Sir Lucius O'Brien, Flood, Hussey Burgh, Foster, and Hely Hutchinson stated their views in pamphlets and treatises—all agreeing that, unless the commercial restrictions were speedily removed, Ireland could no longer pay her way.[1]

Hely Hutchinson's *Commercial Restrictions* was by far the most remarkable contribution presented to the Government on this occasion. It was a piece of sound and creditable work. Having done excellent service to Ireland in its day, it still possesses a vivid interest and high value for the student of history. Already the work has been several times quoted or referred to in this paper, and it would naturally call for special notice at this part of our story, only that its rare pages have been just reprinted and reissued under singularly able editorship. Henceforth it will be no longer out of the reach of general readers.[2]

Whether the eyes of Europe were on the Emerald Isle at this juncture or whether they were not, certain it is that America was not heedless of what was going on in the old land, and equally certain that the consciousness of American sympathy inspirited the patriots to a high pitch of courage and resolution. Benjamin Franklin watched the progress of events with deep interest. He had visited Ireland and formed friendships with her sons, and he was well informed of her wants and her wrongs. Writing to Sir Edward Newenham in this very year (1779), he says: "I admire the spirit with which I see the Irish are at length determined to claim some share of that freedom of commerce which is the right of all mankind, but which they have been so long deprived of by the abominable selfishness of their fellow-subjects. To enjoy all the advantages of the climate, soil, and situation in which God and nature have placed us, is as clear a right as that of breathing, and can never be justly taken from men but as a punishment for some atrocious crime."[3]

[1] *The History of England in the Eighteenth Century*, vol. iv.

[2] The full title of the reissue reads thus *The Commercial Restraints of Ireland, considered in a Series of Letters to a Noble Lord, containing an Historical Account of the Affairs of that Kingdom.* Dublin, 1779 By John Hely Hutchinson, Provost of Trinity College, etc. Re-edited, with a sketch of the Author's Life, Introduction, Notes, and Index, by W G. Carroll, M.A., SS. Bride's and Michael le Pole's. Dublin, M. H. Gill & Son (1882).

[3] *Life o* [illegible], vol. iii. (1833).

Meanwhile the volunteers seconded their demand for free trade by giving the best practical encouragement to the industries of the nation. They clothed their regiments and troops in Irish manufacture, and the brilliant uniforms of the different corps at their reviews and military gatherings throughout the country showed what could be done by native artisans with materials of home growth. They encouraged by their approval and supported by their patronage every undertaking which had for its object the extension of trade. Associations for the use of Irish manufactures sprang up in every part of the country, to the serious alarm of the English clothiers, who left nothing undone to compel or induce the small traders throughout the provinces to take their goods at reduced prices and on long credit. "The volunteers and the leaders of the movement were equally active on their side. The press, the pulpit, and the ballroom were enlisted in the cause of native industry. The scientific institutions circulated, gratuitously, tracts on the improvement of manufacture, on the modes adopted in the continental manufacturing districts, and on the economy of production. Trade revived; the manufacturers who had thronged the city of Dublin, the ghastly apparitions of decayed industry, found employment provided for them by the patriotism and spirit of the country; the proscribed goods of England remained unsold, or only sold under false colours by knavish and profligate retailers; the country enjoyed some of the fruits of freedom before she obtained freedom itself."[1] The volunteer guns were made to express the national sentiment and advocate the cause of Irish wool. Around the necks of the cannons were hung labels with such inscriptions as, *Free Trade or This! Free Trade or speedy Revolution!* Even the drums lent their aid in intensifying patriotic ardour. With more point, perhaps, than poetry, words had been fitted to a stirring march-tune adopted by the regimental bands, and the moment the roll of the drums was heard the popular memory suggested the verses—

"Was she not a fool,
When she took off our wool,
To leave us so much of the
Leather, the leather?

[1] [illegible]

> It ne'er entered her pate,
> That a sheep-skin well beat,
> Would draw a whole nation
> Together, together."

In the month of October the Irish Parliament met, and unanimously resolved to address the Throne, and represent to His Majesty that it was not by temporary expedients, but by a free trade alone, that Ireland could be saved from impending ruin. The Speaker, accompanied by the patriot leaders, carried the addresses of the Lords and Commons to the Castle, the streets being lined with the Dublin Volunteers drawn up in arms, under their commander, the Duke of Leinster, and thronged with a rejoicing multitude. This action was followed by a proposal to withhold the supplies, or to limit the duration of the Money Bill, until free trade was yielded by England. During the debate on this question, the Prime Serjeant, Hussey Burgh, delivered the famous speech in which he declared that, if Parliament were weak enough to grant supplies for two years, it would thereby destroy the fair prospects of commercial hope, and lead the British Minister to treat all applications for free trade with contempt. "The usurped authority of a foreign Parliament," continued the orator, "has kept up the most wicked laws that a jealous, monopolising, ungrateful spirit could devise to restrain the bounty of Providence, and enslave a nation whose inhabitants are recorded to be a brave, loyal, and generous people; by the English code of laws, to answer the most sordid views, they have been treated with a savage cruelty, the words penalty, punishment, and Ireland are synonymous, they are marked in blood on the margin of their statutes, and though time may have softened the calamities of the nation, the baneful and destructive influence of those laws have borne her down to a state of Egyptian bondage. The English have sowed their laws like serpents' teeth, and they have sprung up as armed men."[1]

During the delivery of this speech, Hussey Burgh, in reply to someone who had observed that Ireland was at peace, thundered forth these words: "Talk not to me of peace. Ireland is not at peace; it is smothered war." Extraordinary excitement was produced both within the House of Parliament and outside its walls by the Prime Serjeant's courageous

[1] ([illegible])

words.[1] He ceased to hold his office under the Crown; but the Money Bill was passed for six months only. By this time the temper of the parent State had undergone some change. Mute alarm had taken the place of outrageous clamour. The British Parliament met in November, and the signal for a new departure was immediately given. "Severe censures were thrown out in both Houses upon the Ministry for endangering the loss of Ireland, as they had already accomplished that of America, by delaying to grant what it would be no longer in their power to withhold, whereby they were now reduced to a necessity of yielding, as a matter of right, much more than would have been thankfully received as a favour if granted with a good grace at a proper time. At last the Minister was roused to take up the business in earnest."[2]

Let the sequel be told, even at the risk of some repetition of statements, in the words, first, of a distinguished writer and gifted Irishman of our own day, and, secondly, of the greatest man that this country has ever produced.

Mr. Lecky, in the course of his ably-condensed history of this momentous year, thus writes: "Lord North, as we have seen, had been already disposed to grant a very liberal measure of commercial relief to Ireland, though he proposed to except the capital article of the wool trade but he had been intimidated by the clamour of the manufacturers of England. Now, however, the danger was too extreme for further delay. The fear of bankruptcy in Ireland, the non-importation agreements, which were beginning to tell upon English industries,—the threatening aspect of an armed body which already counted more than 40,000 men, the determined and unanimous attitude of the Irish Parliament, the predictions of the Lord-Lieutenant that all future military grants by Ireland depended upon this course, the danger that England, in the midst of a dangerous and disastrous war, should be left absolutely without a friend,—all weighed upon his mind; and at the close of 1779, and in the beginning of 1780, a series of measures were carried in England which exceeded the utmost that a few years before the most sanguine Irishman would have either expected or demanded. The Acts which prohibited the Irish from export-

[1] See Webb's *Compendium of Irish Biography*. Article, "Hussey Burgh"

[2] *Annal.*

ing their woollen manufactures and their glass were wholly repealed, and the great trade of the colonies was freely thrown open to them."[1]

Edmund Burke, speaking as a member of the British Parliament, conjures up a vision of the Irish people, resolute and armed, demanding a free trade, and thus describes the result: "They (the Irish) interdict all commerce between the two nations. They deny all new supply in the House of Commons, although in time of war. They stint the trust of the old revenue, given for two years to all the king's predecessors, to six months. The British Parliament, in a former session frightened into a limited concession by the menaces of Ireland, frightened out of it by the menaces of England, was now frightened back again, and made an universal surrender of all that had been thought the peculiar, reserved, uncommunicable rights of England — the exclusive commerce of America, of Africa, of the West Indies; all the enumerations of the Acts of Navigation, all the manufactures; iron, glass, even the last pledge of jealousy and pride, the interest hid in the secret of our hearts, the inveterate prejudice moulded into the constitution of our frame, even the sacred fleece itself,—all went together. No reserve; no exception; no discussion. A sudden light broke in upon us all. It broke in, not through well-contrived and well-disposed windows, but through flaws and breaches, through the yawning chasm of our ruin. We were taught wisdom by humiliation. No town in England presumed to have a prejudice, or dared to mutter a petition."[2]

Good grace, it is pleasant to record, characterised the last act of the drama. English traders, albeit sadly, maintained a becoming silence. Lords and Commons for once displayed unanimity in yielding to a just demand. The king exhibited a royal graciousness in assenting to the measure which repealed the prohibitory statutes of William III. Lord Hillsborough, in a letter dated the 23rd December 1779, thus communicates the tidings of the royal assent to William Sexton Pery, the Speaker of the House of Commons, Ireland.—

"The King is this moment returned from giving his Royal Assent to the Irish Woollen Bill, and I take the liberty to

[1] [illegible] *England in the Eighteenth Century*, vol. iv.

[2] ([illegible])

enclose to you a printed copy of it thus early, that you may not unnecessarily lose a moment of that pleasure which I am sure it will give you. I most sincerely congratulate with you upon this happy event for Ireland, as I flatter myself I shall very soon after the recess have the pleasure of doing upon the Export and Import Act to and from the Colonies, etc. It is a very agreeable circumstance in the passing this Bill, that there was not the least opposition in either House of Parliament, and that His Majesty, to whom a Commission was proposed, was pleased to say he would go to the House in person upon an occasion of so much importance to his faithful kingdom of Ireland."[1]

Signal as was this triumph in the repeal, after eighty years, of the statutes which had ruined the woollen trade of Ireland, the patriots were not so dazzled by success as to forget that the victory had still to be secured. The cause might again be lost unless the power of England to make laws for Ireland were surrendered. Therefore, they pushed on to the attack of the inner stronghold. In 1782, after a tyranny of nearly three hundred years, Poynings' Act was annulled, and the commercial freedom of Ireland established on a sound foundation.

It has been said that the freedom of trade, thus fought for and obtained, did little more than put an end to smuggling. Certain it is, however, that a great impetus was given to the woollen industries in Ireland by the inspiriting effect of the volunteer movement, and by the substantial encouragement bestowed by the Irish Parliament on the premier trade. The manufacturers met the demand for home production by increased energy and improved skill, and many thousands of hands were kept at work all over the country. Less wool was exported than formerly, but a larger quantity of manufactured goods was sent out. Despite of vicissitudes, occasioned by war and other causes, the woollen trade prospered during the twenty years that followed its liberation.

Then came the Union. It cannot be maintained that the Act of Union inflicted any injury on the Irish woollen trade. On the contrary, it removed disabilities which the repeal of 1779 had left *in statu quo*, and placed Ireland on an equal footing with England in regard to the staple manufacture. But what ensued? There ensued, first a gradual and then an

[1] [illegible]

accelerated decline in manufacturing industry throughout the country. The woollen trade, always spoken of in the eighteenth century as destroyed, was actually at that period in a flourishing condition when compared with the state it was reduced to in the nineteenth.

At the date of the Union there were, it is calculated, between 5000 and 6000 persons employed in Dublin and its vicinity in the various branches of the woollen manufactory. In 1868 the number so employed in all Ireland amounted only to 1374, according to a return in Thom's *Official Directory*. To the ruins of castles, abbeys, and lordly mansions that strewed the land, were added, in this our century, the ruins of mills In almost every direction mouldering monuments and sad traditions survive to testify to the existence, up to a period not long gone by, of a trade that, with all its limitations, deserved to be called national. Completer ruin could hardly be imagined.

Here no attempt shall be made to inquire into the causes of this calamity. It would be a tedious task, and certain to lead to the most disheartening reflections. Fortunately at this moment there are hopeful signs of a revival, on an extensive scale, of woollen industries in Ireland The Exhibition of Manufactures, which has recently been opened in Dublin, affords gratifying proofs of renewed activity in different parts of the country, helps to make more generally known the fact that even during the worst days some relics of a manufacture so ancient, so national, and so rich in interest, were preserved; and, furthermore, shows that in one branch of high-class woollens, Ireland has, in our own day, bid for and obtained a world-wide reputation for excellence.

The manufacturers who, at this juncture, endeavour to restore the lost trade, undoubtedly merit the most liberal encouragement; while those who represent establishments dating their foundation from pre-Union days, assuredly deserve not only this but the thanks of the nation.

THE END

A SELECT LIST OF

M. H. GILL & SON'S PUBLICATIONS.

Mary Aikenhead: Her Life, her Work, and her Friends. Being a History of the Foundation of the Irish Sisters of Charity. By SARAH ATKINSON. Second and Cheaper Edition revised. With a Portrait. Crown 8vo, cloth extra, 7s. 6d.

Gems for the Young. A Selection of Poetry. Edited by ROSA MULHOLLAND-GILBERT. With Six Illustrations. Crown 8vo, cloth, 2s. 6d. Also in Parts. Fcap 8vo, cloth gilt, each 1s., cloth, red edges, each 6d.

Prince and Saviour: The Story of Jesus simply told for the Young. By the same Author. 16mo, with Twelve Illustrations. Cloth, 6d., cloth gilt, 1s.

Life and Adventures of Robinson Crusoe. By DANIEL DEFOE. Edited by ROSA MULHOLLAND-GILBERT, Author of "The Walking Trees," "Prince and Saviour," "The First Christmas," etc. With Illustrations. Crown 8vo, cloth, 3s. 6d.

The Walking Trees, and other Tales. By ROSA MULHOLLAND-GILBERT. Illustrated. Crown 8vo, cloth, 3s. 6d.

Linda's Misfortunes. By CLARA MULHOLLAND. Fcap. 8vo, cloth gilt, 2s. 6d.

Percy's Revenge. By the same Author. Cloth gilt, 2s.

Cardinal Franzelin (S.J.). A Biography and Study. By Rev. N. WALSH, S.J. With Portrait. Cloth, 3s. 6d.

Persecutions of the Irish Catholics under Cromwell and the Puritans. A Historical Sketch. By His Eminence Cardinal MORAN. Cloth gilt, 3s. 6d., boards, 2s.

The Story of Ireland. By the late A. M. SULLIVAN, M.P. A New Edition. Cloth gilt, 2s. 6d., cloth, gilt edges, 3s. 6d.

A Concise History of Ireland from the Earliest Times to 1837. By P. W. JOYCE, LL.D. Cloth, 2s.

Outlines of Irish History from the Earliest Times to 1837. By P. W. JOYCE, LL.D. Cloth flush, 9d.

Love Songs of Connacht. By DOUGLAS HYDE, LL.D., M.R.I.A. Paper cover, 2s. 6d. net.

Folk Lore Stories in Irish. By the same Author. Paper cover, 5s.

True Men as We Need Them. A Book of Instruction. By Rev. B. O'REILLY. Crown 8vo, cloth gilt, 5s.

Harry Dee; or, Making it out. By Rev. F. J. FINN, S.J. Crown 8vo, fancy cloth, 3s.

Claude Lightfoot; or, How the Problem was Solved. By the Rev. F. J. FINN, S.J. Crown 8vo, fancy cloth, 3s.

Percy Wynn; or, Making a Boy of Him. By Rev. F. J. FINN, S.J. C[illegible] f[illegible] cloth [illegible])

A Select List of M. H. Gill & Son's Publications—
continued

Tom Playfair; or, Making a Start. By Rev. F. J. Finn, S.J. Crown [illegible]vo, fancy cloth,

Cromwell in Ireland. A History of Cromwell's Campaign in Ireland, with Map. By Rev. Denis Mu[illegible] S.J. [illegible]

Ancient Irish Music. Comprising 100 Airs hitherto unpublished. Collected and Edited by Dr. [illegible] By Profe[illegible]r Glover. Quarto, wrapper, [illegible]; cloth [illegible]

Irish Music and Song. A Collection of Songs in the Irish Language set to Music. Quarto, wrapper, [illegible]

Pat o' Nine Tales and One Over. By M. M'D. Bodkin, Q.C., M.P. ("Crom-a-Boo"). Cr[illegible]wn [illegible]vo, cloth [illegible].

The Old House by the Boyne. By Mrs. J. Sadlier. Crown 8vo, cloth, 3s. 6d.

Occasional Sermons, Addresses, and Essays. By the Right Rev. George Conroy, D.D., late Bi[illegible] of A[illegible]. New and Cheaper Edition, demy 8vo, cloth, 3s. 6d.

History of Clare and the Dalcassian Clans of Tipperary, Limerick, and Galway. With Map. By [illegible] Very Rev. P. White, P.P., V.G. 8vo, cloth, 1[illegible] 6d.

History and Antiquities of the Diocese of Kilmacdaugh. By the Very Rev. J. Fahey, P.P., V.G. [illegible] With Illustrati[illegible] 8vo, cloth, 8s.

Annals, Anecdotes, Traits, and Traditions of the Irish Parliament, 1711-1800. By J. R. O'Flan[illegible], B.L. [illegible] "Lives of the Lord Chancellors of Ireland." Crown [illegible] d.

Poems. By Denis Florence MacCarthy. Second Edition. Crown 8vo, wrapper, 1s.; cloth, 2s. 6d.

The Hermit of the Rock. By Mrs. J. Sadlier. New Edition. Crown 8vo, cloth, 3s. 6d.

Moore's Irish Melodies. Words and Music. Cloth, extra gilt, 3s. 6d.; or leather, extra gilt side and back [illegible] gilt edges, 6s. 6d.; best morocco, 15s.

Moore's. A Selection of Popular National Airs. The Symphonies and Accompaniments by Sir John Stevenson and Sir Henry Bishop. 4to, very handsome, extra cloth, gilt edges. New Edition, 5s.; best morocco, extra, 15s.

The Lectures of a Certain Professor. By the late Rev. Joseph Farrell. Crown 8vo, cloth, 3s. 6d.

Irish Pleasantry and Fun. A Selection of the best Humorous Tales by Carleton, Lever, Lover, and other Popular Writers. With Illustrations from Designs by J. F. O'Hea. New Edition. Crown 4to, boards, 3s.; cloth gilt, 4s.

Irish Poetic Gems from Clarence Mangan, Moore, and Griffin. 18mo, cloth, 2s.

** *A Complete Catalogue of M. H. Gill & Son's Publications sent post free on application.*

www.ingramcontent.com/pod-product-compliance
Ingram Content Group UK Ltd.
Pitfield, Milton Keynes, MK11 3LW, UK
UKHW021852070425
457202UK00005B/408

9 781016 282451